AMERICAN PRECARIAT

AMERICAN PRECARIAT

PARABLES OF EXCLUSION

EDITED BY ZEKE CALIGIURI, FONG LEE, B. BATCHELOR,
C. FAUSTO CABRERA, WILL ANDERSON, WARREN BRONSON,
DAVID JANISCH, KENNEDY AMENYA GISEGE,
MARK "RED" ALTENHOFEN, RONALD L. GREER II,
JEFF YOUNG, LAVON JOHNSON

COFFEE HOUSE PRESS
Minneapolis
2023

Coffee House Press books are available to the trade through our primary distributor, Consortium Book Sales & Distribution, cbsd.com or (800) 283-3572. For personal orders, catalogs, or other information, write to info@coffeehousepress.org.

Coffee House Press is a nonprofit literary publishing house. Support from private foundations, corporate giving programs, government programs, and generous individuals helps make the publication of our books possible. We gratefully acknowledge their support in detail in the back of this book.

LIBRARY OF CONGRESS CATALOGING-IN-PUBLICATION DATA

Names: Caligiuri, Zeke editor.
Title: American precariat : parables of exclusion / edited by Zeke Caligiuri [and 10 others].
Description: Minneapolis : Coffee House Press, 2023. |
Identifiers: LCCN 2023020612 (print) | LCCN 2023020613 (ebook) | ISBN 9781566896955 (paperback) | ISBN 9781566896962 (epub)
Subjects: LCSH: Prisoners' writings, American. | American essays—21st century. | LCGFT: Essays.
Classification: LCC PS683.P75 A44 2023 (print) | LCC PS683.P75 (ebook) | DDC 814/.60809206927—dc23/eng/20230624
LC record available at https://lccn.loc.gov/2023020612
LC ebook record available at https://lccn.loc.gov/2023020613

PERMISSIONS

"The Last Days of the Baldock" by Inara Verzemnieks first appeared in *Tin House* 15.1, © 2013 by Inara Verzemnieks. Reprinted by permission of the author.

"For a Solidarity of Condition and Position" by Anonymous first appeared in *It's Going Down* as "All We Have Is Us," © 2020. Reprinted by permission of the author and *It's Going Down*.

"Debt Demands a Body" by Kristen Collier first appeared in *Longreads,* © 2021. Reprinted by permission of the author and *Longreads*.

"Saskatoons" by Angela Pelster first appeared in *Hotel Amerika* 12, © 2014. Reprinted by permission of the author.

"Can We Move Our Forests in Time to Save Them?" by Lauren Markham first appeared in *Mother Jones,* © 2021. Reprinted by permission of the author and the Foundation for National Progress.

"Shape of the Wound" by Lacy M. Johnson first appeared in *Orion Magazine* 41.1, © 2022. Reprinted by permission of the author and the Orion Society.

"There Are No Bars in Rush City" by TM "Redd" Warren first appeared in *J Journal* 12.2, © 2019. Reprinted by permission of the author.

"How to Slowly Kill Yourself and Others in America" by Kiese Laymon first appeared in *Gawker,* © 2011. Reprinted by permission of the author.

"Tell Me How It Ends" by Valeria Luiselli first appeared in *Freeman's,* ©2016. Reprinted by permission of the author.

PRINTED IN THE UNITED STATES OF AMERICA

30 29 28 27 26 25 24 23   1 2 3 4 5 6 7 8

r/evolution is love.

—ASSATA SHAKUR

Table of Contents

Foreword

by Zeke Caligiuri

The book you're holding in your hands is the culmination of a special partnership between Coffee House Press and the Minnesota Prison Writing Workshop (MPWW), with an editorial board starting with twelve writers from the prisoner-created collectives of the Minnesota Correctional Facilities at Stillwater, Faribault, and Moose Lake.

For the past decade, MPWW has provided a first-of-its-kind ongoing writing program within Minnesota state prisons. What started from a single creative writing course taught by the organization's founder, Jen Bowen, has expanded from one facility to every prison in the state. The program offers a wide range of writing classes at all levels of the learning spectrum, as well as an extensive mentorship program. The workshop has become a model admired by potential prison writing programs across the country.

Before MPWW, there was already a burgeoning community of talented, but mostly unrecognized, artists and writers incarcerated in the state of Minnesota. MPWW's presence offered opportunities and resources to meet and take instruction from the larger literary community in the state, helping us to grow into a stronger community and to develop as individual writers. The relationship between MPWW and the incarcerated writing community has produced numerous awards and countless publishing credits for many of the workshop's students, as well as for many of the incredible writers that make up the MPWW instructor staff and mentor program.

The twelve members of this book's editorial staff are a small group of the much larger collectives that have grown up in our state, and throughout the country, in the sense that writers and artists always find each other in these kinds of spaces. There are creation stories that connect to make this community possible.

It would make sense that any history would begin at Stillwater Prison, where so much of the story and mythology of prison in Minnesota also begins. It is where Cole Younger of the famous James-Younger gang did their time, and where they spent their own money to start the *Prison Mirror*, the world's oldest and continuously run prison newspaper.

My first experience with a writing community came when I was still near the beginning of my sentence, decades ago, and was welcomed into the Stillwater Poetry Group (SPG), the first place where I felt that art was something to be taken seriously. As part of the SPG, we met with so many interesting local writers: Desdamona, Wang Ping, Ed Bok Lee, and J. Otis Powell, among others. It was exhilarating, until decision-makers in the facility realized the threat that artists and poets pose to the ideas of the captivity business. After only a year and a half, the group was disbanded. It was my first lesson in how easily good things in prison get discarded. Watching art and culture go away can create a bleak and hopeless landscape that will jade and obscure a person's faith in creative community. It was a pattern shown to us repeatedly.

Several years later, after a long education shutdown and budget cuts, and years into Minnesota's own mass incarceration expansion era, a new wave of incarcerated writers/thinkers/persons were emerging at Stillwater. Dr. Deborah Appleman and Dr. John Schmidt volunteered to teach courses on linguistics, literary theory, and creative writing. Out of these classes, a semblance of a new writer's community was created and a book was published. *Letters to a Young Man and Other Writings* offered us both the gratification of seeing our words in print and a renewed sense of purpose. Then, collectively, we waited, just as before, for the facility to let the professors back in to cultivate our new community. Again, we were reminded of how good things in these places are rarely allowed to come back once they've left.

During those early classes I formed a friendship with Chris Cabrera, a genius young artist with whom I shared similar lofty aspirations for both our work and our lives. We spent hours conversing and arguing over the creative and intellectual visions we had. I would sit with him in his cell while he sketched complex, dark images. There were always people around remarking on how impressed they were with his work. His room was a mess of books, easels, in-progress paintings, and stacks of canvases wherever he could make them fit. Cabrera would shout these big, abstract rhetorical questions at me, one after another, as we tried to figure out what so many more years as artists in prison would look like without fundamental change. We argued whether art was enough to free us, and to what extent we might go to make our dreams reality—or if it would even make a difference in a system that had pretty much always disregarded our work and our humanity. In the end, I think we agreed that neither of us wanted to disappear without the chance for our work to be realized, or at least the chance for it to be recognized and embraced by the people about whom we cared most. Chris envisioned an ongoing writing program facilitated mostly by a collective of incarcerated writers. Ideally, it would harness resources so that it could offer writing classes and opportunities throughout a writer's incarceration. I thought it was a great idea, but our experiences with administration and abandonment in the past made me suspicious of programming in these places. I wanted to publish and to have a career, even if it had to be behind these walls. I was working on a book project and was constantly worried something administrative would mess it up. We both argued that a collective couldn't work unless we were ultimately reconnected to the greater, free-world literary community to which we had very little introduction. It was lofty thinking for guys who had sparse writing credits between them, and who really had no formal writing instruction outside an early creative writing course. Our experiences with Dr. Appleman, though, had empowered much of our thinking. Why not think big? Another writer from our community and I had just won PEN Prison Writing Awards. Why shouldn't we believe our work and our community had a right to be cultivated?

It was from these conversations that the Stillwater Writers' Collective (SWC) was born, out of an agreement that our power was as a community, and a realization that if we didn't support each other, who would? We also realized that it was hard to get our peers, even when they are threatened, to write when there aren't instructors to read and validate their work. Historically, there just hadn't been enough support or success in our prison system to warrant that kind of confidence.

The SWC was also created because our small cohort agreed that, at some point, someone or something was going to come along with opportunities that we had been waiting for throughout the long stretches of our collective incarcerations. There was agreement that as a community we would need to be ready so that the blessing we felt was supposed to be ours wouldn't get passed along to somebody else. We believed it would be a crime for the story of writing in the Minnesota state prison system to be told, or written, without us. Just as the foundations of these old structures had been laid by the hands of the imprisoned, we were trying to lay a new literary and intellectual foundation. We were fortunate to have the support we needed from our then-education director, who introduced Jen Bowen and MPWW to us, and whose own vision made for an ideal partnership for the community at Stillwater, and throughout the state, to grow into what it has.

Most of us on the editorial board of this project recognize how exceptional it is to have the opportunities MPWW provides. It affords us agency in our work that most incarcerated writing communities in the country do not share. Writing communities have and do exist in other prison systems that don't have the same kind of programming infrastructure that we have in Minnesota. Ever since human beings began using confinement as a means to control other human beings, there have been writers imprisoned. Writers have risked their safety and their futures to find ways to sneak their words out into the world. The written word matters. Just as likely—and for just as long—writing and intellectual communities have existed in those spaces. Just like we did, artists will always find each other. It's like a law of nature—if you put a thousand people in a single space, the artists, even with their own divergent energies, will gravitate toward each other.

Time in the life of a writer, or a prisoner, is an emergency. Incarcerated writing communities provide for us what we can only assume they offer to non-incarcerated writing communities: peer support, friendship, competition, rivalry, and shared stakes in the success of their members. These communities offer reminders of time and the emergencies time represents. Classes get canceled and cut. In 2005, our whole education department shut down for months and every computer in the joint was wiped and scoured. Stories, essays, poetry, and even an anthology of our work disappeared from the universe. There are lockdowns, seizures of materials, intentionally, and sometimes collaterally. There are surprise transfers that leave us without computer access, and we must figure out how to keep the things we need most. We, who are working hard to mend some of the wounds in the social and familial fabric of our lives, live with a stopwatch to create evidence that will show something redemptive within us.

I published my first memoir after seventeen years in prison with the support of my small but unified family unit. Less than a year later, my mom passed away. She was my last living blood relative. Deadlines, story and book completions fulfill the need to have whole pieces of writing that can speak for the incomplete parts of our lives and families. They are our main emergency.

We build community because we can't expect, demand, or control the machinations of the captivity business. Likewise, we can't be sure that the politics of confinement will provide the spiritual and artistic resources we need to transcend our encagements. These collectives are our expression of both community and art. They provide our agency. The carceral state will not feed the kind of hunger an artist in these kinds of places experiences. So, we find ways to feed each other. There is a ceiling to the kinds of programming corrections provides, and this includes education. A member of the collective (and this editorial board) connected me with the right people to be able to finish my bachelor's in English when the prison system was unable to help me. Most of the computer labs in the system were originally proposed, and in many cases set up, by members of our community who knew their value. There is a constant nourishing in the books and magazines we pass around. There are the friendships—the several successions where one member will encourage the work of a newer writer to keep revising, because they see the genuine value, and then, later, they see these stories win awards or find publication in reputable journals. There are also the rivalries, so strong and ingrained into the history of collectives. They have driven some to become the writers they were never sure they were supposed to become. We join forces because individually we are writers and poets and artists, but collectively we are power and possibility and refutation of the hypocrisy of the carceral complex.

Does your life matter? Does your art matter? I hope so. I know that I could never rely on an ever-constricting prison system at a pivot point of mass incarceration to answer these questions for me.

In so many ways, prisons are secrets hidden from the rest of the world. Society has always hidden its most disturbing transgressions. Yet, culture still matters in these hidden spaces. We, the incarcerated, are the caretakers of it. If a prison is old enough, it remembers the prisoners that quarried the granite for its walls, or laid the bricks for its cell blocks that we have spent a century inhabiting. The incarcerated have always been more expendable than the buildings that house us, but our ideas echo long after we have left our initials scratched into old slabs of inmate-laid concrete, or scribbled on the walls of holding tanks. The state may maintain the institutions, but we nurture the culture, always—we, the artists, students, musicians, and writers. Prison writing communities are proof of a force stronger than single unread poems or stories. They are proof that there are more of us coming!

There is great significance to a panel of incarcerated writers editing an anthology on the precarious class in 2023. We, the editors, are the same population who have been tweaking and revising our work so that our voices might gain acceptance into the journals and anthologies we've hoped would validate our efforts. We are trying to make greater sense of our place in the larger, broader world. It matters that this is a volume edited by the imprisoned, because the history of class hasn't always been written by the powerful, but they have always been its editors. We are a group of human beings who sought out community to consolidate the power of our own work; we, the incarcerated, are editing this most recent chapter on class. As a group, we have come to understand, or have tried to understand, power and class distinctions through the ways we have, as an incarcerated community, categorized and divided ourselves. Incarceration is the extension of the same mechanisms of power and marginalization that Black, brown, queer, and impoverished human beings have been manipulated and oppressed by through the institutions of our society. We are the depository of that pipeline.

Just as the largest of corporations believed that they could drop sewage into nearby rivers, or bury our human footprint in a landfill or in a plastic swirl in the oceans, without the earth spitting its truth back at all of us, we dispose of human problems into the chasm of the penal system without confronting the socioeconomic circumstances that created the problems in the first place. The power dimensions that are at once manipulative, deceptive, and plain old mean are also cowardly and speak to the fragility of the human place in the ecosystem. We have felt for so long—and our social and economic systems support the belief—that human beings must control each other to control the world.

As a broader, new American society in the wake of a global pandemic, we've now felt the soft incarceration of being sequestered, a fear of being trapped, and a fear of catching invisible sickness with uncertain consequences. The trapped analogy is obvious. The pathologies in all forms—viral, bacterial, psycho-sociological—well, we've been passing them back and forth unknowingly for generations until we are too sick to know any better. We watched, from inside and out, as a knee pushed on a neck and the stop-clock-emergency-of-time ran out, and then, like so often in our history, we have watched the fire and the rage. We bite down because we know that the violence of taking a person's time and all their hope can't be represented in a short video clip on TV, or even elicit the flash or rage such violent taking should.

During the course of this project, our editorial board went through two cohorts—the first, pre-pandemic, totaled twelve individual editors in three separate correctional facilities while the second consisted of a much smaller concentration of editors. COVID-19 did just what time in these places does—change and complicate things further. There were expected and unexpected transfers, incongruent security priorities and lockdowns that made it impossible for our cohorts to meet, so we had to depend on individual institutions to relay memos and manuscripts. Institutions have never been known for an ability to make adjustments to benefit the humanity of their inhabitants. In the pandemic, prisons reverted to the answer they knew best—tightened security. Our project went from finding its purpose and personality to frozen indefinitely—and that continued well beyond when the rest of the world started to open and venture out again. Significant effort was made to keep up momentum, but it was extremely difficult to keep twelve humans, all separated in different carceral compartments, connected to each other and to a changing outside world. When we did come back to this work, we were without members from both cohorts and access to the entire group from Stillwater was cut off. We were left with the cohort from Faribault, with participation from a couple of transferred editors in an entirely different facility in Moose Lake. And by that time, the entire world had transformed. Editing a book about class looked, felt, and tasted exponentially different.

We are now a community that has grown up, inside and out, with so many individual careers and successes. There is a pathway for young artists who believe in their work and in their ability to live a creative life in and outside of prison cells. We are also a community that is hyper aware of its own precarity. We're here—curating, editing, and presenting a series of essays edited by twelve complicated, unique, human writers at different stages of complex lives and incarcerations, with different personal goals and philosophies of the world, working in community, and confronting and arguing over the invisible and not-so-invisible lines that shouldn't mean anything, but too often draw the borders around what we are all afforded in this lifetime. As an editorial board, we now represent twelve different voices, split between three prisons. We are made up of African American, Kenyan-born, Hmong, and, not unexpectedly, white males, unfortunately without women because of the structure of prison—except the constant steady and realistic voice of Jen Bowen, who made sure it didn't all blow up. There were plenty of voices missing from our tables as there are too many voices missing from any table when we discuss class in America.

Introduction

by Eula Biss

A little over a decade ago, the British economist Guy Standing identified a growing class of people he called "the precariat."[1] The defining feature of this class was, and continues to be, a lack of stability and security. Members of the precariat cannot feel confident in ongoing work, housing, or bodily safety. Their lives are dominated by uncertainty.

This is not a tiny class, not anywhere near as small as the top 1 percent who hold 30 percent of this nation's wealth, or the top 10 percent who hold 45 percent of the real estate. At least a quarter of the population of many countries belongs to the precariat. In his 2011 book *The Precariat,* Standing made his claims before a global pandemic brought greater uncertainty to more lives.

This class, the precariat, represents the most vulnerable among us, and the most criminalized. The precariat is not the equivalent of what we used to call the working class. That antiquated term belongs to a society, as Standing writes, "consisting mostly of workers in long-term, stable, fixed-hour jobs with established routes of advancement, subject to unionization and collective agreements, with job titles their fathers and mothers would have understood, facing local employers whose names and features they were familiar with."

That kind of work, and that kind of stability, is increasingly rare. More common now is the gig work described by the anonymous delivery driver whose essay is included in this anthology—work with no set hours and no potential for advancement, work done through the interface of an app by workers who don't know the people for whom they're working. These workers absorb all the risks of riding bicycles through the streets of New York, for example, to pick up items that might be out of stock, in which case they won't be paid for their trouble.

Like many essential workers, gig workers tend to have low incomes, but it's their exposure to risk that locates them in the precariat. The

---

1 Guy Standing, *The Precariat: The New Dangerous Class* (New York: Bloomsbury, 2011).

precariat is not an income bracket per se, as this anthology so bril-
liantly illustrates. Precarity may intersect with poverty, but poverty is
not the only condition that produces precarity. The American precariat
includes Ivy League students and convicts, artists and refugees, people
who own houses and people who live at rest stops along the highway.

This book gives voice to a precariat that cuts across conventional
notions of class, which, particularly in America, tend to be both sentimental and inaccurate. Our politicians routinely evoke the working
class of another era and address themselves to a middle class so poorly
defined that the term is meaningless. Barack Obama's 2012 definition of the middle class included any household making less than
$250,000. Congress later expanded that to any household making less
than $450,000, which was all but the top 1 percent of earners in this
country. Meanwhile, 40 percent of Americans would struggle to pay
an unexpected expense of $400.[2]

Kristin Collier's essay exposes what hides behind many middle-
class salaries—enormous debt. In this essay, a teacher with a college
degree, and who works days, nights, and weekends, is still unable to
pay off the student loans that were taken out in her name but not used
for her education. She leads a life that is technically middle-class, but
marked by precarity and bankruptcy.

Then there is Jose Luis Razo, the subject of Michael Torres's essay.
Razo comes from a Mexican immigrant family and was accepted to
Harvard on a scholarship. He had gained admission to an exclusive
institution, but he still felt excluded, and he ends up in prison, on
the other side of someone else's laugh track. Precarity loops and
spirals, with one form of insecurity leading to another. Defying
gender norms can be more difficult and dangerous if you don't have
money, as Alice Paige argues in her essay, and openly defying gender
norms can make it harder for a person to earn money. The stresses of

---

2 Amy Brundage, "Extending Middle Class Tax Cuts for 98% of Americans and
97% of Small Businesses," National Archives and Records Administration, July 9, 2012,
https://obamawhitehouse.archives.gov/blog/2012/07/09/extending-middle-class-tax
-cuts-98-americans-and-97-small-businesses.

precarity can lead to mental illness, and mental illness can make a life more precarious.

Where did this cycle begin? What produced the precariat? One answer would be the economic and social policies of the late twentieth century. This is how Standing tells the story: "In the 1970s, a group of ideologically inspired economists captured the ears and minds of politicians. The central plank of their 'neo-liberal' model was that growth and development depended on market competitiveness; everything should be done to maximize competition and competitiveness, and to allow market principles to permeate all aspects of life."

Yet, in the wealthiest nation in the world, the wealthiest ever in human history, many people lead lives that are unstable and insecure. Security is not a right in this society; it is a commodity, something that must be bought, though not everyone with money can buy it. Security is sold piecemeal, with its availability determined by the fluctuations of various markets including the housing market, the health insurance market, and the investment market on which most retirement savings depend.

This is all a continuation of a much older story, a parable of exclusion. As Standing observes, many members of the precariat do not enjoy the full benefits of citizenship. This makes them more like denizens than citizens. In ancient Rome, denizens were granted the right to work, but not the right to participate in political life. In medieval Europe, denizens were resident aliens, granted some but not all the rights of native citizens. In the antebellum United States, denizens were free Blacks, non-citizens in the country of their birth.

A Black man today might go out for a fish fillet, as in Kiese Laymon's essay, and find himself the subject of a police state, under threat of arrest for having caught the eye of the wrong cop. He is permanently on parole in the state where he lives and at the school he attends, permanently at risk of having his rights revoked, of having his enrollment suspended.

Many members of the precariat are disproportionately denied the right to vote. In some cases this is because they are not citizens of the country where they live and work. Some are migrants, including refugees and asylum seekers. Others are citizens on paper, but cannot vote because they have been convicted of a crime, or because their vote is obstructed by laws designed for that purpose.

All this leads, inevitably, to a "thinning of democracy," as Standing puts it. The more people belong to the precariat, the fewer vote, and our elected officials increasingly represent the interests of a monied minority. All of us suffer the effects of this thinning, citizens and denizens alike. And all of us, at some point in our lives, may find ourselves living lives dominated by precarity. Many members of the precariat were not born into it. Some entered through a disability brought on by old age, others entered through illness, or unplanned pregnancy, divorce, war, or natural disaster. It is possible to be living comfortably in a house with fruit trees in the yard one day, as Lacy M. Johnson's essay reminds us, and the next day to be huddled in the cold, with no water or electricity, the pipes bursting, the ceiling buckling, and the fruit trees dead. "The precariat is not victim, villain or hero," Standing writes. "It is just a lot of us."

A Note on Conversations

by Jennifer Bowen

This collection was compiled and edited by writers who have devoted their lives to the written word for over a decade, and whose prison sentences range from twelve years to life. These artists, despite their talent and devotion, rank among the most precarious of America's citizens. While incarcerated, they do not have the right to vote. The state, to which they are legal property, takes a portion of their earnings, which average fifty cents an hour. It is not up to these artists what they eat or even when they do so. And so, as you might expect, while they created this book about the precariat, their conversations about instability rang with insight. I know this because I sat in the room with them for every single meeting, per DOC policy.

Each essay in this book sparked conversations that meandered and maddened, energized and exhausted us. We are, after all, in the middle of what Guy Standing calls "a global transformation," and the shattering that comes with such a shift. Make no mistake, such shifts are felt in prison too. These editors' perspectives are thoughtful and challenging, but too often—it must be said—invisible by design. And so, we decided to record them. They're shared between the pages of these essays with humility.

This project spans three years, many facility transfers, constant lockdowns, segregation, and a global pandemic. Every editor involved had COVID twice; one was hospitalized. One was badly injured on the yard. Six family members died. Toward the end, but still in the middle of a pandemic and lockdown, one of the three facilities granted me physical access, and the editors the ability to gather. Those are the editors you see in conversation through this book: Chris, Will, Kennedy, Warren, and David. Zeke, who wrote the foreword, was released just before the recording started, but after years spent building this book and the arts community. Add to the mix Ruby, our intern, who helped transcribe and edit these conversations, and who showed up with a young person's perspective, just when we needed it.

Though you'll miss the funny, wise, thoughtful, macabre, resigned, humble voices of Bino, Jeff, B, Red, Fong, and Von, they shaped the anthology from the first day, and, when possible, through PDFs that resembled smeared mascara. Their brilliance, artistry, and integrity lives in this book even if their stated opinions do not.

Space to talk about change, solidarity, suffering, and beauty, with community and among friends, is rare *anywhere,* including prison, and yet it's one of the only things in fractured times that keeps us whole, and helps us heal. Our conscious goal was never to dissect the essays, but to share what grew in one shared space after reading the authors' words, and by extension, what maybe grows from all art. We hope our talks—edited for length and clarity—stimulate your own conversations, joining minds and voices rarely heard from the inside, with you, wherever you are.

AMERICAN PRECARIAT

Piñatas

by Michael Torres

Jose Luis Razo Jr. is a name I'm reaching back for from the end of the 1980s. I want you to have it, though I don't know what you'll do with it. I'm not even sure what to do with it. Still, his name sits with me, as it has for a while. *Jose Luis Razo Jr.* As if he's a homie I haven't talked to in years but whom I would call to if I saw in a crowd of people.

Here's what you should know. Jose Luis Razo Jr. grew up in a hard-working, blue-collar Mexican immigrant family in the southern California of the 1970s and '80s. He was a great student, volunteered in his community, and was offered scholarships to attend Columbia and Harvard. Sounds good, right? His mother told him that Harvard symbolized the American Dream. So, he chose Harvard. Jose Luis was one of about thirty-five Latinx students in his freshman class. Then, while visiting home on spring break that first year, Jose Luis robbed several fast-food restaurants. Later, he would confess to the crimes, be found guilty, and go to prison.

✤✤✤

I once wrote for my undergraduate university's Latinx newspaper. It happened when I first transferred to the University of California-Riverside, after seven years at community college. I only wrote two articles. One of the reasons I wrote anything for them was because I knew no one at the school except for a third cousin who ran the paper. The other reason—I wanted to be involved in anything related to the Mexican side of my Mexican-Americanness. I think that's what happens to a lot of students of color who enter higher education—they wonder where everyone who looks like them went.

✤✤✤

On the news, reporters called Jose Luis Razo Jr. "The Harvard Homeboy." It was catchy, and perhaps the alliteration put the audience at ease. It seems to create a sort of box inside of which to place him. Close the box, move it to the corner of the room, and you forget it's there. You can stack the rest of history above it, around it.

As quoted in a *New York Times* article after his arrest, Jose Luis's mother spoke about her son's experience at Harvard, saying, "He said that he felt so guilty knowing that he had everything and his family had nothing . . . I told him there was plenty of time for the family, and not to worry. But he was so lonely back there."[1]

⁜⁜⁜

In the 1950s, Charles Douglass was tasked with creating a sense of community. Because TV producers were looking for a successful way to smooth audiences' transition from live performances to their television sets at home, Douglass went to work on what would become known as the Laff Box. Similar to what radio programs had done with laugh tracks, Douglass recorded hundreds of laughs and built a machine about the size and shape of a blue USPS mailbox with a sort of typewriter keyboard on top that, when engaged, would produce a given laugh. You could play so many laughs at once. He even installed a pedal to fade laughter in and out.[2]

All those ways to articulate humor, to turn people toward the belief that something's funny.

⁜⁜⁜

In college, after I'd made a few friends, my theater professor invited a few students to see a performance of Luis Valdez's *I Don't Have to Show You No Stinking Badges!*, which hadn't been performed in Los Angeles in over twenty years, not since its premiere in 1986. *Badges!* is a drama about a Mexican American family, the Villas, and their struggles with assimilation and the American Dream.

1 Robert Lindsey, "Worlds in Collision: From Barrio to Harvard to Jail," *New York Times,* late edition, July 26, 1987, https://www.nytimes.com/1987/07/26/us/worlds-in -collision-from-barrio-to-harvard-to-jail.html.
2 Mike Sacks, "Conversation 5: Ben Glenn II, Television Historian and Expert on Canned Laughter," *McSweeney's,* August 18, 2009, https://www.mcsweeneys.net/articles /conversation-5-ben-glenn-ii-television-historian-and-expert-on-canned-laughter.

That night was the first time I saw someone like me, a Mexican American, portrayed onstage.

Sonny, the Villas's only son, becomes a focal point when he returns home from Harvard prelaw to pursue acting, like his parents. However, Sonny wants more than what his parents achieved—extras who were cast to play Mexican stereotypes throughout their entire careers. Sonny wants to write, direct, and star in his own films. *Badges!* takes a turn when Sonny desires a taste of "real life" as a Mexican American and decides to take his father's gun and rob a fast-food restaurant. He wants real-life experience. In turning away from the embarrassment he feels for his parents, who played housemaids and gardeners, Sonny embraces yet another stereotype: the Mexican American gang member. What resonated with me the most was a brief moment of admission of the loneliness Sonny felt attending Harvard, and the adjustments that he couldn't make that led him to these actions.

After the play was over and I went home, I kept thinking about Sonny. Days later, I found an article where, in discussing *Badges!*, Luis Valdez mentions how "life imitated art . . . when a young Chicano named Jose Luis Razo Jr. was arrested for holding up a fast-food restaurant, much like the Chicano character of Sonny Villa in my play."[3]

✛ ✛ ✛

In his essay "Always and Forever: On Being a Brown Body in a Red State," Ángel García explores how his presence becomes magnified in the white Midwest of Nebraska he moved to for school. How unsafe and (un)seen he feels walking around, especially when he compares it to his upbringing in a diverse southern California community. Near the essay's end, García remembers Anthony, a fifth-grade classmate who would jokingly say, "It's 'cause I'm Mexican, huh?" after being called out or called to read in front of the class. The children would laugh, García recalls. I agree with what García says, that Anthony is

---

3 "'I Don't Have to Show You No Stinking Badges' on Stage in Boyle Heights," *The Rafu Shimpo*, February 15, 2013, https://rafu.com/2013/02/i-dont-have-to-show-you-no-stinking-badges-on-stage-in-boyle-heights/.

"making sense of his reality." The boy's reaction is a sad showing of hands. In his own childish way, Anthony is acknowledging the self, as it's perceived in the United States, which, ultimately, is how he must also understand himself, and not in some small way. Laughter is a last resort, a sort of plea.

✢✢✢

From the 1987 article "From Barrio to Harvard to Jail" featured in the *New York Times:* "several [people] noticed that [Jose Luis Razo Jr.] became increasingly preoccupied with his Mexican heritage and angered when other students sometimes jokingly called him a 'wetback.'"[4]

✢✢✢

In "Laughing Together?: TV Comedy Audiences and the Laugh Track," Inger-Lise Kalviknes Bore explains that laughter is capable of two things: first, of offering "individual viewers a sense that 'we' are all watching and laughing at the program together, as a collective audience"; second, of ensuring "that comedy feels like a 'safe' space where it is okay to laugh at people's misfortunes or transgressions. In this way, viewers are reassured that everything is just a joke, and we are all laughing together."

✢✢✢

I refuse to call him the Harvard Homeboy.

✢✢✢

The Laff Box stayed with Douglass at all times. He made it a family business. I can picture Douglass arriving at the studio during or in postproduction with his small team of employees, the Laff Box being pulled on a dolly behind him. In a *Slate* article "The Man Who Perfected the Laugh Track," Willa Paskin, in talking about Douglass's crafting of laughter, says, Douglass "played his Laff Box like it was

---

4 Lindsey, "Worlds in Collision."

an instrument." Paskin describes laughter from the *MASH* pilot and Douglass's expertise:

> I especially love the laugh that trails off at the end. It tells a story. There's a joke, but one guy in the audience doesn't get it right away. He's a split second late, and then he laughs a little bit longer. Charlie Douglass wasn't just a sound engineer; he was a psychologist.[5]

I think that I'm trying to find reasons to hate Douglass. I want to blame someone for making the idea of a Mexican something just funny or at least not serious. I want to fight Charlie Douglass but he's dead. God rest his soul. I want to fight his son, who now owns his deceased father's laugh track company, Northridge Electronics. In my research of Douglass, I discovered that he was actually a Mexican-born American. I wanted to call him a traitor and be done with it.

✛ ✛ ✛

In an *LA Times* article from 1989, after his arrest, Jose Luis is quoted saying, "I am a homeboy now. I don't sell out my own ethnic identity."[6]

I'd never thought about a homeboy as a type of ethnic identity. I guess it could be. It's always seemed too narrow a category to be its own ethnicity, so difficult to describe to someone outside of the culture. Maybe that's not the point—what someone else wonders. I always associated myself with being Mexican, perhaps much like Anthony. Mexican was whatever I was, because that's what I knew, that's what I was told, whether that was a reason to take pride or to laugh.

✛ ✛ ✛

---

5 Willa Paskin, "The Man Who Perfected the Laugh Track," *Slate,* April 30, 2018, https://slate.com/culture/2018/04/charlie-douglass-and-his-laff-box-invented-the -laugh-track-as-we-know-it.html.

6 Bob Schwartz, "Ex-Harvard Student Faces Trial: La Habra 'Homeboy': 'Why' Still Baffles," *Los Angeles Times,* March 5, 1989, https://www.latimes.com/archives/la-xpm -1989-03-05-mn-615-story.html.

In a promotional video uploaded to the YouTube channel of Casa 0101—the playhouse that staged the *Badges!* performance I saw— there's a clip of the show that begins and ends with laughter, as if the show were a comedy, and I wonder now if the play was actually funnier than I remember. Or if there's something I missed. Or if its impression cast a more serious light in my mind.

✛ ✛ ✛

Jose Luis, maybe, like me, you wondered where all your homeboys were on your first day at the college.

Here's what I want to say. The first week of school, outside a building, waiting for my next class, I stood and watched small circles of friends gather. And I wanted to know, in that moment, how they did it: how so many friends got into any college, let alone the same college. And how they arrived at a sense of belonging that emanated from them.

On lunch break that week, knowing no one, I sat on a bench near the transfer office—the only building I was familiar with. I watched people pass. I looked down at my food. I thought about Friday afternoon, after my last class, and about being around my homies, who were all at work then. Where would we go out? Really, I thought of not having to talk about school. Later, as the weeks passed and classwork began to pile up, I canceled nights with them, told them I had to study. And in this way, I told them, without telling them, that I believed there were more important things waiting for me on campus.

Jose Luis, I want to know if this means we are together in how we had to grasp being lonesome?—in the fact that we felt the choice was a binary—higher ed or the homies?

I wanted to take every Chicano Studies special topics course, just for answers, or perhaps as a way to stay connected. In one, I remember the textbook: *Critical Race Counterstories along the Chicana/Chicano Educational Pipeline* by Tara J. Yosso. Early in the text was a chart to illustrate the Chicanx education pipeline statistics from the start of the twenty-first century. The pipe-work-styled chart begins with one hundred Chicanx students on their educational path. It states that

"54 drop out of high school and 44 continue on to graduate." I traced my journey through the pipeline. Out of 100 students, I was going to be 1 of 7 to graduate with a bachelor's degree. At the time, not knowing I would move to Minnesota for a master's in fine arts, I wondered, of the 1 of 2 to earn a graduate degree, which I would be.

I scanned and made copies of the chart, gave them to people I knew; I kept one behind the plastic cover of my binder. I'm looking in that textbook right now.

✢ ✢ ✢

In another article, written by Razo's friend and former Harvard peer in 1989, Ruben Navarrette Jr. seeks an explanation for the unraveling of Razo Jr. but only finds that, "Psychologists offer simplistic theories about self-destructive 'sun children'—bright minority students who excel beyond expectation and then turn away from the guiding light of success to burn out like a shooting star."[7]

If what we're told about ourselves is a type of light, then perhaps laughter is its intensity. I think of Anthony, who wanted his classmates to laugh *with* him, not *at* him, and so redirected the spotlight's intensity. It's not enough to know that Jose Luis burned out. Here is his name—Jose Luis Razo Jr.—and I want it to mean more. I want it to have another chance out in the world.

✢ ✢ ✢

In the early 2000s, social psychologists in Australia wanted to learn more about how people interpret and react to canned laughter in relation to social influence. They believed that a person wouldn't laugh along with the laugh track if the one listening perceived the recorded laughter to be coming from an audience whose views differed from their own, or was from what they called an "out-group." The researchers thought someone would be less inclined to join in if the group

---

7 Ruben Navarrette Jr., "Harvard Homeboy: A Chicano on the Fast Track Now Heads for Prison," *Los Angeles Times,* August 5, 1989, https://www.latimes.com/archives/la-xpm-1989-08-05-me-337-story.html.

laughing was not recognized as from within their own social group, or the "in-group."[8]

✛ ✛ ✛

After watching that Casa 0101 YouTube video, I decided to revisit *Badges!* by reading it for the first time. I learned how much I didn't remember or understand from being in the audience that night. Noted in the script: "The entire set sits within the confines of a TV studio" as if for a "live studio audience at a taping."[9] I didn't remember there being a prologue and epilogue that featured the voiceover of a director character. I just remember Sonny, and how the entire time he seemed so close to losing his sanity, and how I was right there with him.

✛ ✛ ✛

In 2011, Charlie Douglass's Laff Box was appraised for $10,000 on an episode of *Antiques Roadshow.* In the clip I found online, after host Gary Sohmers tries to explain the Laff Box's significance—pointing out the shows Douglass worked on, such as *Cheers*—the seller, a Latino man says, "I don't know some of these shows," and laughs nervously. Sohmers responds, "They're historical, important shows." But throughout this scene, the brown man only nods, only offers, "Okay." He just wants to know how much he can make off this storage unit find. He's wearing an off-white button-up and jeans, and keeps his hands in his pockets. He looks like the husband of one of my homie's older sisters. The clip ends with both host and seller pressing keys on the Laff Box. A laughter plays in celebration of the appraisal.[10]

---

8 Michael J. Platow, S. Alexander Haslam, Amanda Both, Ivanne Chew, Michelle Cuddon, Nahal Goharpey, Jacqui Maurer, Simone Rosini, Anna Tsekouras, and Diana M. Grace, "'It's Not Funny If They're Laughing': Self-categorization, Social Influence, and Responses to Canned Laughter," *Journal of Experimental Social Psychology* 41, no. 5 (September 2005): 542–550.

9 Luis Valdez, *Zoot Suit and Other Plays* (Houston, TX: Arte Publico Press, 1992).

10 *Antiques Roadshow,* "San Diego Part 2," PBS video, 53:54, January 31, 2011, https://www.pbs.org/wgbh/roadshow/season/15/san-diego-ca/appraisals/1953-charlie-douglass-laff-box--201001A13/.

✤✤✤

I can't stop imagining an audience laughing at something I don't find funny, me there, being twisted into belief, having to adopt different ears.

✤✤✤

There's a moment in Act 2, Scene 2 where Sonny, who's evading police after the robbery, seemingly on the brink of a mental breakdown, questions his reality. He speaks to his girlfriend Anita, saying, "You can almost imagine a studio audience out there . . . sitting, watching, waiting to laugh at this cheap imitation of Anglo life. Superficial innocuous bullshit that has to conceal its humorless emptiness with canned laughter." Then the stage directions read, "(SFX We hear more police cars coming up, sirens blowing. Street sounds, traffic, voices of men. Then canned laughter.)" Sonny then says, "¿Órale? Did you hear that?" He is, however, the only one who can hear the laughter.[11]

✤✤✤

This is a silly story, so silly I don't know why I remember it, nor why I'm telling you, but it's on my mind right now. That first fall I was living in Minnesota, there was a birthday party for the girlfriend of a friend I'd made in my cohort. She was Dominican American and my friend was white. Whenever all of us hung out, I would notice that she and I were almost always the only two people of color in the room. For her birthday celebration, I volunteered to buy a piñata at the town's only party store.

At the store, I picked one out that looked like a red chili pepper, thinking it was on sale for ten dollars. The teenage cashier told me it cost fourteen. I remember she didn't look up at me to say this. I remember having the sense of being condescended to, however irrational that feeling might've been. I was certain that if I wanted to buy

---

11 Valdez, *Zoot Suit and Other Plays.*

back this bit of my culture (despite the fact of its appropriation into white, American culture) she would make me pay full price.

I turned around and walked back to the birthday party aisle looking for another piñata. I picked one that looked like a sombrero. Something about this one made me laugh, or I told myself to.

Back at the register with the sombrero, the worker explained that that one was fourteen as well. I don't know what I said but I bought the sombrero piñata anyway, walked out, and threw it in the back seat of my truck and drove back to my apartment.

That night, hours after coming home from the party store, and when it had gotten dark out, I walked outside to retrieve the sombrero from the back seat.

�֎ ֎ ֎

Jose Luis, I want to know if there was a laugh track playing over you. Maybe what I seek to know is if you, too, imagined always being watched, if you imagined yourself a performer. If there was a spotlight there, its hot glow burning a loop over you. Maybe I'm talking about how lonely academia makes us. Maybe all these things are obvious, but saying them here makes them less, somehow. Or, at least for me, that I can make the memory of that loneliness less powerful by remembering you.

✖ ✖ ✖

Researchers in the Australian laugh track study asked twenty-seven La Trobe University students to listen to audiotapes of comedy sketches. Half were labeled "La Trobe University" while the other half were labeled "One Nation Party," a political party with which researchers found La Trobe students didn't identify. The results were what the researchers' hypothesized.

> Participants' overt smiling and laughter . . . were greater only in response to hearing in-group laughter . . . the laughter of our participants, in response to an audience's laughter, was not an automatic, thoughtless process . . . people actively attend to who is

laughing, and laugh a lot themselves only when they have heard fellow in-group members laughing.[12]

It is not important who owns the laughter but rather, who owns the rented-out silence around it, which you, the audience, the reader, inhabit, and what you do with that silence, which is a sort of prompting. The inevitable question laughter presents—laugh along? Or be illuminated in the disparity it presents?

✛✛✛

Every so often, on *Latinos Who Lunch,* a podcast that "discusses everything from pop culture and art to issues of race, gender, and class in Latinx communities,"[13] hosts FavyFav and Babelito, answer listener letter questions. During these episodes—which are among my favorites—there's at least one question-asker pondering their own Latinx identity. Usually, they want advice about how to be more Latinx, but in a way that's authentic and real.

And each time, in this podcast that I've come to appreciate for how honest and funny it is, FavyFav and Babelito talk their shit before ultimately advising the listener not to worry about what Latinx identity, as a whole, looks like. "There's not a wrong way to perform your Latinidad," I've heard FavyFav say. Both of them want us, their imagined Latinx listeners, their audience, to consider our cultural/ethnic identities in specificity, through personal experience, which could in turn add a facet to the whole, and thus disrupt the stereotype. Sometimes, while running the neighborhoods of vastly white southern Minnesota, I think, "No one would guess what I'm listening to."

✛✛✛

The simultaneity of me. Inside here: the Moreno boys from down the street who all wore Pumas through grade school. And Gerardo in

---

12 Platow et al., "'It's Not Funny If They're Laughing.'"
13 "About," Latinos Who Lunch, accessed February, 14, 2023, http://www.latinoswho lunch.com/#band-section.

eighth grade whose black windbreaker read Adiaas instead. Do I read his name "Hair-are-doe" or "Jerr-are-doe." The phrase, "this foo." Your homie with the clippers, giving fades in his front yard. Lowrider bikes but Gt Dynos as well. A Mongoose painted to match the sky. Okay, yes, fuck it: aspirations to own a Pendleton. Cortezes when you're a kid until your tia tells your mom they're for cholos. Chile y limón on everything. The word *y*. All the pride and embarrassment wrapped in the Spanish language. Witnessing the loud italics of the language everyone thinks you know. Boxing in the street with gloves, but also your subscription to *Disney Adventures* magazine. Building skate ramps. Burning shit. Powder from the Piccolo Pete placed in a sandwich bag and set in an empty two-liter. The fuse lit. All the brown kids running behind cars. A schoolyard game called suicide that all the boys who wanted to be tough played during recess in fifth and sixth grade.

The one white boy on the block who had A/C and a swimming pool. The impossibility of your identity in a vacuum, and thus its development as a result of what you're in proximity to.

The Black kids who rolled with you. RJ and his brothers. And the Black kids you didn't really know. The ones who followed you and your homie home after school in eleventh grade because earlier in the day they had jumped your homie's little brother, failing to find your homie first. Because the day before that, whatever your homie did to one of them he didn't talk about, and you didn't care to ask.

The rottweilers you had growing up, and the Disney character names you gave them. A framed photo of you that hangs in the living room wall, the one where you're on a donkey, crying. And next to it, a picture of your grandparents, young, in love, and still alive. And below that, an end table where your grandfather's American flag sits folded into a triangle-shaped wooden box.

All the accent marks you forget or don't know the directions in which they settle. All the times you're not forgiven for not knowing Spanish, for not saying hello, for not shaking hands. Corridos y cumbias. And hip-hop. Fuck it. Modelo y Corona. But Bud Light too. House parties and the homies. Studying for the SATs. Not studying for the SATs. All the graffiti names you remember. The word *homegirl.* The homegirl you liked but didn't know how to start a conversation with. A silver chain and your sweaty palms. A Brenton Wood *Best of.* Bike pegs and hopping fences.

Fold-open tables and chairs rented from the señora down the street who gave you a good deal. The castle-style jumper her husband and son delivered. The taco man. The clown who paints faces but who also keeps masks of former presidents to use during his show. Everyone laughing. The piñata the birthday girl takes a photo with. A line of kids like kernels, popping. Broom handle and blindfold. Adults counting to five. The rough yellow rope and someone on the roof yanking too hard. The piñata all pendulum, about to tear from the wire.

✦ ✦ ✦

What's on the other side?—if I surrender all this?

✦ ✦ ✦

The week before I left California for Minnesota, my homies came over to see me off. I stood on the bed of my truck, fixing boxes in the bed, when one of my homies joked from below, chanting *Speech! Speech!* We all laughed for a moment.

✦ ✦ ✦

In Minnesota, I spend a lot of time running. I learned disappointment about *Latinos Who Lunch* through a sci-fi story podcast I listened to during a couple of morning runs. I liked the premise: in a distant future, a crew of space travelers are on a mission to save another crew who'd lost contact with everyone after crash-landing on a mysterious planet weeks before. However, after a few episodes of not being able to distinguish characters' voices, I wondered why there weren't characters who sounded like from where I grew up. Not even in this imagined, futuristic world, could I hear anyone like me. No Spanglish, no hood shit, no slang. Everyone's voices sounded like how I imagined voices on radio shows from the '50s probably sounded like.

✦ ✦ ✦

I did, after all, give a speech that day loading my truck. Rather, I thanked the homies. Told them how lucky I was to have them as homies despite the fact that I hadn't been around much over the last few years and had missed birthday parties, holidays, and backyard BBQ gatherings. I knew I could not close whatever gap—which took me years to realize—that academia had wedged between us. But I wanted to let them know that I was aware of its existence and persistence. The least I could do, I thought, was recognize the rupture.

✢✢✢

Jose Luis, sometimes I like to think we would've been homies if the timing was right, that we would've found each other in a Chicano Studies class. But I don't know. Your classmate, Ruben, who wrote about you in the *Times,* can't stop thinking about the diverging paths you both had, how easily he can swap your respective futures.

✢✢✢

The fact that there's always a statistic for us to be a part of.

✢✢✢

I want to say something about the endurance expected of us.

✢✢✢

I am simultaneously disturbed by the gauntlet of higher education and proud to have overcome its challenges. All of this bothers me.

✢✢✢

I wanted to tell you a story about a brown man in college, who fell away, who was dismissed. I wanted to tell you his name. I wanted Jose Luis to remain there, in the mind—mine, yours—precious, somehow. Is it enough to give you his name? Not the loneliness it's associated with, but the silence that surrounds it and the opportunity to fill that silence.

✢✢✢

Jose Luis, I don't want to be afraid to remember your name forever—
the kind of light it catches. In another article, one of the many I've
read over and over, it mentions the tattoos you had done. Everything
you loved, everything carved from isolation: *Razo. La Habra.*

✛ ✛ ✛

What Valdez leaves the audience with are more questions than answers.
Responsibility. In the introduction for the book that includes *Badges!,*
Jorge Huerta says the play "does not give a distinct ending, but rather,
leaves the solution up to the audience members to decide."[14] All of it—
the robbery, the returning home after quitting Harvard, the desire
to be a movie star—could be coming from Sonny's mind. Or, the
play could be the pilot for Sonny's sitcom. We, the audience, might
be there for a taping. We (I) must decide if the sombrero-shaped fly-
ing saucer Sonny's father Buddy imagines at the beginning of the play
is real when it returns at the end to beam up Sonny and Anita. Does
this happen? Or is this all dreamed up? Are there Latinx space travelers after all?

✛ ✛ ✛

Nowadays there are various sets of laugh tracks for the purpose of
serving different countries and cultural groups. But when I think of
what I grew up on—all those syndicated shows of white families, and
their white lives, and their white jokes, that I learned to laugh at and
feel for—I think of a screw being turned to fit into place. Assimilation
and something larger than me at work. A machine. Douglass pressing
down on the keyboard. All the corners in which I searched for someone who looked or sounded like me. The feeling of being observed.
Thinking, seeing, believing someone was there to make sure I learned
what to find funny.

✛ ✛ ✛

---

14 Jorge Huerta, Introduction to *Zoot Suit and Other Plays,* by Luis Valdez (Houston,
TX: Arte Publico Press, 1992).

The summer between tenth and eleventh grade, my homie Miguel Diaz moved from down the street to Chino Hills, the next town over. His father had worked up to management at a *fabrica* that did business with department stores, building their display cases. He made good money, became successful. After high school, Miguel and his brother would both work for their father full-time and for many years. Even my homie Jesse and I would work for Miguel's father the following summer, to make some money for senior-year school clothes.

How we saw Miguel's move was the way everyone else understood it—he got out of the hood.

The first time we went to visit, Miguel told us about a neighbor, this Mexican guy, who after introducing himself, gave Miguel the "Don't forget where you came from" speech. All these years later, after we've all taken jobs and moved away to start our own families and ways of life in different cities, I've never forgotten about this conversation, despite only receiving it secondhand.

I think about how odd the rich, white neighborhood must've seemed to this Mexican man before Miguel and his family moved in. The ways in which this Mexicano became a good neighbor, despite not being able to fully be himself. What he let go of, and how excited and perhaps desperate this man was to talk to my homie, to hand off this piece of wisdom. What the old man regained. I remember that day when, Miguel pointing behind us toward his house, I saw the Mexican flag the man planted on his own porch.

✤ ✤ ✤

I haven't stopped thinking about piñatas. And if I'm not the one who pulls the tissue-paper-plastered cardboard star back into the air, then I must be the piñata itself, swinging wildly, being reached for, with everyone wanting something sweet from me to make them smile.

Piñatas: The Conversation

JEN BOWEN   I remember when we first read this essay, one of you said, "You're an outsider *everywhere* if you're in prison." And someone responded, "Every time you enter a new community, it's a process of migration."

DAVID JANISCH   Yeah, that was Will. Can you talk about the migration comment, Will? Because that was interesting to me.

WILL ANDERSON   Sure. Michael Torres described his experience in college being, you know, with a backpack, and looking around and not being one hundred percent sure where he fit. What I saw in my mind was actually the plaza right up in front of the community college, because I remember when I started taking classes there it was 2003. I'd been out of prison for the first time for a couple of years. And I went to prison literally the summer after I graduated from high school. So, all my friends went to college earlier. [When I got out] I was still college-aged, but my "education" had been in incarceration, both culturally and literally at that point. I experienced it as a kind of migration. And it's something that we all go through, but, as a culture, seem to want to push off. Every time you go into a new school, if you've moved around [for] a new job, when you move to a different town, you're in a constant state of migration. We all have that experience. It's intrinsic to motion, especially with the mobility that's in our society, not upward, mind you, but lateral mobility, geographic mobility. And then, in particular, prison is absolutely a migration. Incarceration is an experience of exile because we were citizens, and we're not now. There's a whole bunch of rights that were taken and stay taken that we never got back.

DAVID   Okay, we're experiencing a period of migration. I like that term when I'm in a new situation. It makes you wonder, though, when do you feel that you're no longer migrating? Like, "Now I'm part of the community?"

WARREN BRONSON   I've never really, you know, I've never really fit wherever—high school, military, family, prison. I've never really met any of the expectations that were there. And the part I picked up specifically from [this essay] was the role of ethnic identity and how you filter and rate that as something important in your life.

CHRIS CABRERA   I mean, prison cultures are made up mostly of minorities. Do you feel like your whiteness is spotlit?

WARREN   Well, Michael Torres was able to find a way to not really assimilate, but to keep *himself* as he fit better into the mold of the greater Upper Midwest society when he had no clue what he was walking into. And Razo, he got there and lost himself. Now, there have been times when I have just wondered, what exactly do I need to do to get myself to fit into someplace or to carry my own identity?

CHRIS   Kennedy, coming from Kenya, do you feel the same type of pressure to assimilate?

KENNEDY GISEGE   I don't think I've assimilated to anything in prison. You know, I hate prison culture. I hate the way they do things. I think you finally feel that you're no longer migrating when you're comfortable with the culture that you moved into. For example, when I came here, the first three months, I really hated broccoli. But everywhere I went, that was the easiest meal to find. Also, white women did scare me. However, you know, after about six months, you get used to them. So, there are these different levels, I think, of the comfort that you achieve after you've been in a place for very long.

DAVID   So maybe the strategy of going into a new environment is finding something that makes you comfortable.

KENNEDY   You know, back home, we have a lot of mushrooms. I think maybe because of too many dead animals out there. Yeah, but when I came to America, I really liked mushroom soup. Because back home, my grandmother used to make it a lot. I used to go out and hunt for the mushrooms. We bring them in, she cooks them. After we milked the cows back home and boiled the milk, she would always take the top cream and just use it as a spice, as the finishing touch for the mushroom. So, when I came here, without even thinking, I'd open the Campbell soup, pour it. It's the cheapest meal when you're in college. It's very safe, doesn't rot. And it's one of those things that you can't, just can't, let go. And so, there's always that reaching back. And in that sense, maybe I'm a little like the Harvard homeboy.

The hardest thing, I think, when you're in a new place, especially when you migrate alone, [is that] there is always that sense that you're a cultural orphan, and you feel it more intensely because there are some assimilations that you just can't avoid. You know, for example, when I was at the university, it was comfortable for me to be around other international students. And there was a girl from Saudi Arabia and we would go to the diners in Dinkytown for breakfast. You know, she's a strict Muslim, but she could never avoid eating bacon, no matter how much she wanted to, because no matter how many times you told the waiters, okay, "Don't let bacon touch my eggs," she knew, and we all knew, that our eggs were cooked right next to bacon. That is to me like forced assimilation into the system. And the funny thing is, and this is why I think the Laff Box might tie to this kind of thing now, you know—lives are uncomfortable, but we just laugh, and that eases everything.

WARREN   Do you think that honesty, that realization that you hold your standards a little bit differently than what, you know, what is expected around you, you think that contributes to you not really conforming, but maintaining your own standards, your own expectations, irrespective of what the society expects of you, and [do you think that] allows you to be comfortable where you are?

KENNEDY   I would think in our society, there are people that don't conform so much. And I mean, it's okay to conform for peace, but I think that when we conform too much, we forget what is better, and

I don't think that we place that over making a difference. It's the same thing we're doing in here—we are in a suffering place. But what we're doing with this anthology is trying to polish the world out there, so that it can shine a little better, maybe not for us, but for our fellow humanity that is sitting out there.

WILL   There are some things that I think I've made adaptations to, as far as acculturation from a survival standpoint, like, for literal survival. There are some things I still hate about this place, and it has surprisingly little to do with the bars, or the concrete, or the fence, or the razor wire. It has to do with the culture. I think some people work to change and evolve over time. And [there are] people who struggle to improve, to make a difference in people's lives around us, with tutors in here and health aides. Those are the jobs that we do in the facility, that I hope can make a difference. But there's a solid contingent of people who are caught in this revolving door of incarceration that is just an extension of where they came from in the world. They are super resistant to change. And they still want to do things and see things the same way that they have always seen and done them because there aren't enough opportunities for them to depart from that. I consider myself largely assimilated [here], but I don't ever forget that this isn't necessarily who I am.

DAVID   I think a person has assimilated when there's just a couple of people in their lives that they're happy to see and that are happy to see [them]. I think once you have that, even in a culture like prison, you kind of have your own subculture. I think what's challenging, what's almost scary, is when there's only one culture that has the power in the country, and you have all these other subcultures that don't have any power.

CHRIS   I think there's a difference between cultural appropriation and assimilation or belonging. You guys are all confident in your own identities enough to come into a culture. [But for Razo] there are stakes involved. So, he's going to Harvard. And he's got this inherited culture.

Where does culture come from? Most of it's an inheritance. And I love that tie with the laughter [in this essay] because I feel like laughter is not a chosen thing. Like you don't choose to laugh, right?

WILL   Unless the Laff Box is telling him to laugh?

CHRIS   Yeah, that's the argument. That's the parallel. So, your cultural identity in many ways is inherited. But then you have an option to tweak it and understand it and make choices. But with Razo, he's going into a culture and having to assimilate. When we're talking about prison culture, and assimilation, I think, what's different is that—I don't know if any of you code switch . . . ?

DAVID   Do you?

JEN   Why did you ask, Chris?

CHRIS   Because I code switch. Because I'm from the city, I'm from the suburbs, and I'm Black, Cuban, and white. So, I was raised with my white family. The white side of my family is Swedish and Irish, so I didn't have just one cultural identity, and I've never had just one cultural identity. I feel confident, but I code switch. It's [the] same thing if you see somebody that speaks the same language, you speak that same language. It's a bonding thing. And my mom used to code switch with the Cubans. She wasn't fluent in Spanish, but she'd get this heavy accent. So, I learned it from her early. So, you're taking something that you like, and you can appreciate, and you're finding that relation[ship] and it becomes yours, it becomes part of your identity. Torres was saying about higher ed or the homies—all his homeboys had jobs and had different aspirations. And the guy that was saying, you know, "Don't forget where you came from." There's this different element when you're a threat, or [when] you're perceived as a threat going into a different culture. With Harvard homeboy, *homeboy* is signaled as a threat. Like, "Oh, there's the Harvard homeboy. He was good enough to go to Harvard, but he still couldn't break his bad habits."

JEN   Do you think you've just decided [that] you don't care if you fit, or because you actually have a more complex background, it's easier for you to fit in a lot of places?

CHRIS   I think it's a little bit of both. When I was younger, obviously I had my inner turmoil. And I was always, no matter what, I was an outsider. So, you become a chameleon to a degree. But in the beginning, none of us feel right in our own skin. I think that's the human condition. We all start out like that.

WILL   Once the initial introductions and boundaries are crossed in prison, and you're talking about versatility, one of the biggest indicators [for assimilation] is, How comfortable are you in your own skin? How confident are you to just say, "This is who I am"? It's hard to do that, because so much of prison culture is shame-based. Person X feels, "I'm ashamed because I've screwed up my life and here I am in prison, and I feel like garbage. How can I find someone else to make them feel shittier or to identify them as worse, because of something that they did, because of something that they are, because of something that they aren't, so that I can, for five minutes, ten minutes, whatever, feel better about myself?"

CHRIS   But even that's a statement of otherness. You reference the fact that white people even have the option to reject homogeny and to identify as simply human [and that] is a massive privilege. White people get to choose the cultural conflicts with which to engage, whereas to be racialized as anything else, is to be drafted into a conflict by virtue of the color of your skin. But at what point do you start deciding your own boundaries? And I think that's just part of your own personal cultural identity. I mean, you start out with these things, and you get to mold them. The whole thing is about equality in these other races, getting the autonomy to be who they want to be without the cultural restrictions that we put on them. There's white kids that come from the cities, you know, that are part of Black gangs and then assimilate to white supremacist ideologies here. But I have a lot of white supremacist friends. And most of it is this—they're just looking for the most audacious shit to say, to make them look tough.

WARREN   Talking about odd juxtapositions, I'm a white farm boy and I was in prison for twenty-six years. And Kennedy, who is not from the United States, not a white guy, was the first person that I was actually able to laugh about chickens with. For all the "rural" white guys who seem to think that that's their ideal, that's where they get their conservatism from, he *knows* chickens. And I will actually cherish that for a long time because it shows that things do not have to fall into distinct categories. Part of that goes back to the speculations that I brought up in the beginning: *how much do the cultural expectations affect us and how, how much do we affect cultural expectations around us?* And that's what Torres was getting to, and I think that's part of what doomed Razos—the cultural expectations were so mismatched from his expectations. He gave more weight to his culture than to his dreams.

A GenderPunk Love Letter

by Alice Paige

The punk show kick drum hammers like a piston as I sweat off a layer of cheap makeup in the middle of a mostly sitting crowd. This feels like an apt metaphor for being a former homeless queer youth. Against Me! is opening for Green Day and most of the people around me could not care less about the first band and its transgender frontwoman, Laura Jane Grace. They do not scream the lyrics to "Transgender Dysphoria Blues"; they do not jump to the beat of "True Trans Soul Rebel"; and they do not understand the connection between fear and makeup. With my all black lips and eyeshadow matching a leather vest bought at Goodwill, I am nothing but a blur of limbs and leather beneath the sweeping stage lights. It's a relief, as I do not have the money to arrive fully formed as what most people would consider a woman—my transition is messy and must claw its way toward femininity, split-lipped and black-eyed. My transition counts quarters to afford fishnets.

The word *transition* comes from the Latin root *transire,* meaning to go across or beyond. The first nights of homelessness involve a lot of late-night transitions between scratchy couches, including one seven-hour drive from the suburban hell of Illinois to the small-town hell of Iowa, a necessity of survival, but one that perpetuates new traumas. Then comes the transition to constant police harassment and then the transition to finishing high school in the midst of food and housing insecurity. And then comes the transition after gender transition with its cycles of settle and bloom.

The isolation feels like death. I trade survival sex for a place to sleep. I trade a violent home life for a violent homeless life. The words "former homeless queer youth" cannot encapsulate the whole of every night woken in a cold sweat. I go across and beyond myself. I leave myself behind, floating somewhere in a bedroom with windows covered by garbage bags.

Somewhere in 2013, I stare up at an Iowa sky dotted with stars forever invisible in a suburbia left behind. Borrowed clothes hang loosely on a body—my body—begging for change as the winter chill sets in and grays the grass beneath my feet. A dog barks in a frozen field beside a leaning warehouse full of farming equipment. In the night no one stares at me, and the clamoring noises of a too full, temporary home seem so far away, being nothing but a dim ring of chaos in the background.

And the kick drum hammers away with my heartbeat. Between the sweat and the tears, every sliver of makeup washes away into the night. Caedyn dances away next to me, throwing their arms out in wide arcs. They crash into me and I into them. We practice a measured violence—one that moves in time with the strum of an acoustic guitar.

I come through clean and new somewhere in the winter of 2017. It is the first year where I feel more a person than a loose collection of coping mechanisms in skinny jeans. It begins a time in my life full of folkpunk, dirty bars, and house parties. An escape spurred on by addiction, music, and writing, but it is the first time I escape toward myself. There is no sweet moment of staring at myself in the mirror considering how soft I would look in a dress. There is a blur of nights twisted into genderless shapes as queer bodies slam into each other on a dance floor. Knuckles dig into my back in a pit and propel me toward a me that is unafraid. This is both metaphor and wonderfully literal.

There is an innate desire in these kinds of conversations to pull gender and class apart and dissect them separately—to understand them as distinct problems. It is easier that way, less full of the mess of nuance. My gender would follow a more stereotypical path in that story—a slow realization that I never fit into the shapes of boyhood. And the story of homelessness would be free of all the complications and violence involved with being transgender. Perhaps the wellness checks would not have been as often or as full of police who look and smell like my father. Boot polish and the same haircut standing in the doorway of a house that I do not belong to threatening to drag me back to my father. Every interaction a chance for queerness to be turned back on me as a weapon.

That first night of homelessness is spurred on by parents bristling at a connection with allyship, let alone with queerness. There is no room for a slow realization in a childhood spent hiding from parents raging through unaddressed traumas. Realization comes when I am finally alone and all at once, like the speakers are blown out on my childhood. It is all static and I am crowd-surfing with every other queer kid with no home to stumble back to at the end of the night. We reach for each other at every punk show, hands soft as clouds.

In the first year of homelessness, I settle into identifying as non-binary. It is an existence as "other" but feels some level of safe. It does not come with expectations of femininity or surgery. The questions are not as invasive, the statistics of violence less well defined. This first year is spent questioning what it means to be a person. Interrogating it, like I can reason myself into feeling again. It will take years to settle into a comfortable, stable identity of woman.

The first time I hear Against Me! it is on a shitty speaker at the base of my phone in a dark bedroom paid for with student loans and I cannot catch my breath. I learn that femininity can be all rasping voice, knuckle tattoos, and piercings. "Woman" tumbles out of my mouth in a hushed whisper between songs and, *holy shit,* is that terrifying. What a thrill to discover your gender just on the other side of a fading song. There is a freedom in accepting the possibility for violence and joy in a future you want.

The time to move up the waitlist for gender treatment at the University of Iowa is approximately six months and is the only option if you are too poor to pay out of pocket at a clinic. This is also enough time to realize my first therapist in Iowa would not write the required letter of recommendation due to her own unfamiliarity with trans people. Her unfamiliarity becomes inaccessibility, another hurdle that requires jumping in order to access a version of myself I have only dreamt of—a version of me that can look in the mirror without flinching. Too many trans people have stories like this. Too many have years of their lives shaved away by a waiting game that no one wins. I offer to answer questions, to guide, to explore, but ultimately, I have better luck with the second therapist. She has at least met other trans people and she is kind.

A handful of months before the concert, I sit in a shining waiting room at the University of Iowa with my partner, Blue. They drive me the entire way, smiling and laughing to distract from the slurry of anxiety beneath my skin, to distract from the worry that I am not trans enough to be given hormone replacement therapy (HRT), despite the obtuse number of hoops I have already jumped through to make this appointment. Their car smells of pine, and the sky overhead rumbles with a barely contained thunderstorm. On the drive home, I cry while looking at a few tiny pills that will change my life.

This is the best way to understand the overlap of class and gender— messy snapshots of joy and panic, the pendulum wildly swinging from one extreme to the other. In one moment, a therapist who takes Medicaid is refusing homeless queer youth the chance to shapeshift, and in the next, a partner is cradling my face between their palms and calling it joy.

In one moment, I am running out of meds because my insurance has lapsed, and my skin feels uncomfortable once more. In another, a friend smiles and sends money so I can buy HRT for the month. We ignore each other's legal names on PayPal. So many of us have so little to give yet still try. The trying is one of the most important things I learn from the queer community. We always try to save one another. Our impermanence demands this constant attempt to give whatever we can; we all know the statistics for suicide among queer youth.

The Trevor Project estimates that every forty-five seconds one of us tries to erase ourselves. I can't help but watch the clock with hope that every minute is a survival, someone outliving the things in their head trying to kill them.

We all know this impermanence comes from a lack of structural support—the hours spent driving to unnecessary appointments; the explanation after explanation of gender to gatekeepers who do not really believe us anyway; the rejections for treatment from insurance companies that don't care about how quickly our bodies disappear. This rejection then leads to hours spent on the phone with people insisting they cannot help, they cannot help, they're sorry, but it is just the insurance policy. The therapist's letter wasn't good enough.

Another letter is needed. The doctor thinks you aren't ready but won't say that out loud. Conversations about our own health and wellness exclude us. The system's gears turn as ineffectually as intended. It wears on us—us, a collective of bodies in flight.

So, we push together in dim bars and run-down apartments, trying to build community as best we can. We search for the warmth in each other. Every forty-five seconds spent together is forty-five seconds not spent alone begging for an escape.

The next year, my pockets full of dollar bills from bartending, I buy somebody else their meds. I transition to keeping queer bar rats alive. I transition to being kept alive by queer bar rats. I am hungry, and pizza appears. I am thirsty, and a round of whiskey slides across the bar counter like wind chimes. I spend a night on my knees becoming too familiar with the smell of porcelain and toilet bowl cleaner and someone holds my hair back. Every night is full of new miracles. Look how many of us survive. Look how many of us return from near death.

A chosen sibling overdoses, so I sit on the floor of the bar bathroom and hold them through the rush of stomach blood. I've never seen a person look so gray. They come to consciousness long enough to sign a refusal of treatment form so the EMTs don't take them, and I don't think I have ever been so pissed at somebody. They tell me they do not have insurance. I hold them sweat-drenched and curled against my chest. I stay with them while the threat of death too slowly slips by like the seconds hand of a clock. One day we will laugh about this. We will message each other from opposite sides of the country and say, "I miss you," which means "I have more time because of you."

I'm fucked up and making out with someone in the back of a dimly lit bar and the portrait of a dead boy stares at us from a wall nearby. I remind too many people of him.

I go out for dinner with my partner and a man across the restaurant stares at me the entire time.

Everything about class and gender is a mess of survival. So often the public sees trans people arriving fully formed. They have the money to purchase a new wardrobe and to overcome the barriers to gender-affirming surgeries. Often, such people disappear and then appear matching expectations of gender—a magic trick done to escape violence. Most of us aren't so lucky. Some of us are more interested in preventing violence than escaping it.

A man follows me from one bar to another to ask if I'm really a woman. He refuses to make eye contact. I spend the rest of the night with the uncomfortable feeling that everyone is watching me, judging how I perform femininity.

Passing comes with so many costs. New clothes. New makeup. New voice. I know we're experts at shapeshifting, but few of us can pay all the costs. And if we don't pay them, other costs come quickly, like a ripple in a crowd. The pressure of depression mounts incredibly quickly. Some of us slip back into the closet for survival. Others are fired from jobs because they are not able to pass as their gender. There is little ramification for this in states that maintain at-will employment.

I raise my fist into the air as "FuckMyLife666" claws its way from the stadium speakers and a handful of people shuffle to their feet. The lights drop low, and the spotlights flicker out into the crowd with each electric strum. I scream the lyrics until my throat is raw. Something about this feels so freeing. In this moment, I can only be seen when the lights sweep over me. What a relief to only be seen briefly. What a relief to be myself.

It is 2022, and most days, especially with makeup, I pass.

Passing has never been the goal. To be in the crowd and never be seen, that's not the goal. So, I write and speak loudly about being transgender. I fly trans pride flags. I wear buttons with my pronouns. I refuse to be anything but proud of my identity. There are already far too many shameful years of my life. I will not pass because I refuse to hide my identity.

It is 2022. I google my friend's poetry and their obituary fills the search results.

We both have written so much about queer love and transness and I am alive, and they are not. Everything about their absence screams of isolation. Forty-five seconds can last forever.

The lack of structural support results in isolation and the luck of being alive looks a lot like grieving. More states are passing anti-trans bills after years of a pandemic have once again taken so many from our community. They tell us what bathrooms we cannot use. They ban children from life-saving medical and psychological treatment. They pass bill after bill and I pass out on a couch, trying to fit this rage into a decipherable shape. At times, this rage is a punk show. Fist still in the air but goddamn do I need the band to play louder. At times, this rage is a couch—a space in which I exist but barely live.

The few well-off trans folks existing in the public eye are fine, but the rest of us are drowning. Their wealth does not find us huddled at house parties. Their wealth does not find us visiting friends' graves. Their wealth finds its ways into my rage. It takes so many shapes.

It is now and then and forever, and I am reaching for every queer kid stumbling somewhere that could never be called a home. Forty-five seconds is no time at all.

This is a story both about me and not about me. The intersection of class and gender slamming together like a mosh pit gone wild. The clamor of a community for liberation. The recognizable sound of loss caught in a speaker's static haze. The pit breaks like a fever and I am so lucky to be alive. My friends go across and beyond. It is a magic trick with no payoff.

It is 2022, and I look at the last message I sent my friend. Their name was Bennett. In that message, I tell them to reach out whenever they need. I think about messaging them again, like the silence would reverse itself. This last year has been so full of silence with all these closed punk venues.

I worry about the deepening of the violence trans bodies have faced during this pandemic. Public figures have become bolder in their attacks on trans voices. Structural barriers have increased. The pandemic has made the realities of homelessness even harsher. Food and housing are even scarcer. What little support there was has atrophied in many ways. How many of us have been forced back into the closet to survive? How many more of us have traded parts of ourselves for couches to sleep on? There is no way to measure this silence.

And yet, I am still here. I have traded pieces of myself. I have bargained for beds, couches, and food. I have choked down whole bottles of whiskey. I have faced down too many cops who remind me of my father. I have stood on train tracks and thought about slipping into the rust-coated night. Through luck, the privileges I do have, and a whole lot of good friends, I am here.

It is 2022, and I go to my first concert since the start of the pandemic. I stand on a balcony overlooking a crowd of bodies rushing to meet each other. I stand next to my date as the queer punk band takes the stage—their faces glowing with dark makeup and colorful hair. The lead singer screams their pronouns into a mic and threatens anyone who would misgender them and then kicks off a song about therapy. My date and I laugh and dance in place, appreciating the movement of bodies in a crowd. Our community is still here through it all.

I yell, "This is breathtaking!"

And my date grabs me by the beltloops and pulls me close. Hair dye and hips swivel in time with the beat.

I have so much love for the queer community around me. In a mosh pit, if somebody falls, you pick them back up. This community of poor queers picks each other back up. We lack so much in terms of resources, but we try our damned best. When one of us disappears, we grieve together. The stage lights flare.

The week my friend dies, their Facebook page floods with testimonials of their fight for queer liberation. Their funeral is a symphony of once more with feeling. The week my friend dies, my partner cooks me chocolate chip pancakes. The week my friend dies, I read every testimonial from the AIDS Memorial. It lets me know there is joy in survival. Memory is the antithesis of loss. Every queer body that has slipped away dreamt of my survival. Death is not a wall.

I carry with me the weight of class, gender, and dead friends. Every support system that is lacking is made up for by a mad rush of love-struck queers trying to hold each other up. Class and gender are messy; my friends are messier. I love them for it. I love them for all the ways they don't pass because they don't have that kind of money. I'll love my friends whether they're here or not, because the silence can always be broken with joy. This community of queers is so full of love.

It is 2017, confetti and makeup mingle on the floor. Caedyn and I wander with the crowd and out to the parking lot, hearts still hammering quickly. We recount what we found on the other side of a fading song.

In this memory, I find pieces of Bennett and other ghosts. How sweet that all this music can still be felt thrumming in the body. How wonderful it is that this parking lot can hold my sweet dead.

It is every moment all at once and I am so glad to be alive and queer.

My friend and I have so much in common. I think that is what makes their passing so difficult. Our closeness makes me a ghost and it is not the first time I have been the ghost of a dead queer. It probably won't be the last. And, at some point, someone will be my ghost.

But goddamn, please play the music louder and keep moving.

A GenderPunk Love Letter: The Conversation

RUBY HAACK   So, I grew up with the presence of Riot Grrrl culture all around me. Riot Grrrl is a punk movement that was started by bands like Bikini Kill, Team Dresch, and Batmobile; it's all about all girl-bands taking up space. Kathleen Hanna of Bikini Kill would call out on stage, "All girls to the front," because so often, punk was dominated by a kind of white male rage. And it felt very exclusive. A lot of women were relegated to the backs of venues and, you know, mosh pits might be way too aggressive. So that was what Riot Grrrl is and was. It started in the 1990s and it has since dissolved a bit. But that's what I grew up with, and there is more and more discourse right now about the exclusions that are inherent to Riot Grrrl, because for those who either don't identify as women or don't identify with the Riot Grrrl aesthetic, Riot Grrrl—even though it had maybe more of a feminist agenda—was still dominated by middle-class white women. There's now new discussion about gender in punk. Take the Linda Lindas, for example: young women of color that are now dominating the pop punk Riot Grrrl-esque scene. And so, I thought that this was coming at a really appropriate, interesting time. Because even though Riot Grrrl values are still really important to punk scenes around the country, people are looking at [that] like, what is the new Riot Grrrl? How can it be more inclusive?

WILL   Just to clarify something, you're talking about how Alice identifies with the punk movement, but as a transgender woman, may not necessarily be included?

RUBY   I think Riot Grrrl was kind of inherently queer, but [growing up, I never heard] transness really ever talked about. So, it's interesting to think about, how, just because you don't really have the vocabulary for the nuance of it, we just decided to assign it as "a women's movement."

KENNEDY   The thing that touched me was kinda different. It was the forty-five seconds, and the idea of suicide. Suicide, to me, represents the death of hope. You know, it's the point where despair just takes off and forces an individual to declare war on their own body. You know, that is a very agonizing thing. Look at the way Paige talks about it. If you look at the lives of the trans community and what they have to experience, you know—bad politicians, bad insurance, bad therapists, parents who don't understand, the church although she doesn't mention it, difficult employees, and ignorant public, police, poverty, and everything else. Imagine an individual having all those forces against you, you know, those are the things that kill hope. And I think that society has never really paid attention to that, and that people believe the silly notion that [suicide is] an easy way out really disappoints me. And I think that is what, it's what Paige brought close to home for me. You know, when I was reading this article, as the only conservative in the group, I was really hoping every conservative politician or every conservative individual in America could have a chance to just read Alice's article, just from a human interest point of view. Because there's just too much misunderstanding and lack of understanding in the world, and it's leading to a whole lot of our troubles. And as a conservative, I would think that somebody deciding what to do with their bodies is the ultimate goal of anybody who's conservative. Women deciding to do whatever they want with their bodies . . .

JEN   You would think, right?

KENNEDY   Yeah, that should be our ultimate goal. And I think most of us totally forgot about that. I know, there's a few people like me that still stick with the old ways [and want people to] have as much freedom as you can, with as little interference from outside as possible.

WILL   To connect with the conversation about suicide, and it connects with other mental health issues that we discussed as part of the anthology in general. It's the experience of—especially being younger and being assailed from all directions—all things garbage in our culture and our society. And especially being of an age talking about going back to Riot Grrrl and punk movements, at a time when everyone just gets sort of herded into a group. And if you can't say, "Oh, you know, I'm a dyke," or you can't say, "Oh, I'm gay," but that's not really what's going on, and not having the language to articulate and express your own experience. It's like unconscious hopelessness because you don't understand what's wrong; you just understand that something is [wrong], and so you say, "I'm just fucked up. I'm just broken," without having any sort of resolution to any of that experience.

WARREN   Parents have huge insecurities for, you know, someone close to them not leading the life that they expect. If they're not going to be what you expect them to be, which is another version of you, that has to be wrong. In the world I grew up in, this is about as wrong as you can get, because God made you the way you are. And anything other than that is, you know, pure blasphemy.

WILL   The thing that fascinates me is people who fiercely defend, not what they sincerely believe or experience as themselves, but what they have been conditioned to believe. These constructs serve a social order of oppression, or patriarchy, or domination, you know, the structures that people live in, because they've been conditioned to identify with those things, they fight for the things that are actually oppressing them. They've repressed all these different aspects of who they are to the point that they're terrified of it. They're conditioned to feel terrified of pieces of themselves.

JEN   Language does have power, right? Yeah, I was gonna say, on the optimistic side, it's amazing how quickly norms can change. I grew up in rural Texas. The word "gay" was not even spoken aloud; it was just alluded to.

WILL   The love that dares not speak its name.

JEN   The precarity of the trans community is so near the danger of death. Yes, by suicide, but also by violence from others. That felt visceral to me in this essay.

WILL   Most of what we take for granted as being natural and scientific, when it comes to biology, was constructed by Victorian era British men in a language that was Latin that is inherently gendered, you know, and it's constructed. When we get into the whole, what's nature . . . well, it was invented by a bunch of Western men.

JEN   Let me, here, quote Darwin. "I hate a barnacle as no man ever did before."

The Last Days of the Baldock

by Inara Verzemnieks

Given the chance, the more sentimental among them would probably return in summer. Summer was when it seemed as if all the residents of the Baldock threw open the doors of their homes to the bronchial, hawking churnings of the passing semis and wheeled their coolers out to the picnic tables that had not yet surrendered to rot. There they would sit, cans clutched in cracked hands, as their dogs whipped smaller and smaller circles around the trunks of the Douglas firs to which they were chained. In those moments, it was possible for them to imagine that they had merely stopped there briefly on a long road trip, that they were no different from the men and women with sunglasses perched on the tops of their heads who trooped in and out of the nearby restrooms, mussed and squinting.

Sometimes they walked over to the information kiosk and collected travel brochures, and then rustled the pages and pretended to plan journeys to state attractions they knew they would never reach. *Crater Lake is the deepest lake in the United States . . . Shop Woodburn Company Stores!* When it grew dark, they crumpled the sun-warmed paper in their fists and used it to start fires in the barbecue pits. After the flames died, they would toss whatever leftovers they had to the dogs, leaving them to thrash beneath the trees. Then they climbed inside their cars, stuffed blankets in the window jambs, reclined their seats, and let the freeway's dull squall, constant and never-ending, gradually numb them to sleep.

Without any kind of written record or historical archive to consult, the question of who first settled the rest stop must be answered by one of its oldest former residents, a vast, coverall-clad man named Everett, who claims to have arrived in 1991, after years of wandering the bosky wilds along the interstate with his pet cat. Together, they set up house in the secluded farthest corner of a rest stop named for Robert "Sam" Baldock, "father of Oregon's modern highway system" and an "honor roll member of the Asphalt Institute." They began in the bushes in a rough hut assembled from scrap, and then moved into a ragged van that remained more or less parked in the same place as one decade turned into the next. In that time, dozens more joined Everett and his cat, drawn by stories circulating among those versed in a certain kind of desperation about how there was a place off Interstate 5, about fifteen miles outside Portland, Oregon, where someone with nothing left but a car or a camper and a tank of gas could stay indefinitely.

Screened by thick stands of evergreens planted under Lady Bird Johnson's Highway Beautification Act, this backlot settlement grew in relative isolation, its residents largely invisible to the outside world as they pursued the dystopian task of making a life in a place where no one was ever meant to stay. By the time I stumbled upon their community in October of 2009, they were a population of fifty, give or take. No formal census was ever attempted—or deemed necessary, for that matter—since they all knew perfectly well who they were and the myriad ways they passed their time. Seniors waited on social security checks. Shift workers slept. Alcoholics drank. A single mother knocked on truck cabs. A one-eyed pot dealer trolled for customers. Others sat locked in their compacts, fingering sobriety tokens.

"We call each other Baldockians," said a woman who introduced herself to me as Jolee.

Jolee had been at the rest stop for going on three consecutive years when we first met, though she had lived there off and on for much longer, using the location as a winter retreat when it became too cold to pitch a tent in the foothills. When she was growing up, Jolee's dad had taken her to an elk camp each year, and taught her from the time she was just a little girl how to survive on her own in the woods. "And then he's all pissed off that I take that knowledge and use it to live like I do," she said. But in recent years, Jolee had grown tired of testing herself for such long stretches, of being at the mercy of the elements, and so she and her boyfriend were residing at the Baldock in a rusting van that ran only occasionally and that periodically needed pushing across the parking lot to a new spot in order to appear in compliance with the rest stop's posted rule that a vehicle remain parked on the premises for no more than twelve hours at a stretch.

Jolee took it upon herself to keep an eye out for the strays, like me, people who needed the Baldock explained to them. Strays were different than visitors, like Jolee's kids, who came on Mother's Day or her birthday and sat for an hour with her at a picnic table, the grandparents who raised them waiting nearby in a running car. Strays were those who drifted into the community's territory by accident, but once they'd become aware of the Baldock's existence, the strays couldn't stop thinking about what they'd seen. The residents of the Baldock were used to strays, preachers, social workers, strangers with extra cans of kerosene and bags of groceries in the backs of their flatbeds, people who kept coming back with questions and concern, but who never stayed.

I first came to the Baldock in an old school bus driven by a man whose job it was to bring hot meals to people living in the region's more rural areas, people for whom it is not an easy matter simply to drop by a soup kitchen or food pantry. I was a reporter at the time, working on a story for the local paper, and shadowing the man's efforts. When he told me that our last stop of the night would be at a rest area, I could only imagine that he meant we would be taking a break, or perhaps offering food to down-on-their-luck drivers. But then we parked, and a crowd began to gather, and Jolee appeared. "Let me show you our home," she said.

And that's how I became the accidental chronicler of the Baldock's last days. In truth, it seemed as if they'd been waiting all along for someone to take an interest.

"People normally look right through us," Jolee told me. "Or they might ask, 'Where are you from?' like how people make small talk, and if we say, 'We're from right here,' they'll get this scared look on their faces, and then they'll rush away."

The access they gave me didn't seem to depend on my being a reporter, or on any perceived authority that might have granted me. In fact, soon after I met them, I signed paperwork accepting a voluntary layoff from that job. Instead, I suspect, they were judging me by a more subtle rubric, reading me for clues that would help them gauge my capacity to understand.

I came to learn that the orientation of all permanent arrivals was typically left to a man everyone called "the Mayor." I could never get a fix on just what it was he had done to earn the title, whether it was due to a general sense of grudging respect for the fact that he was said to have once let a gangrenous toe rot in his boot because he was too cussed to see a doctor or the rumors that he kept a pistol in his RV. Either way, the Mayor saw it as one of his principal duties to greet the incoming residents. "I don't have money, booze, or cigarettes to give you, and don't give me any shit. But I always have food to share. Ain't no one out here gonna starve," he would say.

Baldock etiquette discouraged questions, and this allowed most people to maintain a presence as blurred and unfixed as the reflections cast by the bathroom's unbreakable mirrors. No one asked about the swastika tattoo that crept just above a collar's edge. Or why a police scanner rested in the pocket of a car's door where insurance papers were sometimes kept. In his own more talkative moments, the Mayor liked to remind anyone who cared to listen that "you meet all kinds here, the bad and the good. Mostly good. Still, best advice I can give is to look out for yourself. Don't trust anyone." What he meant was that all the residents of the Baldock, himself included, had versions of the truth they preferred to keep to themselves, maybe even from themselves.

In Jolee's opinion, the most important person any newcomer could meet was the man who lived in a 1970s Dodge motor home known as a Vaquero. "This here's Dad," she said as she motioned to a man of ashen face and hair who was trying to chase a tiny, tawny-colored dog back into the battered rig. "Sweetpea, Sweetpea, come on now, sugar," the man coaxed as the dog jumped and nipped at the air, trying to catch circling flies with her teeth.

Addressing me, Jolee said, "I call him Dad because he's done the most to help us out here. He shared his knowledge about how things work, explained everything we need to know. He looks out for people."

What she meant but did not say, I would learn, was that Dad had once pulled her aside and pressed one hundred dollars into her palm. "Use it to leave him," was all he said. And that had been the last of it. He never brought it up again and Jolee never told her boyfriend, who wandered over to the Vaquero every morning to suggest a run to the convenience store to get more beer. And Dad always obliged him.

Dad's name was Ray, and he seemed pleased that Jolee had mentioned him so prominently, over the Mayor. For as long as anyone at the Baldock could remember, Ray had been saying he had six months to live, smoking his days away beneath a sign that warned oxygen tanks were in use, while Sweetpea splintered bones on the floor of his motor home. Ray was born in Kentucky, he said, but moved to Oregon when he was fifteen or sixteen and over the years had felled trees and labored as an auto mechanic. Somewhere along the way he had done irreparable damage to his lungs and now had emphysema. "All that asbestos in those brake pads," he figured.

Sometimes Ray would bring up wives, children. "Buried," he said, in a voice pumiced by all the years of smoking. But it was never clear what he meant by this, whether he meant them or his memories of them.

Sometimes Ray said he had fought in Vietnam. Other times he said he'd never been. He had lived at the Baldock for going on fifteen years. Twelve. Thirteen. He didn't seem to know anymore, one day so much like all the rest, mornings with the paper, coffee on the hot plate, and then when the shakes set in, a nip or two, on through the day, until his voice feathered at the edges and his eyes bobbed and pitched behind his glasses.

"It's not that we want to be here," he told me the night we met. "It's just we can't get out of here. I'm sixty-eight years old. I get $667 a month in social security and some food stamps. That's all I've got except for what I can make panhandling or rolling cans. Everyone here's the same, figuring out how to get by on less than nothing. But I'll tell you, I don't know how much longer I can make it. Last winter was a bearcat. It was hot dogs on Christmas. I was snowed in for three days, icicles from top to bottom." He pulled out a pouch of tobacco and some papers and rolled a cigarette as he talked. "I'm too damn old for this anymore."

He'd been of a mind lately to light out for the coast—he was sure he could get a job as a park host somewhere—and so Ray was rationing gas, trying to save some cash. He'd even picked a day for his escape: "First of the month, I'm fixing to be gone."

He said this in October 2009. He said it again in November and in December and in January and in March and in April.

He was, in fact, among the last to leave the Baldock.

Jack was among the last to arrive, driving in the night after the Fourth of July, his gas gauge near empty, the trunk of his little white Ford four-door loaded down with what he had managed to take while everyone was gone, as his wife had asked him to do, so the kids wouldn't see: a Route 66 suitcase packed with clothing, including his good church suit; an old camping cooler; a pile of books; a sleeping bag; a tent; and a scrapbook his wife had made that contained the boys' baby pictures and photos from the barbecue they threw in the backyard the day he got his union card.

He'd told himself that he'd leave the rest stop come morning, but the truth was Jack had nowhere else to stay, not on $206 a week in unemployment, not with his wife and kids needing money whether he lived with them anymore or not and the debt collectors lining up. None of his family would take him in, and, for a long time, he felt it was no less than what he deserved for what a fool he'd been. He'd known, after all, as someone who'd been raised in a strict family of Jehovah's Witnesses, and who had married a committed convert, that secret strip club visits and hours of adult movies downloaded from the Internet rank up there on the list of the faith's most grievous sins, right along with lying about it all, repeatedly. Still, he couldn't stop. According to the church elders, who referee such matters, excommunication was the only fit punishment. "Disfellowshipping," they call it. And while a part of Jack wanted to believe that maybe it was a bit out of proportion to the offense, he did, as he put it in his more contrite moments, "regret the crap I put my wife through, and I really did put her through crap—it's not as if I was an angel, and then got kicked out." And so, Jack accepted the elders' pronouncement of his exile, if only because he did not know of any other way to express his sense of humiliation appropriately, other than to make himself disappear.

At first, he pitched a tent at the state campground, but at fifteen dollars a day, the campsite fee added up quickly and he was left with less than one hundred dollars a week. It was there, in passing, that another man mentioned the Baldock.

Jack resisted the idea initially, but then, one day, driving along Interstate 5 on his way to a job interview, he decided to pull off at the rest stop exit. He was stopping only to use the bathroom; that's the reason he gave himself. But when he still had some time to kill before his appointment, Jack found himself following the man's directions, guiding his car past the rows of mud-spattered semis and the volunteers dispensing Styrofoam cups of grainy drip coffee, until he reached the invisible line separating those who were simply passing through from those who had nowhere else to go. He sat for a few minutes and watched through the windshield, his engine ticking. He watched the dogs, running and rucking the earth beneath the trees to which they were tethered. He watched the people hunched around the picnic tables, sunburned and knotty-limbed. Their laughter, loud and muculent, beat against the sealed windows like birds' wings.

It took three more days for his resolve to build, then take. His first night, Jack parked as far as he could from all the other cars, which were gathered close, fin to fin, as if in a shoal. For much of the night, Jack sat bolt upright, certain he could hear voices, the jangle of dog collars outside his door. But in the morning, he couldn't think of anywhere else to go and he wanted to conserve what little gas he had left. And so, he'd remained there, just sitting in his car, in the oppressive heat, and tried hard to look as if he wasn't looking. He could sense everyone was looking at him too, though not in an unfriendly way. Sometimes someone would wave, or nod at him, like an unspoken acknowledgment of something shared. It made him uncomfortable, the way they seemed to recognize something in him before he saw it in himself. At the time, Jack didn't yet feel he had anything in common with anyone at the rest stop; he still believed he would be there only temporarily.

No one else thought he'd be long for the Baldock, either. "I get the feeling this place is going to blow his mind," Jolee told me. "Short-timer," Ray predicted. "You mean he's not another volunteer?" a visiting social worker asked me one night. Jack worked hard at cultivating the appearance of normalcy, or what passed for it in the world beyond the rest stop, anyway. His clothes looked freshly pressed, though he had no iron. "If you take them out of the dryer and fold them just the right way while they're still warm, you can make it look like you've creased them," he later explained. He spit shined his shoes. Although he had only a high school equivalency degree, he regularly worked through stacks of books and, in careful handwriting, filled pages of a journal.

The childhood Jack described, when I asked about it, sounded isolated. Few friends. A life that revolved around the family's faith. At some point, though, he'd become possessed by the idea that he would like to live in a world that offered experiences more expansive than those he'd known. After years of working variously as a pizza delivery man and a swing-shift worker at the local dairy, he decided it might be wise to learn a trade, like carpentry, and had been fortunate enough to apprentice out just as a condo-building boom swept through Portland, industrial wasteland giving way to "planned urban communities." Suddenly, Jack was framing walls in million-dollar penthouses with Mt. Hood views.

He recalled how once, during that time, he had taken his wife to a restaurant near a development in downtown Portland that he was helping to build. Up until then, he and his wife had only gone out to places like Applebee's and, months later, Jack still remembered the white tablecloths, the white flowers, and the way the food came out on white plates, "like paintings." Looking back, he realized it was the first moment he had allowed himself to think that he might be different, that all along he had been living the wrong life. But then his work started slowing. Then the housing bubble collapsed completely, and the condos men like Jack had been working on were left to stand empty, their interiors an expanse of white.

The layoff came not long after he and his wife bought their first house. In response, Jack thought it made sense to enroll in school again, to learn another trade, like driving a truck, so he'd have something to fall back on. The school told him he could take out loans, and he figured if he found work quickly he could pay them back before long. He graduated with his CDL at the time gas prices spiked and trucking companies started slashing their fleets. He'd added another $5,000 in debt to his name. Soon, they had to let the house go, the minivan, too.

Now, at the rest stop, Jack reads Dave Ramsey's book *The Total Money Makeover* by flashlight at night, marking passages that seemed particularly relevant. On Ramsey's advice, Jack had started to portion his unemployment money into envelopes that he marked "bills," "gas," "savings," "fun," and "allowance" for his two boys, even if it was just a couple of singles. Later, he would make an envelope for "child support." By the time we met in October, he had been out of work for six months and had been living at the rest stop for three. He was thirty-six.

Jack carried copies of his resume in the front seat of his car, just in case an opportunity arose to hand one out. Once, he flagged down a maintenance crew working at the rest stop and pushed a sheet in their hands, but that failed to yield any leads, as did the applications he filled out through the unemployment office. He did not have a criminal record or a problem with drugs or alcohol, though he had joined a twelve-step group, hoping, as he put it, it would help him "fix whatever's broken in me." He'd even tried to continue going to services at the Jehovah's Witness Kingdom Hall in the nearby town of Aurora, although, in keeping with what is expected of the excommunicated, he sat in the back and did not speak to anyone.

In the context of the Baldock—where a convicted pedophile with a habit of luring little boys into his vehicle, driving them to out-of-the-way places, then forcing them to have sex at knifepoint, happily lived out his last days; where, a few years ago, the decomposing body of a fifty-six-year-old man believed to have been murdered was found in the underbrush not far from where vehicles parked; and where, more than once, the grip of a pistol could be glimpsed peeping out from under a seat—Jack, with his resumes and scrapbooks and savings envelopes, seemed remarkably naïve, impossibly good, even. "Just a baby," Ray told me.

Of course, it all depended on your perspective. Jack knew his parents and his in-laws and, most importantly, his wife had plenty to say about him and what he'd done. Or not say. Sometimes when he called, they hung up on him. Once, his mom took a few whispered seconds to say that she shouldn't be speaking to him, not after what he'd done, that those were the consequences of his excommunication, and he shouldn't call again. And he couldn't argue with the opinion his family now held of him. Jack was everything they thought he was. He was nothing. He had tried to come up with a list of good things about himself in his journal. He wanted to be honest.

Finally, he wrote, "I am alive."

They had their own ways of measuring time. One month had passed when the medical delivery truck arrived to drop off a new set of oxygen tanks at Ray's Vaquero. It was fall when the school buses came to fetch the children. Saturday was when the church group came round, offering pancakes and prayers. Thursday was when the bus from St. Vincent de Paul pulled in with its onboard kitchen and cafeteria tables where the seats should have been, a place out of the cold where they could eat plates of fettuccini and turkey melts. Night was when the jacked-up pickup came through the lot, its driver tapping his brake lights, waiting for one of the semis to wink its high beams back, the signal that he should park and climb inside to name his price.

They marked the persistence of loneliness by the frequency with which a knackered blue van appeared, groaning its way through the parking lot, the driver waving gently like a beauty queen on a float. It was Everett and his cat. A local social service agency had managed to get him into a low-income apartment complex that allowed pets before he and the cat had to face a nineteenth winter at the Baldock. Still, the van coasted past nearly every day. "Too quiet in my new place," Everett would explain and then launch into his latest theories about the causes of unemployment and homelessness to anyone who stood outside his window long enough to listen—NAFTA, globalization, illegal immigration. He never required any kind of acknowledgment, except to be heard, engine idling, cat perched unblinking on the passenger seat.

Soon, they felt the weather turn, winds wailing cold out of the Columbia River Gorge and turning the condensation that accumulated inside their windshields while they slept into streaks of ice. Mornings, they followed each other's footprints through the frosted grass to the restrooms, where they washed and shaved beneath the industrial lights.

On one of those cold nights, after most of the other residents had retreated to their cars, Jolee stood with me in the wind by the picnic tables with an insulated coffee cup in her hands, watching the receding taillights of cars bound for the freeway on-ramp. "All any of us want is to get back over there one day," she said, her eyes following each car as it left. "We want to be over there with them, doing normal things. Like paying taxes. I'm serious. The day I pay taxes is the day I know I've made it back to the mainstream. That's what I want, to feel normal again."

By mid-November, she was gone. Jolee gathered her things from the floor of the van and stuffed them in a backpack, then walked over to Jack's car to borrow his cell phone, which she pressed against her bruising cheek. "I'm sick—I need to go somewhere to get better," she said. Her boyfriend watched silently from the open door of the van with the dogs, his own face welted and swollen. Eventually, Jolee's father's pickup appeared and she climbed inside the cab. When it disappeared onto the freeway, her boyfriend got up and walked over to a sign directing patrons to the restrooms, and he drove his fist into the metal as hard as he could. Finally, he spoke. "Time to go to the store," he said. "Who's going to give me a ride?"

He went on a bender that lasted days, stumbled around in a fog. He accidently locked one of the dogs inside the van, the pit-bull mix who'd loved Jolee, and by the time he remembered and opened the door, the dog had torn the stuffing from the two front seats, shredded all the clothing strewn about, then snapped at his reaching hand. No one knew what to say, and one of the cardinal rules of the Baldock was that no one was in a position to judge, so they all kept quiet, and let him go on saying that the tears he wiped from his red eyes were because of the dog.

Jack for his part had given up his silent visits to the Kingdom Hall and had stopped talking about one day reconciling with his wife. He felt embarrassed when he thought about his uneasiness that first night at the rest stop, how he had imagined he could somehow hold himself apart. After four months at the Baldock, he'd seen enough of "what people do to survive" to realize that he had been deeply misguided ever to presume he'd known what it was to endure. Like the woman who often left her ten-year-old son alone in their motor home while she visited the rows of parked semis—and even the rigs of her neighbors—creeping back hours later, sometimes with what looked like bite marks on her chest. Or the people who stood by the low wall near the rest stop bathrooms, which they called just that, "the Wall," flashing signs made from the cardboard backs of empty half racks at all the weary travelers emerging from the cocoons of their cars, road tired and bladder full, hoping to part some change from them. They organized their panhandling in shifts in an attempt to maintain some kind of order and equity, but there were often fights when they tried to chase off anyone who didn't live at the rest stop, the tweakers who had homes or hotel rooms, but who would parachute in just long enough to beg money off tourists for a hit. In the hierarchy of the Baldock, those who came to beg but who had somewhere else to stay were openly disdained, cursed as cheats and liars, not because of their habits, but because they presented themselves as homeless when they had somewhere else to go.

As a rule, the police tended not to bother the rest stop residents, unless someone called in a specific complaint. Although officials had long been aware of the community living there, and the local district attorney's office certainly made its position on the matter clear when it began referring to the Baldock as "Sodom and Gomorrah," the unspoken policy, at least on the ground, appeared to be one of benign neglect, so long as the residents kept themselves out of the run sheets.

But then, one day, a particularly ambitious state trooper came through and ticketed a number of vehicles for lapsed tags, and rather than watch their homes disappear on the backs of tow trucks, those residents quickly disappeared. The whole scene had struck Jack as unbearably unfair, and he couldn't stop thinking about it, like a pawl clicking over and over again into the grooves of a gear. He sat at one of the picnic tables for hours, trying to organize his thoughts. Finally, he got in his car and drove to the local community center. There, in front of the public computer, he began to type.

Baldock residents often spoke about how much they feared breakdown—as in, "My car's broken down on me twice now and I don't know what I'll do if it happens again." Impounds were an altogether different matter, however, and represented perhaps the most frightening possibility of all for someone whose car was his final vulnerability, the one thing left tethering him to any illusions of stability. Losing a car to impound almost certainly meant losing that car for good. Or as Jack wrote at the computer that day: *How can we afford to get them out? . . . [W]e cannot pay for towing or impound lot fees. Even if we pull all our money together, this is an expense we cannot afford.*

He typed: *We have a very difficult time paying auto insurance, gas, and food. Many of us are looking for work and have to travel long distances in search of employment. Gas prices are high and food stamps are good but not enough people receive them. None of us can afford a home, an apartment, hotel, or even campgrounds.*

He typed: *We are homeless!*

And he typed: *All we seek is a safe place to live, until we find better options. The rest areas provide us a place to sleep, help each other out, and have access to the rest rooms 24 hours a day.*

Jack kept going until he'd filled the whole page. He imagined it would be a letter of grievance, written on behalf of the entire community. He ended with the line, *Thank you for your support.* Later, Ray read a copy at his dinette, holding it close to his glasses. "Boy can write!" he said, speaking as if Jack was not standing next to him. "Fancy. There's even semicolons!"

For Jack, the biggest declaration in the whole letter had come down to a single word.

We, he had written.

It was a word drawn from the nights they made communal meals, pooling their ingredients to stretch emergency food boxes and food-stamp allocations. Someone would always fix up plates for those who slept during the day and did shift work at night, balancing leftovers and thermoses of coffee on the hoods of cars for the drivers to find when they woke. From the way they bought each other presents from the Dollar Store, socks and singing cards *(Wild thing, you make my heart sing).* From the time they climbed onto Ray's roof to fix the leaks that soaked his bedding, or when they helped Jack change his oil, or lent one another cooler space or propane. But also from the moments when the dogs wouldn't stop barking, and someone was screaming for them to shut the fuck up, and when the trash cans overflowed with all the garbage they'd dumped, and yet another person was asking if he could get a ride to the Plaid for more beer and smokes and only offering pocket change to cover the gas, and from the old timers who would grouse about how the young had no work ethic, just wanted to smoke dope and have everything handed to them, and then they'd ask if they could take a shift at the Wall. It was Ray, pawing women's asses, braying and frothing at the Mayor that he was nothing more than an imposter, that he, Ray, had more right to appoint himself sovereign of the Baldock. And the boy who spent his nights alone in his motor home, waiting for the sound of his mother at the door—he did not go to school, but no one said any-thing, just as no one said anything about the abrasions on his mother's chest that turned purple, then green. In a single word, Jack had writ-ten himself into the Baldock, and he'd meant it unequivocally—the whole kind, desperate, resourceful, ugly truth of it—without denial or defense.

Thanksgiving marked the turning, the point at which time and mem-ory began to pull away from them, though no one recognized it as it was happening. They were all too preoccupied with the planning of a Baldock-wide turkey feast; a list had been drawn up of ingredients to procure, and, while everyone seemed to agree on mashed potatoes and gravy, some people disagreed over the value of stuffing and yams.

People decided to lose themselves in holiday preparations rather than focus on a disconcerting little story that had begun knifing its way through the populace. Apparently, a few days before Thanksgiving, one of the rest stop cleaners told someone who told someone else that as of the first of the month, the Baldock would have a new landlord, and this one was not likely to be tolerant of the current laissez-faire living arrangements. Rumor had it there were all sorts of plans to spruce the place up—artist demonstrations, fancy coffee, solar panels, nature trails. (Ray had harrumphed over this one: "Nature trails, my ass; if there was any nature to find here, we'd have killed it, gutted it, and eaten it by now, had a big old barbecue.")

But disbelief gradually gave way to paranoia. Whether it was the maintenance-worker-cum-informant who was the first to mention the possibility of police sweeps and mass banishment, or it was the result of the residents' own grim future casting, soon the rest stop was frantic with speculation of an impending eviction. And so it came to pass that the inhabitants of the Baldock found themselves in a curious and unexpected position: after telling themselves for as long as they could remember that they couldn't wait to leave this place, they now realized they wanted nothing more than to stay.

They tried to talk about other things. On Thanksgiving morning, the early risers crammed into Ray's motor home, downing cups of coffee and taking turns putting the soles of their shoes on the propane heater until they could smell the scorched rubber, savoring the burn of their numb toes. "You know what I love most about Thanksgiving?" Jack said. "Football. It's been months since I've actually seen a game on a TV, not just listened to it on the radio." Everyone nodded and they talked about how luxurious it would be to sit on a sofa again, stupid with turkey, tasked with no other concern than whether to flick between the college or pro games. It struck them all as the height of decadence, of insanely good fortune.

And then the man who looked like a gnome and hardly ever socialized knocked on the motor home window, faced flushed. "Did you hear they're going to kick us out?" he shouted.

"You're late to the party," Ray barked through the window. "We've been hearing that for days now. All bullshit. Just scare tactics. They want to make the panhandling stop. I've been here for thirteen years and this one always makes the rounds, but it's all show."

He raised his cup of coffee to his lips, but his hand was trembling.

"Anyway, I'm leaving. Come the first of the month, I'm outta here. I'm sick of all the drama. The doctor tells me I got six months to live and gotdamned if I'm gonna die at the Baldock."

His face was red and the cords of his neck had stretched taut, and no one spoke for fear of winding him up even more. He reached down, took a beer from the case he kept under the motor home's dinette, and poured some into his coffee as though it were cream.

And at this, the day began its slow slide into drunkenness for everyone except Jack, who didn't complain when he was asked to make a run to the convenience store when provisions ran low. He came back with five dollars' worth of Powerball tickets, bought from his "fun" envelope. The jackpot had reached nearly $200 million. "I figured if we won, we could all buy houses, maybe even the rest stop," he said.

Eventually, the main rest area, which had been heaving with holiday travelers, slowed to a few scattered cars. Afternoon tipped toward evening. The food remained uncooked, the air inside the motor home brackish with smoke. Ray, who had been brooding over his mug for some time, finally spoke. "Some people would say they wouldn't be caught dead living like this, in this nasty old RV," he said. "But you know what, I consider myself so fortunate to have this. Because when you've had nothing—and I've been there—living like a no-good, dirty bum, low as you can go, in the streets, and people won't even look you in the face, like you're an animal or something and you don't have shit, you're thankful for whatever you can get. Let me tell you, I've never been so thankful."

He jabbed his face with his fists, trying to hide the tears.

"I don't know what I'll do if I lose this. I can't live like that again."

No one spoke.

Abruptly, Ray collected himself and motioned for another beer. "You know, when I leave here on the first, I won't miss a single one of you fools, stuck in this place. Now if you'll excuse me, I need the pisser."

The dreaded December 1 arrived without incident. Outwardly, at least, each day resembled the next. Ray's Vaquero did not budge. The blue van traced its lonely revolutions. Jack dropped money into his envelopes. He had finally found a job, working the graveyard shift at a manufacturing plant for $9.30 an hour, making "plastic injection molded components." And while at first he was relieved to be receiving a paycheck again, he had been doing the math and it had dawned on him that it would never add up to the kind of money he needed to move into even a modest apartment—first, last, and a deposit. He'd toured a complex in Wilsonville—"They had microwaves built into the cabinets; it was beautiful; I'd give anything to live in a place that nice"—but they wanted to see proof of income of at least $1,400 a month. He made just under that. "It's like a merry-go-round you can't get off," he said. "I don't know how I'm going to get out of this."

So, he continued to sleep in his car at the rest stop and hoped each day that it would not be his last. Everyone did. Some people urged a discussion of contingencies, the way some families speak of fire-evacuation plans or designated meeting places following natural disasters. What about forest service land? Was there a remote wooded space where they could all caravan? Too cold this time of year, the pessimists argued. Think of all the food and propane and water you would need to stockpile.

Others, like members of any neighborhood group upon hearing rumors of possible planning changes, turned to the public computer at the community center for reconnaissance. As a result, they now knew the name of the new landlord: Oregon Travel Experience (OTE), a semi-independent state agency, as the online literature put it. It had been granted the go-ahead by the legislature to take over the operations of five rest areas that had previously fallen under the purview of the Oregon Department of Transportation. And though none of what they could find was written in what one would call plain, unadorned speech, one phrase in particular—about helping the rest stops achieve their "full economic development potential"—seemed to them to translate as having something to do with money, be that making money or saving it. Either way, it was not a concept that they suspected would live comfortably alongside homelessness. Intuition told them that much.

Then one day, a woman appeared in the back lot. By the pristine condition of her vehicle, they knew she wasn't a new arrival. As it turned out, she was the new landlord, head of the OTE. Her name was Cheryl, she said. She'd stopped by because she wanted to personally reassure everyone that OTE was not just going to kick people out of the rest stop, but they should know that things were going to change at the Baldock. She had been talking to people from the community center where many of the residents received assistance, and she hoped that over the next few weeks they all might be able to work together to find a way to help everyone move on to something more stable.

"We're not stupid," Ray said later, after she had left. "It was just a different way to say the same thing: you're out of here."

Jack was not ready to embrace Ray's cynicism. He wanted to believe that the promise made to them had been sincere, that no one would be kicked out of the rest stop until he or she had somewhere else to go. But where would that be? Whenever he tried to trace a clear path out of the Baldock for any of them, it always came out confused, occluded, unmappable. No sooner had he considered a possible exit route than his mind would throw up a fact that directly contradicted this option, and so it went, fact upon fact, one after another, like a thicket of construction barricades choking all conceivable ways forward.

Fact: There's not a single homeless shelter in this particular county.

Fact: What if you have a criminal record or are living with someone with a criminal record? What if you have an eviction in your past? No one rents to you.

Fact: Most RV parks won't rent a spot to rigs ten years or older, yet that's what most people at the Baldock owned.

Fact: Most one-bedroom apartments in the area rent for $750 a month.

Jack rehearsed his arguments on me, and on anyone else who would listen, and when there was no one to listen, he repeated them to himself, until he was losing sleep. It had reached the point where he was reporting for his graveyard shift bleary, his thoughts smudged, sluggish. He blocked his car windows with sunshades to keep out the daylight, but still he winced and churned at the sounds of his neighbors, who seemed to be tuning their voices to a pitch that matched the collective anxiety level.

They grew irritated with each other. It was easier to cloak fear with anger. Ray, for one, announced that his motor home was henceforth off limits to any more coffee klatches. He locked himself inside and did not speak to anyone, though they could see him, glowering at them all through the blinds. He should have been happy. The Mayor had abdicated, putting the Baldock in his rearview mirror. As it turned out, he was not homeless, merely restless, prone to long cooling-off periods when confrontations arose at home. After carefully considering his options, he'd apparently found the idea of returning to the missus preferable to gutting out another day in the uncertain climate of the Baldock.

In this way, they welcomed spring, agitated and aggrieved. Finally, in March, a meeting was called at a local church. Cheryl from the OTE promised to be there, along with the man she had recently appointed as the rest stop's new manager, as well as local politicians, a deputy district attorney, and a trooper from the state patrol. A good number of people from the Baldock showed up, even a few people who no longer lived there, including Jolee, whose new home was a camp trailer on her parents' property, and Everett. Ray had said he would boycott the meeting.

"Ornery old fart," Jolee said, and she called Ray on his cell phone until he relented and showed up, late, smelling of drink, his face gray. Jolee pressed a mint on him.

They sat at tables set with tablecloths and formal place settings for lunch and bouquets of lilacs and bulb flowers and bowls of pastel-wrapped candy. Someone had set up a whiteboard at the front of the room. The Canby Center, the social service agency that had worked most closely with the residents over the years, had organized the event, and the center's director at the time, a woman named Ronelle, spoke first.

"We're here so that you can have a chance to speak," she said. "Please be frank about the obstacles and the barriers you face so that the people here can understand what you are up against, and what might help you."

But how to make it all fit on a whiteboard?

They each tried to tell a corner of the story, but it came out fractured, a chorus of elisions:

"A lot of places won't let you have animals and animals are part of our sanity."

"I had to sell my house and move into my motor coach."

"Your *motor coach?*"

"SHH!"

"You have no idea how scary it is trying to imagine where to go to next."

"I never thought in my life I would panhandle, but I've flown a sign to raise money for my tags, my insurance."

"A lot of us have jobs, but they aren't very stable, or we don't have enough hours to make what it takes to get back in a place. I make just above minimum wage, and I have child support to pay too."

"Some of us just slipped through the cracks. We don't have alcohol problems, medical problems, or a mental illness. There seems to be no help for us."

"I've had times where I've worked double shifts, and then I need to catch up on my sleep all at once. I might sleep twelve hours straight in my car. I need a place where I can do that, so I can keep my job."

"You know, if you move us, you aren't going to get rid of us. We just go hide."

"We used to have movie nights in the summer. Jack had this portable DVD player and he'd set it on one of the picnic tables, and we'd all pretend like we were at a drive-in."

Ray said nothing.

Finally, Cheryl rose and spoke. "We understand you're a community, a neighborhood." She respected that very much. She knew they were afraid, but she wanted to reassure them that a "transition plan" was being developed. "We promise to keep you informed every step of the way."

So much said, and yet, in the end, it would be silence that told them the most. The phrase they most hoped to hear—*you can stay*—went unspoken and there was only the scrape of chairs all around, the rustle of skirts and suits departing.

It was time to go, but they dawdled. Everett shook the remainder of the candy into the front pocket of his overalls. Jolee went with her boyfriend off to a quiet corner to talk, their heads close together. And Jack stood off to the side, rehearsing one last speech: "What if I did some maintenance work for you, strictly volunteer. Could you let me sleep there during the day?"

Maybe, in those last days, if they had been different people, more like the people they saw on the other side of the rest stop, those so seemingly certain in their slacks and sedans, counting down the miles to home, maybe then they might have known how to reassure each other, how to spin this into a good thing, a fortunate thing, to be given the chance to leave this place and pretend as if it never existed. Wasn't that what they had wished for all along? As it was, they hid their faces under propped hoods, screwdrivers clenched between their teeth, cussing recalcitrant old engines into cooperating for the drive ahead.

Proffers had been extended to each resident, elaborate relocation plans crafted by a committee of representatives from the county and state, police officers, social workers, and housing specialists, assembled at the request of Oregon Travel Experience.

For Jack, and seven others, there were immediate slots in a six-week class offered through the county that would help them land low-incoming housing. For the more complicated cases that eluded immediate solutions, there were prepaid spots in campgrounds and motels. For one man, detox. For others, there was help navigating social security applications and untangling veterans' benefits.

For Ray, a stall had been secured in an RV park willing to allow his old motor home, but he wasn't having it. "It's nothing but a drug den. Place is full of meth heads and thieves. Sweetpea and I won't go." He was convinced that everyone who agreed to leave the Baldock was just being set up for a fall. "Once they get you alone," he said, "you just become a number. We should hunker down, like a family."

Ray was still refusing to budge, right up until the last day in April, when everyone was asked to caravan to Champoeg State Park, where a block of adjoining campsites had been booked for the weekend, after which everyone would head on to whatever was next. True to its word, Oregon Travel Experience had not kicked anyone out, but now that all the residents had been offered someplace else to stay, that promise no longer held. From this day forward, anyone who remained at the rest stop, or who returned, was subject to trespassing charges should they violate the twelve-hour rule. Or as Ray translated it, "Once you leave, you leave. They've got you."

As the others made their last-minute preparations, packing and replacing flat tires and loading squirming dogs into cargo holds, Ray hunkered down in his Vaquero. "This is gonna get nasty," he promised through the blinds.

His standoff lasted less than two hours. By late afternoon, he'd pulled into one of the empty berths at the state park, next to Jack, who stood shrouded in tent fabric. "Can someone please help me with the poles?" Jack called. This was the campground where he had first stayed when his wife kicked him out. It also marked the first time in nine months he did not have to sleep in the seat of a car.

The sun warmed the leaves of the ash trees and, together, they sat at one of the communal picnic tables, watching the dogs skitter through the underbrush and admiring the trailers of their new, if temporary, neighbors. It was a nice campground, everyone agreed, though they would never venture farther than their assigned row. They would not go where there were birding trails and pet-friendly yurts, or to the field reserved for disc golf. They kept close together, to what was familiar, working their way through their coolers, telling each other this wasn't so different from the Baldock, but then worrying all the while that their new neighbors might think them too loud, too uncouth ("DON'T PEE AGAINST THAT TREE!"), shushing the dogs, trying not to think about the check out dates recorded on their receipts, when they would all head off into whatever it was that waited for them after this, alone.

Once, long ago, this had been a pioneer settlement, the last stop for those who had set off across the plains, drifting west until they couldn't drift anymore. Now, on special occasions, volunteers in period garb demonstrate for park visitors the difficulty of life for those who had once tried to settle on the frontier's edge. Each year, in "a celebration of Oregon's rugged pioneer roots," the curious and the masochistic could attempt the skills those pioneers acquired for daily survival, such as wheat threshing, butter churning, and wool carding. This particular weekend, however, happened to mark the occasion of Founder's Day, when, nearly one hundred and seventy years ago, the settlers had gathered and voted to establish a provisional government. The land where the park now sat was to have been its capital. Already, in preparation for the festivities, men in boots and braces were rigging draft horses to plow furrows in the earth as minivans puttered past.

Such recreation was all that was left of what had once transpired there. Eighteen years after the historic vote, the nearby river tongued its banks, then surged. The settlement vanished beneath seven feet of water, and the pioneers scattered. They never rebuilt. Twelve miles away, for the first night in more than a decade, the back lot of the Baldock stood empty, like a stretch of back shore licked clean by the tide.

Ray disappeared first, pulling out of the campground in the middle of the night. No one heard from him for months, and everyone started to wonder if he might really be dead.

The rest tried to forget the Baldock as they moved into rent-assisted apartments and bought plants and hand towels and carefully positioned throws on the backs of donated sofas, where they sat, absorbing the quiet. Some of them found jobs, and some of them lost those jobs when they failed the drug tests. Those who had not been visited by their children in their car days practiced unfolding hide-a-beds, and stored plastic cereal bowls in the cupboards.

They called each other, until they didn't.

Months passed.

They did not see the workers bent over the long-neglected flower beds of the Baldock, planting local bulbs of peony and iris.

Then Ray finally surfaced, alive, but rig-less and grieving. "I did a dumb thing," is how he said it to me. "Had some drinks with a friend, drove off, cops stopped me. I'm not gonna lie; I had beer on my breath, so they gave me a DUI, took the motor home, and I couldn't get it back."

He had been looking for a place where he and Sweetpea could stay—how he hated to beg—and for a while the joke was it looked like a Baldock reunion, because it was Jolee who offered to help. She had a couch of her own now—she'd managed to get a little rent-controlled apartment in Oregon City that she shared with her boyfriend, though since he'd left the rest stop, he was no longer being called a boyfriend but a fiancé—and she told Ray he was welcome to the living room. Just like old times, they'd said, and crammed into the little apartment. And it was true that it was just like old times, but that wasn't always good. Ray grew restless—"can't stand being cooped up"—and took to walking Sweetpea around and around the apartment complex, until one day he slipped on a patch of ice and shattered his hip— "broke the socket clean through"—sentencing himself to forty-five days in a hospital bed.

"I've got nothing," Ray said upon his release. "I'm seventy years old and not a damn thing to my name." He'd left Sweetpea with Jolee and he hoped to buy a van "come the first of the month, something less than $750, if I can find it." But even if he found a new vehicle, he had no idea where to go. He insisted he had no desire to return to the Baldock. "That's all in the past. Gone now. Buried." But the way he said it sounded as if he wished it wasn't true.

Jack was the one who went back.

"Yes," he'd said, and then he hung up the phone and set it on the coffee table of his apartment, where he now kept his journals and scrapbooks in a neat, angled stack. Then he'd picked it up again to quit his job at the manufacturing plant.

On his last shift, his colleagues presented him with a sheet cake. They had scribbled a message onto the chocolate frosting. "Good luck, Jackass!"

He pulled back into the parking lot of the Baldock on New Year's Day.

It was January 1, 2011, and he had stayed away from the rest stop for a total of six months.

They set him to work mowing the grass, emptying trash, and erasing the graffiti that erupted in the bathrooms. He pruned the trees where the dogs once howled and paced. He made it his special project to tame the overgrown spinneys that romped the edges of the property, only to unearth in his sculptings a decade's worth of discarded liquor bottles, tattered condoms, and needles, all carted away like evidence of an obscene archeological dig. He worked until no signs of the old settlement remained.

Also among his duties was to tend to travelers who might be stranded, who needed a jump or a tire changed or some gas. Sometimes, Jack gave directions. For all this, he made ten dollars an hour and received benefits better than those he had known when he was with the union. It was the happiest he'd felt in a long time, but also, strangely, the loneliest.

For company, he sought the continued counsel of Dave Ramsey, who strongly advised a second job if one hoped to shed debt more quickly. And so, on his days off, Jack returned to the manufacturing plant and his cake-giving colleagues of the graveyard shift.

The borders of his life had contracted to a simple triangulate: work, his boys, and the garden apartment where he hung his sons' framed school photos on the wall and taped a flier for a one-bedroom house for sale at the end of the road with an asking price of $129,000 to the refrigerator. He had been adding figures endlessly in his head, and, although he was so tired he sometimes found his mouth refusing to form whole sentences, he was certain that, if he could keep this up and his car did not break down on him, he would be debt free within the year, maybe even build up an emergency fund.

Sometimes rumors reached him about his former neighbors at the Baldock. Ray had disappeared again, and no one knew where he had drifted to this time. Jolee had lost her apartment and was briefly sighted living with her fiancé in the bushes at the confluence of the Willamette and Clackamas Rivers, where, according to the local parks and recreation department, "the beaches attract both the sun worshipper and the nature lover with sun, water, nature paths, and wildlife!" A notice in the classified section of the local newspaper had recently announced the auction of all the possessions in Jolee's storage unit due to lack of payment.

Mostly, though, Jack lived in silence, quietly and deliberately tracing the same route each day, from rest stop to apartment, and at the end of it, the sound of his key in the door, then dinner at a small pine table with a single place setting and his manager's first review of his work at the rest stop, which he reread as he ate: "Keep up your consistently good attitude and strong work ethic and you'll do fine."

You'll do fine, he tells himself and tries not to think about those days at work when a car pulls into one of the rest stop's parking stalls, belongings strewn in the back, and how he prays it'll leave before he has to be the one to knock on the window and tell whoever's inside it's time to go.

The Last Days of the Baldock: The Conversation

DAVID   You know, we talked earlier about how the Constitution needs to be rewritten? Four rights that I care about, and that should be written into the Constitution, would be: the right to shelter, the right to food, the right to health care, and the right for every human being to reach their full potential. There's no housing! Why isn't there housing? Like, *why*? You look at Americans who dedicate all their political energy into making it known that humans have the right to own a gun, yet, I don't know why that is more important than the four rights I've listed.

WILL   I think people are passionate about the right to have a gun because they have been socially conditioned to believe that that is necessary to their identity as an American.

DAVID   But why haven't we been socially conditioned then to, say there's a homeless person . . .

WILL   Because there's no money in it. Because there's not a military industrial complex that's fed down into the weapons manufacturing and the gun manufacturers. That's what the NRA is.

WARREN   The second leg of the Great American culture is bootstrapping yourself up. This is a nation of self-made people? No, it's not. I grew up in a culture where you work to eat. If you don't have a job, if you don't have a house, if you don't have income to prove your social worth, then you are a parasite, or you have not contributed to the greatness of America. You're destroying the American Dream by taking away from those who have. That's kind of the second leg of the American fallacy.

JEN   So there's a park in my neighborhood, which is not a wealthy neighborhood. And it's a park that's known for having a lot of needles lying around. And a white woman posted [on the neighborhood Facebook group], "I'm curious about all of the tents popping up at the park lately." And someone else replied, "Curious about why you're judging folks who have no home instead of just getting out there trying to get help." The thread blew up, as you might expect. There was bullying. Name calling. There was so much anger, *so* much anger, and she was like, "I was simply making a statement." She was trying to disguise her disgust as curiosity, and some of the neighbors argued that she had a right to a simple question and others suggested ways she could try to help. I'm guessing those same seven tents are still there. I'm guessing very little has changed.

DAVID   The discourse didn't shift into action.

WILL   It didn't change the structural factors that put those people there in the first place.

JEN   What I loved about this essay is how complicated the [Baldock] community is. And I think it's interesting that the people on my neighborhood Facebook group called the unhoused folks *neighbors.* I don't imagine they probably think of us as neighbors, but they might think of themselves as neighbors to each other.

DAVID   Here is what I wonder—do people have a right to be homeless?

WILL   Yes.

JEN   If they want to be.

DAVID   Okay, then do you think people have a right to stop at a rest stop and not have to be confronted by homelessness?

WILL   No, because it's public space.

CHRIS   There's a legitimacy to that and homelessness. I don't think it's bad. It's just, I think what we're talking about is when it starts to spill into other people's domains, or you know, their neighborhoods.

If it's in a park, it's fine. But when houses get broken into, garages, shit comes up missing? Now, it's probably a [problem], you know what I mean? So now it's a cause-and-effect thing.

WILL   Well, I would argue that the people complaining about the homeless in their park are not as far removed from the homeless as they like to think they are. And their precarity, while not as extreme as the people suffering from homelessness and drug addiction, [is still there]. But they [the homeless] are so much farther down the ladder of the hierarchy of true power, [so far from] true absolute agency and wealth in this country.

WARREN   [I'd guess] forty percent of the population is one hospital bill away from bankruptcy.

KENNEDY   I think the thing that always struck me in America, [since] the first time I came here, is that America is the kind of country where there is always an "other." You know, if you're rich, then those ones are poor. If you're a Christian, those ones are atheists. You know, when you look at the Baldock, there's a guy living there really just because of circumstances. He is not lazy. He's done everything you could ask a man to do to succeed. Some have sacrificed. But they threw him out, you know, and the only place he could run to was in the Baldock, you know, and to me, they look more honorable, more noble than any part of America.

If you look at the Christian church, I think a few years ago in Texas, some of the mega churches wouldn't open their doors for people during floods. They have not done their job, you know. I'm thinking: a flood, you know, making people homeless, [maybe it's] God's way of telling these Christians to be more Christian to their fellow people, but they did not. It's like, as long as there's that level of *the other* . . . The problem in America is that the system is designed in such a way that it always takes. You can put in so much, but it takes more out of you, which means for you to surpass the system, then you have to be as brutal and mean, like a Trump, you know, or you have to be smarter than all the smart people around you, like an Obama, to really succeed.

WILL   I used to have this conversation with a guy who absolutely believed that everything was a zero-sum game. It's this idea that, in order for me to be successful, somebody else has to lose. That the only, like, the only dollars that I can accumulate have to be dollars that are taken from someone else that exists. The fact is, that it's just not true. There's enough. But we live in a system that's designed to exploit that mentality and to perpetuate that ideology among regular people. Like, they're not as far away from most unhoused people as they are from the people who are most benefiting from the system existing the way that it does.

CHRIS   You're in a race and you're racing the people who are closest to you.

RUBY   I also think it's important to think about the actual geographical location of where this takes place. This is in Oregon, fifteen miles from where I grew up. And when you look at property and housing costs on the West Coast, it's ludicrous. But particularly in Portland right now, rents are spiking to an unmanageable level. But the folks that are concerned most often about seeing homeless camps pop up in their neighborhoods also tend to be the folks who will not encourage more housing to be developed in their communities.

KENNEDY   The big difference I see like, say, in a country like Kenya versus the US, you know, because when I think of Kenya, I don't think there are that many people that are homeless, because we got like the slums where people can go and live. So, if you walk in Nairobi, you're not gonna see homelessness camps like you see in San Francisco. And the reason you don't have that kind of housing, you know, in a place like this country, is because of the strict zoning laws that they got. Homelessness in America, to me, has always been a function of government, politics, and capitalism. [And there is] the greatest danger of the Baldock—they're always constantly being harassed there because they've made landlords unnecessary; they've made the police almost unnecessary; they have a way of solving their own little disputes. As a community, they've developed this unique system of self-governing.

JEN   I just have a small story. Back in my married days, I lived in a much more affluent neighborhood than the one I'm in now. And the neighborhood council had done some survey and asked, "What does our neighborhood need?" It's a lovely little village. And everyone loves the little village, but there wasn't [enough] retirement housing for folks who were growing old. Around the time the elders began to retire, Luther Seminary realized they don't see many seminary students anymore; the buildings are empty. So, they decided to sell off a bunch of their buildings and lease the land. And folks in my neighborhood voted to put a condo on the land. And at these community input meetings I would say, "What if we made it affordable housing?" But the surveys had been done and it reflected what some people wanted. Keep in mind, this neighborhood has one of the best public schools in the district. These progressive attorneys, artists, professors, all of these allegedly super liberal minded, wealthy, mostly white people decided *we need a place for our retirees to go, aka: for us to go.* I mean, I'm talking to you about vocally liberal humans. As in, this person goes to all the protests. Like, she's carrying all the signs. And long story short, no one wanted low-income housing.

The average price for those condos today is around half a million. The builder is called Zvago, which is Italian for "fun." And so we talk about selfishness, and I wonder, what's the antidote? Because most people know better. It's not that they don't know. Every one of them understands the circumstances. I swear to God, there's probably a professor in that building who taught coursework around housing policies and the poor. There's a lovely hippie artist who grows and shares his organic food, but still voted for a half-a-million-dollar condo for himself and his spouse, as long as they made the roof a little more green. They knew the right answer; they just weren't willing to give anything up. They wanted to stay there, and they did, and they're happy. They're still walking to the grocery store, which is just a block away. They've got little shops that are popping up and all these other places that cater to them. They've got patio furniture out on covered decks, and lots of beautiful flowers, and they had the chance to do something different and they didn't.

DAVID   Are they really happy, though? Are they really happy in their isolated world?

JEN   I mean, yeah. They seem like it.

DAVID   This is why I asked, can there be true happiness when there's that much precarity in the rest of the world? Are they truly happy?

WILL   I don't think they can tell the difference between what they feel about what they have versus what you're trying to describe as a moral condition.

CHRIS   Keep emotion out of it. It's about integrity, and the fact that they won't live their own self-proclaimed ideals.

JEN   They're creative, intelligent people. They express ideals about right living. Do you know how many kids they could have made space for in their zip code? They could have made an impact. All the yards have trees. Some of them have tree houses. Their kids and, later their grandkids, [are going] to make shit out of cardboard and read great texts—banned texts, texts about community, about justice. Their kids and grandkids are well cared for. Before they grow up and grow old in this neighborhood, they play freely and safely in the neighborhood. They're just not playing with poor kids.

The Promised Land

by Sarith Peou

It was the summer of 2015 inside Minnesota Correctional Facility-Stillwater. My supervisor stopped by D-Hall after her Friday group and told me we had a new participant in our transition services program. I was quite intrigued to hear he was from Liberia. I hated to see another refugee stuck in the system, but I was always happy to help one. I knew almost nothing about West Africa, but somehow we foreigners felt more connected to each other than we did to people from our host country. Being a refugee myself, I understood what they had been through.

The young man arrived that afternoon. His face lit up when I introduced myself. "Sarith? Yeah, they told me that you'd be my mentor," he said, shaking my hand firmly. His eyes darted, voice vibrated—signs of disturbance.

"What's your name?" I asked.

He grinned, never letting go of my hand. "Call me Machiavelli."[1]

I was excited that we had connected so well. Walking back, I wondered why he wanted to be called Machiavelli. I hoped it had nothing to do with the author of *The Prince*.

After supper, I took Machiavelli for a walk in the yard. He surprised me with his insight into his mental health issues. He called everything by its first name, delusion, psychosis, and so on. Starting that night, and through many years, Machiavelli told me his story. Sometimes, words were not enough to express our thoughts and feelings. Sometimes, words stirred up emotional turmoil. Sometimes, talking plunged us deeper into despair. Then we would walk morosely in silence.

I understood Machiavelli. We had gone through almost identical traumatic experiences: poverty, war, genocide, refugeeism, crime, and now incarceration. While our stories were on the dark side of humanity, it was still a relief that we understood each other. We were

---

1 Names have been changed to protect people's privacy.

fortunate to have one another. And I was fortunate that he trusted me with his story. He's asked that I share it with others.

Machiavelli was three when civil war broke out in Liberia in 1989. The rebels attacked his town and massacred many people, including his parents, whom he has no memory of. Machiavelli didn't have relatives to take care of him because his parents had been orphans themselves. So, he was raised by soldiers.

Machiavelli grew up listening to war stories: bloodshed on the battlefields, grief back in the village, all set to the background sound of gunfire. On his ninth birthday, Machiavelli was presented with a rifle. Battle after battle, he fought alongside older comrades, his Kalashnikov right by his side.

The Liberian Civil War ranks among the bloodiest of all African conflicts. Through the 1990s, this small nation of 2.1 million people lost two hundred thousand lives, while half of the population fled to neighboring countries. All sides recruited children as soldiers, took no prisoners, and massacred civilians.

Growing up, Machiavelli listened as people who'd known his parents told stories about how they'd overcame adversity. His father had become the manager of a busy seaport, congested with logging and fishing exports and a variety of American imports. His mother had become a schoolteacher. Machiavelli took pride in his parents. He believed that, had they survived the invasion, they would have become respected leaders of the cause, of his tribe, and of the nation. Those stories informed his childhood dream: to become a powerful general, a formidable warlord. He knew the path to such power was paved with money and gunpowder.

By age eleven, Machiavelli's dream had been deferred. In 1996, all factions of the war signed a peace treaty. However, after the election, tribal massacres continued. For many, it was a time for revenge. As an orphan, carrying a gun and belonging to a militia were Machiavelli's only protection. He remained in the militia, even as skirmishes with other tribes became less and less frequent.

For the next few years, Machiavelli took the opportunity to go to school and play soccer on the side. He began to enjoy a child's life, but he was still bound by the militia to one duty: to steal livestock to feed the troops.

People erected voodoo signs on their farms to protect their livestock. No one knew how voodoo worked; some, including Machiavelli, believed it only worked on true believers. One time, when soldiers stole a pig, everyone who ate the meat died. As he had been taught, Machiavelli would first urinate on the signs, to desecrate the voodoo; only then would he kill and bring the animals back for his troops. It worked well for him over the years.

At the age of fourteen, Machiavelli experienced a life-altering event. As he was playing soccer in the rain, lightning struck him. All he remembered was a blinding flash of light. When he woke up the next day in the hospital, the doctor told him it was the one gold earring he wore that had saved his life. After absorbing a good share of the electricity, the earring had melted, leaving Machiavelli with mere burns to his arms and legs. Being struck by lightning was a curse in African voodoo culture.

For the first time, Machiavelli realized there was something mightier than money and guns. Something or someone from above was judging, rendering a different standard of justice. He thought of the African golden rule. When you killed someone, his family didn't need help from the Higher Power—they rendered their own justice with machetes or voodoo. Machiavelli thought of the many goats and chickens he had been sent to steal from people's farms. Survival bore consequences in the form of a curse, and the scars from that lightning would serve as a lifelong reminder.

✦✦✦

When the opportunity presented itself in 2000, Machiavelli escaped to a refugee camp in the neighboring Ivory Coast. Tribal killing followed him to the camp, and he took arms and fought for another year. Where could he find another way of life? He thought of his parents, of who they were and what they had done to succeed. He heard about refugees going to America, which became his new dream. When another opportunity came up, Machiavelli once again escaped, this time to Buduburam, a refugee camp in Ghana. Here he started a new life. He gave the little money he'd saved to a refugee family to adopt him, as a way of redeeming his childhood and the passage to freedom. Now, at fifteen, Machiavelli finally had a chance to get a real education. He started high school.

In 2004, his new family was accepted for resettlement in the US. They arrived in Oakland, California. Two months later, Machiavelli met a new Liberian family from St. Paul who claimed they knew his parents well. They adopted him and brought him to Minnesota. Machiavelli was happy to finally have a family to call his own. Even more gratifying, he was the only man in the house. He started ninth grade in an American high school. He did well in school, socially and academically—not only was he voted "best dressed," but he adjusted so well that he was also voted "most likely to succeed."

One advantage Machiavelli had over other refugee students was that English was his first language. Another was his age. His official age was fifteen; his actual age was eighteen. In the refugee camp, Machiavelli had reduced his age so he could catch up with the education he missed early in life. Here, he also discovered his talents in sports and music. He danced like a robot and rapped. Tupac Shakur was his icon. His popularity soared when he became a soccer star. Finding a date was never a problem. Rene, his first girl, remains dear to him; he also met Shannon online in his junior year.

In his senior year, however, Machiavelli's life began falling out of rhythm. His grades dropped. He fell behind in his commitment to soccer training. He even missed games. The head coach and his teammates blamed his change on dating too many girls and smoking weed. Shortly after graduation, Machiavelli was arrested for domestic abuse. Rene, whom he'd hurt, told him he had mental problems and needed help. When he didn't listen, she left him, leaving Machiavelli broken-hearted. That's when he started hearing voices.

Mysterious speakers took hold of his life. They gave conflicting messages. A voice he called Tim acted as his guardian. Tim spoke most often, warning him of danger, lifting up his spirit, making him feel special. Bee, Ted, and Tee also gave him purpose, and sometimes advice and direction as well, all in distinct voices and styles. Todd, however, always brought bad news that alarmed Machiavelli. Sometimes a mysterious commanding voice would appear in one single event and never return.

In voodoo tradition, a person trades their soul to the devil for success. Sometimes they trade the soul of their son. There is a ritual to extract the soul from a woman. There are taboos prescribed by one's school of witchcraft that prohibit places to visit and food to eat. Violating a taboo will drive a person insane. When one of Machiavelli's adopted brothers became insane, Machiavelli believed it was his fault—he had violated a taboo.

His adopted mother noticed he had become eerily withdrawn. She told him to find a new girl and stop smoking weed, but marijuana helped Machiavelli relieve the chaos (though never the fear) in his head. The mysterious woman's voice told him to run away from his mother. Machiavelli put a few belongings in his '98 Ford Taurus and drove to Portland to live with his older sister Ariana, to start his life over once again.

In Portland, he started community college. Two weeks later, sitting in writing class one morning, Tim told him, "You know the world's gonna end, right?"

"What?" Machiavelli asked.

"Yeah, the world's gonna end. And everyone will die, if you don't rescue them."

"How am I gonna do that?" Machiavelli asked.

"A spaceship will fly you to a different planet. But first you must find your queen." Machiavelli had no idea who his queen was. "Shannon," Tim told him, "your girl from Iowa."

Machiavelli was surprised—Shannon had not been on his mind for a while. He wondered how she had become his queen. "She's the one because she has blue eyes and blond hair. She will bear your children," Tim explained. "Get out of the class, go and drive. I'll show you where to meet her."

Machiavelli slipped out of the classroom and into his car. In his car, Tim told him, "You know you're the king, right? The world is yours and everything in it. Go find Shannon. She has all the papers to your property."

Machiavelli kept driving without direction, while Tim repeated the same messages over and over. He lost track of time and place. In late afternoon, his gas needle reached E. A warning sign flashed as the hotel loomed. Tim told him, "She's waiting for you in that hotel! But don't check in yet. Let me teach you a trick to drive on E first." Machiavelli drove on E until his engine stalled. He abandoned his Taurus on the highway. He flagged down a car and hitchhiked back to the hotel where Shannon would be waiting.

At sunset, the king finally arrived at the hotel for his destiny. Bee told him to check in. "The staff already knows who you are. You're not a guest; you *own* this hotel. Shannon is waiting in the hallway." But there was no Shannon in the hallway. Or in Machiavelli's hotel room. Instead, 50 Cent's music filled the air, and voices tormented him all night. His family told him, "50 Cent took our souls. He won't give them back until you sell yours."

Tim warned him, "Your life's in danger. The government plots to kill you for your wealth." The voice of 50 Cent told him, "You ain't shit!" If he wanted to survive, he had to sell his soul. His family called out, "Come on! Join us; sell your soul so you're rich like us." Obama, 50 Cent, Ariana, and his mother all conspired to buy Machiavelli's soul.

Machiavelli was unraveling. All the voices were present at once, over twenty in total. Some spoke, some rapped, and some beat drums and chanted voodoo incantations boisterously in his head, keeping him frenzied throughout the night. They were with him everywhere and every minute in his daily life, awake or asleep, a coordinated mission to rob him of his soul, to free theirs.

After days of voices and sleeplessness, Tim told Machiavelli, "There's a brand-new car waiting in the parking lot. It will fly you to heaven." Machiavelli, eager for help, ran out to the parking lot. A couple of police cars approached, blue lights flashing. "You are under arrest for trespassing," was all Machiavelli remembered from his encounter with the Vancouver police. The next thing he remembered was stepping out of jail, release papers in hand. Looking at the date, Machiavelli realized that seven days had passed. He didn't remember eating, drinking, or appearing in court. "Where have these days of my life gone?" he wondered through his ride back to Portland with Ariana.

In Portland, Machiavelli began living on the streets. As he drifted through a quiet neighborhood one day, he was haunted by voices in the air, like they were speaking from a microphone. The voice of his best friend, who was making love to his girlfriend back in Minnesota, told him, "We are in the building right in front of you," but Rene howled, "Don't believe him. He lied. We're in Minnesota." As she moaned, Machiavelli's best friend mocked him. Tee told him to head for Minnesota, to stop his best friend from messing with his girl. "Go to your sister's house. Just get the key to your Camaro and leave."

Arriving at Ariana's house, Machiavelli told her husband, "Give me the key to my Camaro!"

"There's no Camaro. I have no key. What are you talking about?"

Machiavelli grabbed a kitchen knife. "Don't mess with me. I'll kill you," he warned, waving the knife. In the midst of the square-off, Machiavelli felt kicked by an invisible force—causing him to fall from a third-floor balcony.

Reports show that an eyewitness saw Machiavelli jump off on his own. His sister and brother-in-law believed he was on LSD, and this is what they told the police. The police brought him to an emergency room. Two days later, he was transferred to a mental hospital. Machiavelli took one pill of Geodon, and his mind went blank every two seconds. A new voice told him not to take pills, because they erased his memory.

He refused the next dose.

Having learned about the incident, his adopted mother flew out with an extra ticket to bring Machiavelli home. Ariana told police that his behavior had changed recently—that he was "crazy" and needed mental health treatment. Officers heard Machiavelli talking to himself, but nothing he said made sense to them. His family told mental health staff that he had been acting erratic over the last nine months, that he had not been eating or sleeping and was hearing voices from angels and from God.

Machiavelli was diagnosed with schizophrenia.

Even though police showed he posed an imminent danger to himself and others, after a seventy-two-hour hold, Machiavelli signed himself out. The mental health providers could not stop him. He was startled to see his mother, Ariana, and Ariana's husband waiting in the lobby. The same voice told him, "You must run from these people. They'll kill you!" Machiavelli told his family, "Let me grab my bag first."

"No. You've got to come with us now. I'll take you back to Minneapolis with me," his mother insisted. They wanted him to sit in the middle of the car, but Bee told him to sit by the door. They fought over seats. Finally, he got to sit by the door. Todd's voice told Machiavelli, "They gonna poison you when they get home."

The wheels rolled. Leaving the parking lot, the car picked up speed. His family began to finally relax. Bee commanded, "Jump!"

Machiavelli opened the door and jumped out as the others screamed in panic. He ran for his life. His family, who could not catch him, notified the police. His mother flew back to Minneapolis but left his ticket with Ariana to have him flown home whenever he was found.

Thus began a period of wandering for Machiavelli. He journeyed aimlessly, rapping, eating from dumpsters, sleeping under bridges. Some days later, the police found and brought him to Ariana. Machiavelli felt sick each time he ate the food Ariana cooked. He believed she was poisoning him with the medicines the hospital had sent with his release. In his sister's custody, Tim told Machiavelli to get himself together and fly back to the Twin Cities to "marry your queen." He needed to get away from the voices. After all, it was his goal to find a place to quiet his mind. Finally, he flew back home to Minnesota.

Machiavelli called Shannon. She'd gotten married and moved to California. She told him to cut off all contact. However, Tim told him that Shannon did, in fact, want to continue their relationship. She would give instructions for how they could meet.

As he walked to the station with the intention of going to Shannon, a mysterious voice told Machiavelli, "Go and jump off that bridge." Machiavelli climbed over the barbed wire to the other side of the railing near the I-94 bridge. While he contemplated the jump, the voice told him, "Wait, don't jump! The bridge is not high enough; it won't kill you."

"It will if I hit an oncoming car."

"Why don't you go and jump off that tall building instead?"

Machiavelli looked to his right. A tall building stood before him. Carefully climbing back over the barbed wire, he went to the building. The door was locked. He tried a different door, and some residents who noticed him called the police. The voice led Machiavelli back to the bridge. The police intervened before he could jump and brought him to the nearby hospital. Bystanders reported seeing Machiavelli hanging his feet off a bridge, talking to himself about whether to jump or not. The doctor described Machiavelli's state of mind during the intake as "acute psychosis." He was so disturbed that he could not be interviewed. Machiavelli was diagnosed with a "psychotic disorder, not otherwise specified." While the doctor's words accurately reflected Machiavelli's danger to himself and others, his actions at the time did not. After a couple of days of observation, Machiavelli once again left a hospital without preventive care, treatment, or therapy.

While his life drifted in and out of reality, Machiavelli believed that what he was struggling with was a problem of a spiritual nature. On one of his good days, he encountered Islam. He participated in a Ramadan fast and experienced connectedness, but when he practiced at home, his mother told him to go back to Portland. Again, Machiavelli returned to Ariana, who helped him to get a job, working alongside her as a personal care attendant. Ariana was everywhere for him, but to Machiavelli she was plotting to hurt him. In his dreams, with his guard down, she and her mother raped him.

There was no escape.

Ted tried to intervene. "Go to Division Corner," he said, "and a spaceship will be waiting to fly you to another planet." Machiavelli did. No spaceship. Instead, the police showed up. They tackled him and repeatedly kicked him in the face, although he didn't resist. For one week in the hospital, he incurred over $60,000 in bills. The police told the judge they had responded to an emergency call and found Machiavelli unclothed, playing with himself. He was charged with indecent exposure and resisting arrest.

Machiavelli called it an outright lie. Machiavelli said he could not have been unclothed because it was a very cold night. He took his case to a hearing. When he told the judge he was waiting for a spaceship to fly him to another planet, the judge dismissed the charges.

Machiavelli's family hired an attorney to file a civil suit against the police, at least to pay his medical bills. Preoccupied with the voices, Machiavelli didn't cooperate with his family. Ted told Machiavelli if he wanted to get rid of the voices, he had to move to LA, where Shannon, his queen, was waiting. Without a ticket, Machiavelli hopped on a bus. On the streets of Los Angeles, he was no longer alone. The whole city was filled with people like him: people running away from something, homeless, hearing voices, enduring their American Dreams, trying to survive.

A homeless man offered to teach Machiavelli the tricks of the trade: panhandling, shoplifting, pickpocketing, living under bridges, showering at the beach, sleeping in a moving train. Machiavelli became a decent hustler. Marshall's was the pair's favorite store; they sold the stolen merchandise in Mexican neighborhoods. When they had no money, his new friend taught him to dine and dash. Denny's was their favorite restaurant.

By now, Machiavelli had developed patterns. Being arrested and thrown in jail became part of his daily life. There were blackouts when he woke up in a hospital or jail. There were good times, when he could perform complex tasks such as driving across states. He visited doctors who would prescribe him marijuana to relax the chaos and reduce the pain in his head. For at least a year, the voices quieted, but he was not free from other symptoms. He felt bugs crawling up his nose and feared being infected through the air he breathed—he would even wear a gas mask while walking on the street. He was clever enough to fool friends into thinking that it was an artistic way of life. He became known as "The Masked Man." He also donned sunglasses, because if people could see his eyes, they could manipulate his thoughts.

Unfortunately, a gunfight over a dispute in North Hollywood reset the course of Machiavelli's life. His attacker fired several shots. One struck his chest. He woke in the hospital the next day, and the doctor told him an operation had saved his life. Machiavelli was glad to be alive, yet he feared the guy would kill him in his hospital bed. Machiavelli slipped away from the hospital that second day. He thought about all the goats he'd killed back in Liberia. The lightning strike. The voodoo curse must have finally tracked him down. Machiavelli made a survival kit: pistol, gas mask, machete, and a bag of marijuana. He hopped a Greyhound back to Portland.

Back in Portland, the voices said his mother had visited Africa to put a voodoo spell on him. His mother flew to Portland to intervene. She told Machiavelli that she had good news for him. It might have been about his citizenship. Machiavelli took it the wrong way—that she had succeeded in getting his soul. He walked away from her with a warning—if it were not for God's will, she would not have lived to that day.

For a month or two, Machiavelli avoided Ariana, fearing she would poison him. He drifted along the city streets. Tim said, "You will never be free from the predatory voices unless you confront your mother in Minnesota." She was behind all those voices in their incessant attempt to get his soul. Machiavelli drove from Portland to Minnesota.

He blacked out somewhere along the way. He remembered being stopped in South Dakota. In the trunk, the police found the pistol, gas mask, machete, and bag of marijuana. They also discovered that the Honda was stolen. Machiavelli was charged with grand theft and remained in jail for several months. He didn't remember being in court, eating, sleeping, or being released. The next thing he remembered was waking up in the middle of a road in Iowa several months later, being tased, and getting arrested.

Court documents showed that, around sunset, a witness saw Machiavelli's car cut in front of hers and roll over. It rolled over three times before landing in a ditch. The driver crawled out. The witness called the police, who soon found Machiavelli a few blocks away. When he didn't respond to their commands, the police tased him. In jail, Machiavelli was told that he was wanted in Minnesota for the double murders of his mother and nephew the night before.

He believed it was a mistake—he bore no memory of being in the Twin Cities at all. At the same time, Machiavelli was horrified by past experiences of waking up in jail or the hospital and having to be told what he had done. No one thought to wonder whether suppressing memory, numbing emotions, and going into denial might be survival mechanisms from his war traumas.

Machiavelli was extradited and indicted on two counts of first-degree murder. He still believed the police were out to get him, until he became overwhelmed by evidence presented to him. The investigation revealed that Machiavelli had indeed arrived at his mother's house in Minneapolis. There were a few people inside. One said Machiavelli had sat on a couch in the living room and appeared upset, but hadn't said anything other than that he was tired. They'd retreated to their rooms. One heard and witnessed part of the attack. He inferred the assailant was Machiavelli. The prosecutor suggested that a machete was the murder weapon.

Machiavelli became convinced that he had killed his mother and nephew. He was terrified, but insisted that he had no control over the act or awareness of it. It must have happened during one of his blackouts. After being pronounced unfit for trial by the court, Machiavelli was sent to the state hospital for treatment and the competency restoration program.

At St. Peter, he was diagnosed with paranoid schizophrenia. He was subsequently civilly committed to the Minnesota Security Hospital at St. Peter. Machiavelli was treated with Seroquel, and the voices quieted down. He learned coping skills through intense group and individual therapies. At St. Peter, Machiavelli also received psycho-education, learning about his own mental illness. He learned to differentiate delusion from reality. When he was sent back to court to face his trial, his public defender chose a one-panel judge over a jury trial.

Three court-appointed forensic experts reviewed Machiavelli's mental history, including three hospitalizations in 2010, his jail record, and interviews. They all agreed that he suffered from paranoid schizophrenia. One, the chief psychologist for the Fourth Judicial District, stated that, at the time of the offense, Machiavelli's "understanding of the situation was significantly impaired by his delusions, hallucinations and thought disorder. While he may have had some very concrete understanding of his action at the time of the offense, I believe his overall understanding of what he was doing was highly unrealistic and irrational because of his mental illness. He was not able to understand his actions and their moral implications realistically or rationally." He concluded that Machiavelli's "behavior at the time of the offense reflected a significant exacerbation of his mental illness. Therefore, it is my opinion that the evidences available indicate that at the time of the offense charged [Machiavelli] was laboring under such a defect of reason as to not know the nature of the act constituting the offense or that it was wrong because of mental illness."

The prosecution opposed these findings and hired their own expert, who diagnosed Machiavelli with substance-induced psychosis, in remission. At trial, the chief psychologist for the Fourth Judicial District testified that Machiavelli knew that he was stabbing his mother and nephew, but due to his mental illness believed his behavior was justified: "I think he had a general vague sense in a delusional way that this was what had to happen, and I don't think he was capable of rationally considering the moral implications of what he was doing." The psychologist concluded that "[the d]efendant's mental state at the time of the offense satisfied the requirements of the mental illness defined under the rule 20.02" and that "the defendant was not guilty, by reason of mental illness."

Before making her finding, the judge asked a lot of questions about Machiavelli's social safety net. He was homeless. What had helped him survive as a child soldier and on American streets as a mentally ill person was turned against him in the courtroom. The judge found Machiavelli guilty of first-degree premeditated murder and sentenced him to two consecutive life sentences without the possibility of release.

The judge failed to recognize all the factors that made Machiavelli who he was. Like all orphaned child soldiers in Liberia, he was forced into a daily lifestyle of violent crime, including genocide. If he, as a child, ever stopped to think, he would be the one dead. Even a child will not limit what he must do to protect his life. Machiavelli didn't choose mental illness either. And at numerous intervention opportunities in the United States, he was always released to the streets to fend for himself.

At the sentencing hearing, Machiavelli told me the judge said something to the effect of, "Many people who are in the criminal justice system have some diagnosis of mental illness somewhere in their past. It doesn't mean they are not criminally liable." If the judge implied that they were sent to prison because they were not currently ill, she was either poorly informed or dishonest. Many people who are in the criminal justice system have some diagnoses of mental illness *right now*. According to the National Alliance on Mental Illness (NAMI), ten million Americans are afflicted with severe mental illness,[2] and two million of them are in prisons.[3] At the Stillwater prison where Machiavelli will live out his life, about 450 of 1,650 inmates are seen by mental health professionals. A few more have never sought help. The state fails its responsibility to provide care and treatment for its mentally ill citizens. Instead of treating them as patients in hospitals, the state jams them into prison to silence their outcry.

Ariana alone was the heroine in this human tragedy. She did all she could to assist Machiavelli throughout his mental crisis and the criminal justice process. In county jail, she sent pastors, telling him that she was with him; she was on his side. In a victim impact statement, Ariana read, "I want Machiavelli to know that we still love him. We will ever pray for him. It is a dream that never ends . . . Peter and Ma, they are in heaven. Wherever they are, they still pray for you. But

---

2 "Mental Health Facts in America," NAMI, accessed February 14, 2023, https://www .nami.org/nami/media/nami-media/infographics/generalmhfacts.pdf.

3 "Criminalization of Mental Illness," NAMI, accessed February 14, 2023, https://www .nami.org/Advocacy/Policy-Priorities/Stopping-Harmful-Practices/Criminalization -of-People-with-Mental-Illness#:~:text=People%20with%20mental%20illness%20 are,%25%20held%20in%20local%20jails).

we just want to tell you on behalf of my siblings and myself, that we forgive you and pray for your forgiveness."

Machiavelli has worked hard to maintain contact with his sister and the rest of his Liberian community. He has continued correspondence with Ariana. They love and care for each other dearly. His Liberian community in the Twin Cities and his adoptive family, who are also his victims' family, asked what they could do to help get him out of prison. They all know and accept the fact that he suffers severe mental illness.

Sending Machiavelli to die in prison will not prevent the next tragedy. War and mental illness are the two abusive parents Machiavelli grew up with. He survived dozens of battles as a child soldier, and then found his way to freedom. He thrived at first in the Promised Land, with a bright future, until mental illness swallowed his life. As a system and as a society, we failed him. He once ran toward bullets; now he runs away from voices.

The Promised Land: The Conversation

DAVID   This one has weighed on me. Can I say something, before we begin? I got diagnosed at a young age with bipolar disorder. It happened the first year I was in college, when I experienced psychosis and delusions. And it was something that I didn't understand, that the people in my life didn't understand. In earlier years I had been suicidal, and we didn't understand that. Throughout my twenties, I started to go through these periods when I thought I had stability, which would lead to mania, then psychosis, then depression, then back to stability, only to have the cycle repeat. And it wasn't until I got to prison that I got on the right medication. It's been almost a decade and a half since I've had delusions, but that hasn't made me forget what it was like to have them.

I had a peaceful childhood. But something like psychosis can develop even when there hasn't been violent trauma in the past, and there are many people out there who have had similar delusions to Machiavelli's due to symptoms related to schizophrenia or bipolar. Though that doesn't mean they always talk about it—life can spiral out of control until they are hospitalized in a psych ward, and when they're released, they might not be able to tell even to the ones closest to them what was happening in their minds prior to being admitted. Young adulthood seems to be a common age when this first surfaces. Not that there is ever a good time, but young adulthood is such a challenging time, because that is when a person is developing their own identity. And even though the vast majority suffering from these types of conditions don't commit violence, their life does get vastly disrupted from whatever path it was on before the illness. And I feel it is not so much because of the restraints of the illnesses but because of the way the medical system is set up. It does not help them fully recover as effectively as it could.

There were two crucial developments in July 2022. One was receiving confirmation that the James Webb telescope launch was a success. And on July 16, the 9-8-8 number was launched for suicide prevention. It's not just for suicide, but for people suffering mental illness crises. And it's a necessary number. Twenty-five percent of police shootings occur because a person is dealing with a mental health crisis. Hopefully, by the time this book gets published, that percentage will have gone down. Sometimes if we try only calling the people who care about us, they might not know how to help. I had really good people. I had loving people. I had intelligent people. But this was a skill set that was beyond them.

Yet you look at a phone number like this and ask—is there an infrastructure that supports this 9-8-8? In recent history, people would go to the hospital, they'd be hospitalized, but then they'd be released back in society, and there wasn't a system in place for them to reacclimate. And so, when people hear the words "psychosis" or "psychotic delusions," they think that maybe a person just has to go to the hospital, get on the right medication, and everything will work out. But in all honesty, there's a next phase when someone has this type of experience; we have to ask, what's the life they're walking back into? And this is where it gets *truly* precarious. By that point, they may have ruined all their friendships; they may have lost their job. If they had a profession, they might never be able to re-enter that profession ever again. Whatever money they had could be gone. Let's say they do get on medication. Everything is stable, then there's this whole new set of challenges. And I speak from experience with bipolar, the way my cycle was—if I went manic, or into psychosis for three months, then that'd be followed up by nine months of depression. And so that's a year right there. And it'd probably take another year to get things where you have a new group of friends, or a new school, or a new job, or whatever. And, I mean, that's tough to deal with. And people don't necessarily know how to handle that. People don't know what the right support system is.

What happened to me was, when I was nineteen I went off to college, and it started to build up, build up, build up. And when someone has psychotic delusions, generally it's pretty obvious that they're not going to be able to function because they believe stuff that's not real. I was hospitalized, and that's when I was diagnosed with bipolar disorder. But, you know, when I think back, if I would have stayed on medication consistently starting when I was nineteen—and let's just say it was the medication that got prescribed to me when I was thirty—the trajectory of my life would have been a lot different. But at the same time, I don't want to demonize people who don't take their medication, because that's hard to accept when you're nineteen years old and you have these conditions, and it's hard to believe the doctors who are telling you, "You need to take medication for the rest of your life." Even with how far medicine has advanced, they can't really cure mental illnesses, but they can manage most, and getting on the right stuff is the difference between night and day. But it can take a long, long time to find the right medication. In the meantime, people with mental illnesses have to deal with all this other stuff. So you don't even know which stage of the process someone is at in their recovery.

In my twenties, I had this one goal: I had to get a college degree. But my life, and reaching that goal, were constantly disrupted for reasons that I mentioned. I got my degree during the five years without a manic episode. I'm not sure what really happened when I graduated from college, but I think I might have said, "Okay, this is behind me now. I can go off my medication. It was something that my brain outgrew." And then I got hit with that final psychotic break, which was the most devasting one. But it's good that I'm at least on the medication now, because if it weren't for the medication, I can't imagine what my prison sentence would have been like.

When I went to jail, there was a psychiatrist who, when he visited, knew that this was his one chance to see me. So, he kind of gave me a new medication regime. I had never been on it before. He knew he had to get it right. And he gave me a Tibetan chant, which was a welcome surprise coming from a doctor. It was one of the chants that meant "life, death, rebirth." And the medication was spot-on. I started staying on it. And then I think my personality started to emerge, something that hadn't happened when I was in my twenties. Not everybody has that experience in prison. I was lucky to have a diagnosis coming into prison, where I think they treated me a little bit more seriously, and so I got the help I needed. But someone shouldn't have to go to prison to get the quality help that they need. And there are many people that need help in prison but don't get it.

There is also the importance of mentorship in helping people recover from a serious and persistent mental illness, which this essay really illustrated. It's a different role than a doctor or a therapist, but it's a role that is often not utilized, and I don't know why that is. It's not as if it takes a huge investment in infrastructure. I'd like to see a world where when people get released from a psych ward, not only are they set up with a psychiatrist and therapist, but they also are *paired with a mentor*—someone who also at one point needed to recover and has. Mentors can help in ways that a therapist and doctor can't or won't. A therapist likely won't go for a walk with you or tell you in-depth stories from their past. Friends, although incredibly important in recovery, might not have the crucial insights or patience. And although social workers do wonderful and necessary work, being visited by one can have an institutional feel to it. But a mentor . . . that's a comrade.

Now, going back to the James Webb telescope, whatever they find out there, it's probably not going to be more complicated than the human brain. Stars, the birth of stars, black holes colliding, whatever it is. Even though something like psychosis or delusions might not make sense, you could say it makes sense in that it seems possible that something as complicated as the machinery that is the human mind could break down within a set of the population. People who have these experiences shouldn't have to feel so isolated. We should be able to talk about mental illness as frequently and as easily as someone who is going through chemotherapy or who has a car accident and needs some rehab to walk again. I mean, it's the same thing. The only real difference is the part of the person that needs help. With psychosis, the difference is just that it is the brain, and we just don't understand the brain as well as we will in the future.

For a Solidarity of Condition and Position: A Report from a Delivery Driver in Manhattan

by Anonymous

Written while in mandatory quarantine on April 9, 2020, after escaping NYC following its declared lockdown.

With all these calls coming out for solidarity among all humanity in the face of the COVID-19 pandemic, I'd like to be specific about where my solidarity lies and to encourage others to do the same. While some of us are risking our lives, others are pulling the strings from above as they ride this pandemic out in comfort. While "we are all in this together," we are not all enduring the same conditions or facing the same risks.

The reality that we have been numb to for so long is coming into focus. It has become impossible to conceal the inconsistencies in the ways that our labor is valued, to ignore all the ways that we are at the mercy of those above us in the hierarchy. They have done everything in their power to make us blame ourselves and each other for our situation, but it's no longer possible.

I am writing from a mandatory quarantine outside of the United States. I spent March [2020] in Manhattan, working as a so-called "essential worker" delivering food to the rich as the pandemic spread through the city. Like so many people in my situation, I suspect that by now, I must have already been exposed to the virus. If I contracted it, I was fortunate enough to have no symptoms. As a lower-class resident of the United States, of course, I never had access to a test, so this is just speculation.

I'm not happy to say "I told you so" about the situation we find ourselves in today. At the beginning of March, many people were still dismissing me as paranoid. It wasn't that I was afraid of getting sick. For weeks, I was trying to explain to friends that they have to understand how the food they eat reaches their plates, where their medications are made, and how the division of a globalized world into consumer nations and producer nations could cause serious issues when it comes to us getting access to basic sustenance. Now everyone is talking about these things.

The first few weeks of March in New York City were like a roller coaster climbing to the top before a steep plunge. The tension just built and built. Every day, I agonized about whether I should flee to the countryside or try to return early to my home abroad. I had to weigh both of those options against the money I was making and the prospect of a future in which it might be much more difficult to obtain employment.

Biking across the boroughs, I could feel something strange building up. Most people who took the situation seriously expressed it by shopping or leaving the city. There was rampant panic buying and an exodus of those with second homes or families to stay with outside the city. Near the projects and poorer neighborhoods, I could still find toilet paper and disinfectant, since fewer people there could afford to hoard. Many distrusted the government; many didn't care; many had witnessed things even worse than a pandemic; and many felt helpless in the face of the confusion and fear that arrives with the unprecedented.

Those who wore masks and gloves were considered eccentric up until the third week of March. People were still promoting parties up to the very last day they could. Those who were able to work remotely were sent home first, while everyone else remained at work. Some of the more affluent private schools were canceled shortly after that. Then the suburb of New Rochelle was put into lockdown, but everyone else went about their business as if nothing was happening. When Mayor de Blasio finally closed the schools and forced the restaurants and bars to shutter, the reality of the situation finally began to settle in. All the reasons for high rent, all the distractions from the stress, all the rationalizations were suddenly gone. Ignorance was no longer an option.

The weather fluctuated the way it has over the last few years, prompting cynical comments about climate change, but everything just seemed dreary to me. Hugs became more and more awkward.

Soon, I reserved them only for people I wasn't sure that I'd see again. I was staying with a friend who tested positive for COVID-19 and has since recovered. I house-sat for another friend whose partner had died of the virus.

Manhattan became emptier and more and more frightening as the tension increased. In contrast to the September 11 attacks, or to Hurricane Sandy, when we saw a blackout of Manhattan on Halloween that I will never forget, the pandemic didn't hit all at once in an obvious way. It was an invisible impact in slow motion—it was hard to grasp what was coming or to what extent it was already underway. It was chilling to see friends who had recently dismissed my concerns as paranoia coming to me for advice. It made my blood run cold to watch people who had always tried to calm me down slowly growing more fearful as their livelihoods were cut off. The biggest, busiest city in the United States was shut down by an unseen force. In the end, I escaped, leaving many of the people I love to wait for the unknown.

During my final weeks in New York City, I was deemed an "essential worker" because I brought food directly to rich people's doors in order to ease their risk of exposure. I see people posting "stay at home" memes on Instagram, never pausing to acknowledge how the fusion meals they post photos of alongside them are still possible during this time.

It's hard not to scoff at the cheers of the rich I see in recent videos taken from Manhattan. Apparently, the ones who didn't escape to their summer homes take a moment each day to appreciate delivery people and other workers who have been taking the risks for them throughout this pandemic. I watch these clips and their petty gratitude leaves me unmoved. My memories of being disrespected, degraded, and underpaid are not dispelled by a moment of flattery from the comfort of Manhattan's luxury buildings. We deserve more than a little applause.

I worked delivery jobs up until the day I took what I feared was my last opportunity to return to my partner and a more affordable life abroad. I knew the risks of travel, but I was more concerned about what the future would bring and what my economic position would be in it. Most of my friends in New York work service and hospitality jobs—or used to. After every job I had intended to work was canceled, the app-based delivery jobs I turned to as my last resort were pretty much all that remained for those of us who lacked the privilege to work remotely. I still get notifications informing me of one-off work opportunities. I wonder if each one I pass up is a meal I won't be able to eat in the future.

So, I resent the applause of the wealthy. I wish I could publish the names and addresses of everyone I had to deliver to, along with the exact amounts of the tips they gave me. I wish I knew the net worth of each person I delivered to so I could calculate my anger precisely.

I delivered to skyscraper condominiums across Manhattan. At first, when I showed up, the doormen would greet me with a smile, assuming I was a visitor or resident because of my light skin. As soon as it came out that I was a delivery person, they would suddenly change tone. The transition was intense. You wonder how they choose these guys.

Other times, I was forced to enter through disgusting, piss-covered "poor doors"—secondary entrances for service workers and low-income tenants. This doubled the time it took me to enter and leave buildings. It also forced me to come into contact with more building staff, increasing my own risk of exposure.

Still other buildings wouldn't allow delivery people up at the request of tenants. I assume they considered us dirtier than the bags we delivered. While this was degrading, it was also a relief.

I delivered to penthouses as high as the seventy-third floor only to receive no tip at all. Generally, the tips were shit. Maybe this was because the rich are nervous about what the future will bring for them. (The *New York Post* has since reported on customers pretending to offer big tips and then cancelling them afterward.)[1] The tips

---

1 Hannah Sparks and Heather Hauswirth, "People Are Bait-and-Switching Grocery Delivery Workers with Big Tips," *New York Post,* April 10, 2020, https://nypost.com /2020/04/10/people-are-baiting-grocery-delivery-workers-with-big-tips-then -reneging/.

were so bad that I was afraid to ask for no-contact deliveries, as some customers scoffed at my requests. As a service worker, how dare I protect myself?

I won't forget one of my last nights delivering. I did my best to reject delivery requests to Walgreens and Duane Reade pharmacies, partly because it was just too degrading to take jobs in which my sole function was to reduce the risk that people wealthier than me had to face, but also because I knew that the products people were trying to order were already sold out.

These apps force you to be the one to bear the consequences when someone requests a product and it is sold out. They don't give you the option to cancel the job when the product is unavailable—you have to say you are unable to complete the order. Consequently, you not only forfeit travel compensation for biking to the location, you also can forfeit delivery consistency for the remainder of your shift.

That night, instead of thermometers and toilet paper, someone ordered fifty boxes of laxatives, a purchase of $250. I bit the bullet and took the order.

I biked through the silent streets of Manhattan's Upper West Side. Even in the eerie absence of traffic, I still had to obey the traffic lights, lest the police ticket me for delivering "essential" services. I miss the old school days of NYC before "quality of life" policing. In those days, riding a bicycle, you felt unstoppable.

I got to the pharmacy and went in. It felt like I was stepping into a giant petri dish teeming with COVID-19. Of course, as at all the pharmacies in Manhattan, everything was sold out, including this person's fifty boxes of laxatives. I called the customer to beg her to cancel the order—my only chance to keep the pathetic $2.36 that I get for the "pick up" part of the delivery process. More importantly, it was also the only way to avoid having to cancel the order myself and risk losing my spot in the app's almighty algorithm.

"*Of course* they are out, ugh!" she answered when I informed her. She demanded that I be the one to cancel, because she knew she'd lose her $2.36, reciting the standard, "It's your job; it's not my fault." She had used me to confirm what she already knew so she wouldn't have to enter a pharmacy in the epicenter of the epidemic, but she had the audacity to demand I cancel so she wouldn't have to give me any money. I ended up begging her, trying to explain that I had biked through a pandemic to check on the product for her. I offered to send her a photograph confirming that I went into the store and saw that the product was out. She replied that it wasn't her problem. I moved on to the next job, obsessing about her selfishness and entitlement. After thirty minutes, she canceled.

She was placing a $250 order and she demanded that I forfeit all dignity so that she didn't have to "waste" $2.36. I am certain that if I had not spoken good English, I would have received nothing at all for my pains. Of countless stories like this, this one remains fresh in my memory—it took place the last night I was working in New York.

This is why, when the wealthy and powerful speak about solidarity, it leaves me cold. I reserve my love and appreciation for those who are not only afraid of getting sick at this time, but who are also forced to risk being infected in order to survive—those who are struggling to figure out how to eat, how to keep a roof over their heads, how to prepare for an even more precarious life in the economic recession ahead. I reserve my love and appreciation for those who have always been underpaid and replaceable, who are on the front lines of the pandemic. *Now* we are essential? *Now* we are heroes? What were we before? What will we be when this ends?

It's shocking how people continue to rationalize the value of leaders and institutions that have utterly failed to do anything to help us survive this catastrophe.

How is it possible that police officers are still getting respect as "emergency workers" when they are running around without masks on, infecting people throughout the city, attacking children on the subway? How can anyone set them alongside nurses and grocery store workers, who are dying dozens at a time so we can eat? Hasn't the role of police in the spectacle of the end of the world shown their true purpose clearly enough, if it wasn't already obvious?

ICE agents have been hogging N-95 masks so that they can protect themselves while they continue disappearing undocumented people, spreading the infection as they terrorize communities and separate children from their parents. Prison guards are spreading the virus to prisoners whose only means of protest is to stage revolts at great risk to themselves.

I saw police pulling over delivery workers for bicycle traffic violations in Manhattan when deliveries surged in response to the virus. This is a typical tactic by which the New York Police Department fulfills their monthly ticket quotas. Grocery workers, agricultural workers, those working in transportation, delivery people, EMTs, and hospital staff helping to keep us alive under what amounts to martial law—all these people are all truly deserving of my gratitude. How can anyone place the police alongside these courageous individuals? What do they do to sustain and care for us?

The United States has passed a two-trillion-dollar stimulus plan. I don't even know if I am eligible for the check or for unemployment, thanks to working gig to gig all these years. I read that only 30 percent of the stimulus goes to individuals ($602.7 billion). The other 70 percent is split between large corporations ($500 billion), small businesses ($377 billion), state and local governments ($339.8 billion), and public services ($179.5 billion).[2] As far as I see—and especially considering that the airlines alone are getting over 10 percent of the corporate bailouts—I see this as a big "fuck you" to me and everyone like me. Just one more reminder that, in this society, my value is conditional at best, determined by the logic of the market and the priorities of the ruling class.

If the way that the stimulus package is distributed doesn't make their priorities clear enough, governments are simultaneously rushing to maintain, reconstruct, and usurp power.

In places like Russia and Israel, authorities are exploring new opportunities in cyber-policing. In places like Hungary, rulers have already used this opportunity to transition to outright dictatorship.

---

2 Kelsey Snell, "What's Inside the Senate's $2 Trillion Coronavirus Aid Package," NPR, March 26, 2020, https://www.npr.org/2020/03/26/821457551/whats-inside-the-senate-s-2-trillion-coronavirus-aid-package.

In places like Kenya, India, and the USA, we see governments containing slums, prisons, and refugee camps as acceptable death zones. In Greece, on International World Health Day, police attacked a gathering of doctors and nurses at Evangelismos Hospital in Athens who were calling for more safety resources. Experiments in martial law are taking place everywhere under the guise of lockdowns, supposedly for our protection—but those in power are seeking to protect their own positions, not to protect us. Nationalists and fascists are using this as an opportunity to advocate for bigger border walls and prisons. We've even seen some scientists calling on world governments to go to Africa or other populations that are less valuable to the global economy in order to carry out the experiments through which they hope to generate vaccines.

So, I want to call for another solidarity. A solidarity between those who have a lot more to worry about than the virus alone. A solidarity among all who have to fear what governments and their police will do to us. A solidarity between everyone who is waiting in terror for even more precarious conditions to arrive as the rich scramble to enter the post-pandemic world still standing on the shoulders of us expendables. A solidarity that includes refugees and others who have lost their homes.

I want to share my gratitude with those who deserve it—those with whom I share *condition* and *position.*

When in our lifetimes has the mathematics of our value been more flagrantly displayed? Politicians, police, and billionaires are struggling to rationalize their comfort and privilege; in the United States, they are being more honest than ever before about what really matters to them.

We need a solidarity that has nothing to do with politicians and plutocrats, nor with the police who protect them. Let us look on those beside us with love and a mutual commitment to protect our humanity. Those who are looting in southern Italy are expressing the same passion for life as those who looted New Orleans after Hurricane Katrina in order to feed their neighbors. These are the people who are setting a good example, not the police, not Governor Cuomo.

Today, my own quarantine period is about to end. But my mother is working in a grocery store at nearly seventy years of age, while my father, who is in a hospital with a compromised immune system, has tested positive for coronavirus. If concerns about the market had not been prioritized over concerns about life, I am certain my father would have been spared this virus, as he was isolated since the beginning of March in a nursing facility. My mother cannot distance. My father couldn't distance. But many can afford to sidestep these risks. They are not facing the same pandemic. They don't deserve my solidarity.

We are not all in this together—but most of us are.

Return to normalcy? Never again.

For a Solidarity of Condition and Position: The Conversation

JEN   Who here has been a delivery person?

WILL   I got out of prison the first time in 1999, and I had gotten to the interview stage at a couple of jobs. And when my record came up, they took me out. And my PO was like, "You need to get a job at the end of the week, or else." And so, I started just calling down the job listings, asking, "Does it matter that I have a criminal record? Does it matter that I have a criminal record?" And it was Red Rooster Auto Stores up in Lexington, Minnesota; they needed a delivery driver. And they said, "Well, no, we don't care about that. Can you drive a stick?" No, I could not. Did I tell them that? No, I did not. So, I'm out driving around with this old guy, he's got to be in his early sixties. And I'm just grinding the fuck out of the gears in this little S-10 Chevy pickup. And one time we were at a green arrow and, because I had it in third, I kept stalling it out. And so, I missed the green arrow for the whole line.

JEN   Been there with a stick.

RUBY   I was never a delivery person. But I was working in food service during, not necessarily the height of COVID, but the summer after the school year had been remote and whatnot, before they opened indoor dining. And so, I was working with a lot of delivery people because, you know, they were the only people who were really able to come into the restaurant and pick up food for folks. And there's a weird incentive system with online delivery apps. They really gamify it, like if you deliver to X amount of people in this amount of time, you'll get a $200 bonus. And so, the folks that are coming in, the delivery people who are coming into the restaurant, they are really under a harsh deadline and under a lot of stress.

CHRIS   It's a hustle, right? America is inherently a hustle. That's what you sign up for if you do that work.

JEN   I mean, the woman in this essay can tip better, or cancel the order. The system does not force her to be an asshole. The system does not force anyone to give a one-dollar or three-dollar tip.

CHRIS   But it allows them to.

JEN   What if we don't look at it in terms of systems? What if we just asked, what does it mean to be a human and to have asked something of another human and have that person come to your door, and to recognize or not recognize that that person is somewhat in danger because of the thing they're doing for you?

WILL   I think the argument of this essay is that to have subjected him to a precarious position by engaging in the delivery app in the first place is to participate as his oppressor.

JEN   Yep, fair. It's a continuum, right? There's always a way to navigate where you fall on the continuum as the oppressor. Did I order groceries during early COVID? Hell, yes, I did. But I tipped so much money, because it felt like that's the cost of saving your own ass.

WILL   Which I think is fair. I think that's reasonable.

RUBY   From my experience—just working in food service and being around folks who work in food service all the time—I definitely have noticed that my friends who are struggling the most financially and who are working as baristas at three different places at once will tip the most. And I think that has always been the case—that a person in a precarious situation engages in mutual aid more often than those who have all of the resources in the world.

DAVID   This is why I think this essay is important. Because how many times did you see essential workers show up in the news? They talked about it a lot, but they never showed this side of it. And when people see essential workers, they should see this side of it. Automatically.

KENNEDY   What you see in this essay is capitalism at its worst. The guy's like a modern-day slave. The app company makes money, and the customers get what they want, but he doesn't. And he gives us a very good example of how he actually has a need—he does actual work, but nobody's going to pay. And that is what makes him mad. You know, that is what makes me mad. I figure like Jen was saying, if you're a human being, when you see a problem or a mistake, the idea is to try and solve it. And his argument is like, "Okay, you guys are clapping and saying thank you to all the essential workers. But when we need you, you don't show up for us." This rich lady sitting at home, just waiting for her food and laxatives, she should have taken the fight to say like, "Hey, these people are doing something good. It needs to be fixed, and here is how we can help them do that." She doesn't do that.

RUBY   What is the example of responsible and well-regulated capitalism? What country could the US look to [in order to] create a capitalistic structure that is equitable?

WILL   I think there are individual programs, amid larger systems, that don't function well, because the entire concept of Western civilization is right now at odds, trying to figure out that late-stage capitalism is problematic. Like what the German manufacturing industry did—open up their immigration policy to allow Eastern European immigrants to come into the country on work permits and to be trained to receive full German citizenship. So, training pathways to citizenship, economic support in exchange for working in one of the better labor environments in Europe, as an example, as opposed to, you know, tenuous permits and border walls for agricultural workers.

KENNEDY   I think instead of looking for a model country to emulate, it's better to fight for everybody to play by the same rules. That is the worst thing—when people say that America is a democracy, it doesn't make any sense in my head at all. Because we don't all play by the same rules, not at all.

Debt Demands a Body

by Kristin Collier

I open the email at 9:30 a.m. in my retrofitted, windowless office on the second floor of a high school in St. Paul, Minnesota. The fluorescent lights are so bright and the walls so white that sometimes I look up from my computer screen and feel as if I'm in a dream. Everything blurs and bends. Here, I shield myself from my students' bodies, from their breath, in between teaching classes. I remove my mask, just briefly, to eat lunch while refreshing a COVID-tracking map. November 3, 2020: 1,040 people died in the US from COVID-19.

I read the email's subject line: "The results of your request are now available in a paperless inbox," before noticing the sender is American Education Services (AES), a private student loan servicer. The body of the email informs me that AES has added a message to the inbox—something about new loan terms that will require me to begin payments in December. I minimize the screen and scan the room quickly, as if the desk lamp and the growing stack of compostable knives can see the message. I pull the screen up and read the email again, willing the language to be different this time, but it's not. My AES account, along with accounts from a handful of other private loan servicers, was settled in 2018 after protracted and painful negotiations that had begun years earlier. What remains, or what I thought remained, is $2,000 in federal student loan debt. But now there appears to be a new loan, something left unsettled. I close the computer screen. Elbows on white table. Head in hands. I cry.

✤ ✤ ✤

The email from AES is the first I have received from them in over six years, part of a halted but lengthy correspondence that began, unbeknownst to me, on July 29, 2004, when I was eighteen and my mother took out the first of many private student loans in my name. That July day was cold in southwest Michigan, a detail I researched years later when I wondered what went on in her world that day. It rained. There was little sun. In the morning, my father drove to his corporate office to design washing machine parts, I drove to a golf club where I worked in their food shack, and sometime that day my mother contacted Bank One, a student lending arm of Chase Bank, and requested $15,000 in my name, using my birthdate and Social Security number. I've never been able to ask her how the fraud was committed—if she told the bank that she was applying on my behalf and would get my approval later, or if, pretending to be me, she filled out an application online. It's unclear if Bank One, who partnered with AES for loan management and collection, asked her the questions they should have, the questions that might have revealed that she did not have my approval or that she was not me. I'm unsure if the bank account she funneled the money to was one she opened in my name or hers. I do know that on the loan application she forged my signature, which I'll see years later—the swoop of the cursive *K* larger and fuller than mine.

Over the course of the next three years, as my mother's gambling addiction escalated, she took out another student loan, and then another, and then so many others that the amounts and institutions from which she borrowed knotted together into something big and impossible to disentangle, but the accumulation of which was about $125,000. It seems that none of the private lenders were alarmed by the rapid acquisition of increasingly large amounts of money—more than I would ever need for my state-school tuition—a record of lending they would have seen when they pulled my credit. It might be that they noticed and didn't care.

While I didn't know about my fraudulent debt in those years, I did know that my mother had her own. At home during university breaks, I often fielded calls from credit card debt collectors, the phone company, or the internet company. I learned to recognize the callers' scripts, and the moment they departed from them, becoming angry with me for refusing to put my mother on the phone, and then threatening to shut off our services if we didn't pay. And there were other signs her gambling problem was growing big and wild. Bounced checks. Denied credit cards at the supermarket. My mother, home late with handfuls of cash, tipsily offering my friends and me $50 because she'd won on slots that night.

In my early twenties, I watched my debt total increase like some people watch an eroding shoreline. The interest rates on many of the loans were unfixed, so some years the shoreline stayed constant. Then, as if overnight, a wave touched my toes. At my debt's peak, when I was thirty, I owed about $386,000, and the water overwhelmed what little land was left. Thirty-five now, I recall the day I first learned of my debt in foggy, tender detail. I was twenty-one years old and graduating from college in two weeks. I was *just* applying for my first credit card, and then an hour later, I was learning that I was a victim of ongoing identity theft by my mother. Debt decides the future for you. At twenty-six, I would be paying $600 a month in loan payments to barely cover the mounting interest. At thirty, I was telling someone I loved that to be with me would mean entering into a life of economic peril. The future that debt chose for me—indeed the future it chooses for many people—included a lot of shame, confusion, and pain.

I walked home from the bank, rejected credit card application in hand, as if walking toward certain death. In place of the steady hum of college students commuting to class, all I heard was the hollow sound of the wind as I slid my boots across the slick sidewalk. Home now, seated on my bed in a new world, frozen still, I held the credit report in front of me, counting the listed debts: $10,000 owed to JPMorgan Chase, $20,000 to ACS Education Services, $15,000 owed to someone else. I didn't yet know that the majority of these were private loans protected by the federal government. This can't be right, I said to myself over and over again. Part incantation, part desperate plea.

When I called my mother to tell her and ask for her advice, she begged me not to call the police. "I'm so sorry, honey. But it was me. All of it was me."

✢✢✢

In late March of 2020, as the first wave of the pandemic spread across the country, Congress passed the CARES Act, a $2 trillion aid package marketed as relief to struggling Americans. While the act provided much-needed relief for those most impacted by the pandemic, it didn't provide enough. The $1,200 received by poor and working-class Americans was spent quickly on essential items, which, sadly, included debt.

As part of that act, Congress included several measures to support student debtors. First, their employers—if they were lucky enough to be employed—were able to provide student debtors with up to $5,250 in tax-free student loan repayment benefits. Before the CARES Act, only about 8 percent of employers were making contributions toward student loans, and as businesses and institutions closed, most employers reduced benefits rather than expanding them. During the first four months of the pandemic, at least four million workers had their pay cut, and nearly six million workers were forced to work part-time.[1] In other words, though this measure could have helped student debtors, there's very little evidence to suggest that it did.

The second measure affecting student debtors was an automatic suspension of payments on federal student loans, a relief extended several times and now set to expire after January 31, 2022. As part of this moratorium, loan servicers cannot collect loan payments, including on defaulted loans, and interest rates remain at zero percent. Roughly 35 million student debtors are eligible for this temporary relief, collectively owing $1.5 trillion. I'm one of them. Of the $14,000 I knowingly took out in federal student aid, about $2,000 remains. It's worth noting that the many millions of borrowers whose debt is privately held are excluded from these benefits. Few private lenders, if any, deferred interest, and most offered only a three-month suspension on collection.

April 2020 marked the first month since I graduated college thirteen years earlier that I didn't pay a portion of my wage, at times nearly half of my wage, toward my student debt: either my own federal debt or the $125,000 that my mother took out in my name. For

---

1 Heather Long and Andrew Van Dam, "Pay Cuts Are Becoming a Defining Feature of the Coronavirus Recession," *Washington Post,* July 1, 2020, https://www.washingtonpost.com/business/2020/07/01/pay-cut-economy-coronavirus/.

many people, the moratorium is a lifesaving pause. Those who are unemployed can perhaps afford a car payment or a home payment or the co-payment necessary to see a doctor. The employed can also make dignified decisions to care for themselves and others. They can fix the broken heater in their car; or buy medication and a working phone; or something more banal and essential still—buy groceries.

Employed as a teacher and earning a living wage, my own debts didn't force me to go without shelter, food, or basic utilities, a fact that was tested in my twenties when I had trouble finding landlords who'd rent to me because of my credit score. When the moratorium went into effect, I increased my contribution to my 401(k), which had recently sent me a message saying that based on my modest savings goals, I would not be able to sustain myself in old age. I also bought a winter coat, the first I'd purchased in seven years. The old one had thinned so much that it was porous, and the Minneapolis wind moved through me in the winter. This was not the first time in seven years I'd had enough money for a coat. Rather, having lived with financial anxiety for so long, I struggle to decide what to spend money on, what's worth depleting my small but growing savings account, even by a couple of hundred dollars.

✤✤✤

I return to AES's message, this time from my home, where I teach virtually the second half of the week. After attempting to log onto the account, I soon realize I no longer have the information. This account, like all of them, was created by my mother and managed in secret for the years I was in college. It was opened after her gambling problem bloomed into an addiction, after she'd spent her and my father's savings, along with the money she'd borrowed from his mother and from her parents, and the money she'd stolen from her employer. It would have made sense for me to reset everything once I learned of the account's existence, but I never did. I wonder now if I conflated this step with an acknowledgment that the debt was mine. Often the tiny protests I waged in my twenties hurt me: I lost paperwork, passwords, loan correspondences. I missed details that would have made managing my mounting debt easier. But I didn't want to manage it. I wanted to pretend that it wasn't there.

After I discovered the debt, the boundaries between myself and everything else became cloudy. At first, it was just my mother begging me not to file criminal charges. She called me regularly in those days. "You can't send me to jail," she said over and over, her voice rushing around me, as familiar as the sound of the wind.

I agreed not to, not so much because I believed that she would be capable of helping me as she promised, but because I didn't have a clear sense of where I ended and my mother began. After she was released from her incarceration for workplace theft only a few months into her sentence, my father and grandparents asked me not to file charges. "Your mother won't survive it again," they told me. "She doesn't deserve it." "You're young. You're strong," they said. "We'll help you figure it out." I didn't want my mother to suffer, and I didn't believe that her criminal conviction was a requirement for my justice and healing. But beyond my love and my politics was the sense that I was beginning to dissolve, and self-preservation felt impossible in the face of this rapid depletion.

Outside in Minneapolis, it's seventy degrees—a warming earth in disguise as a lingering summer. I search through my email for clues to the account information. Nothing comes up in my search, so I make a guess at the username and am diverted to a series of security prompts: name of first pet, paternal grandfather, name of elementary school. I'm not sure if my mother answered as me—Jesse, Jim, Brown—or herself. Sometimes, to navigate my debt is not to imagine myself as my mother, but to imagine myself as my mother imagining herself as me. If she loved me enough, she wouldn't have done it, I thought for much of my twenties. I wore that belief like a warm but itchy sweater. And even though at thirty-five, I now understand that my young belief was not protective, but harmful and untrue, each failed guess feels like a rock in my stomach, a reminder of a personal betrayal within a systemic one.

Alas, I figure it out: she answered as me.

AES explains that I must begin to make payments on my loan, the first of which is due in early December. I'm surprised to realize that, unlike federal loans, private loans such as this one are not covered under the moratorium. More than that, I'm surprised that this loan exists at all.

Looking at the details of my loan feels like looking at a hand that has appeared suddenly before me, attached to my own body, part of me but not mine. The loan is through a private student loan program (ALPLN) that often requires young borrowers to enlist cosigners, locking both parties in for long repayment plans with variable interest rates that fluctuate according to the market, but rarely to the benefit of the borrower. The original balance of this loan was $25,000 (the equivalent of two semesters in-state at the University of Michigan in 2008, or a down payment on a home in a middle-class Minneapolis neighborhood today), but today I owe $30,549.08 (two semesters + living expenses) and were I to finish paying this loan, I would pay in total $40,051.86 (a nicer house, another semester).

For all of my twenties, I worked multiple jobs to keep up with the $600 monthly loan payments. In 2013, for example, I taught sophomore English at a high school in Chicago, working 7:00 a.m.–4:30 p.m. On Tuesdays, I led our school's literary magazine club till 5:30 p.m., and for six weeks each semester, on Wednesdays and Thursdays, I taught night school classes till 6:30 p.m. for students who needed credit recovery. On Saturdays, I picked up ACT administration work, and on Mondays, I picked up ACT tutoring. After I got home at 7:00 or 7:30 p.m., or later, I wrote the next day's lesson plan as I picked at my dinner. If I also had to give students feedback on essays, I worked until 10:00 p.m., falling asleep with the next day's schedule pulsing beside me. Then I was up at 6:15 a.m. to do it all again. By the time I turned thirty, I had paid off about $60,000 of the debt, an amount that barely touched the interest. It was not enough. The debt kept rising, not by $10,000, but by $100,000, and then another $100,000, more than doubling the principal balance.

✦ ✦ ✦

In ancient civilizations, debt repayment was a promise secured by the body. In India, an unpaid creditor could show up at his debtor's door, sit on his doorstep, and stay there, indefinitely, publicly starving to death until he was given what he was owed. In Egypt, a debtor pledged their repayment on the dead body of a loved one.

You could maim someone according to ancient Hindu law, and if that did not yield repayment, you might take his cattle, his sons, or his wife—or simply enslave or kill him. The same punishments were allowed according to ancient Roman law, with an addendum: a debtor who was killed for unpaid debts might have his body divided for creditors, sliced up proportionate to the amount of each one's claims. A severed head for the largest debt, I guess, and just a foot for something smaller. This Roman law would spawn the "pound of flesh" Shylock seeks to collect in *The Merchant of Venice* and all the cultural references it, in turn, generated. Though this grotesque form of accounting has little documentation, debt slavery was common.[2]

So, too, was debt imprisonment, which existed in the barbarian kingdoms that followed the Roman Empire in the West. Still later, as feudalism declined, the Catholic Church encouraged and enforced imprisonment for unpaid debts. Those debtors who died without leaving enough money to cover their remaining debts were denied a Christian burial, their very bodies unwelcome on holy land.

Debtors' prisons followed colonists from England to the Americas, where they remained in practice until the mid-1800s, only to be revived in the South less than twenty years later as part of Jim Crow. According to many of the laws that guided early debtors' prisons, sentences had no fixed length: one could remain incarcerated for a month or years, whatever amount of time satisfied the creditors. While the prisons' upper class debtors were often assigned well-lit rooms where they could write or paint, the poorest prisoners slept in the cellar, sometimes sitting in near darkness day and night, hungry and cold, threatened by disease. In this case, the punishment was not labor or mutilation, but isolation and stagnation: a body left alone to rot.

✤ ✤ ✤

2 Louis Edward Levinthal, "The Early History of Bankruptcy Law," *University of Pennsylvania Law Review and American Law Register* 66, no. 5/6 (April 1918): 223–250.

Living in New York City in my early twenties, I began my first year of teaching, and my mother began her trial for workplace embezzlement. I'd learned of her arrest earlier that summer—standing in a dorm room in Queens where I was undergoing teacher training. Just out of the shower, my wet hair dripped into puddles on the floor as my aunt explained over the phone that my mother had been stealing from the dentist for whom she managed medical billing. When we hung up, I didn't feel anything. I considered what my aunt thought my mother had stolen—around $40,000—and all I could think of was, "That's all?" It was nothing compared to what she owed me.

After my mother began her five-month sentence, I moved through my life as if I were underwater. On land, I was required to participate: laugh with colleagues, cook dinner with my roommates, engage in conversations about the future and the past, both of which I wanted to avoid. Submerged in the water, I was alone, stranded in a perpetual present. For weeks I lived like this, allowing the calls from debt collectors to hover over me like ships on the surface, and then suddenly, I would come in from the sea—awakened by a nightmare at 3:00 a.m., or sitting at a student desk eating my lunch, I would suddenly be thrust back into the bright, loud world. And then I would feel the full weight of it all: hundreds of thousands of dollars that I'd pay until I died.

I slept poorly during those years, plagued by severe stomach pains and recurrent UTIs that sometimes reached my kidneys. Once, after a week of particularly distressing calls with debt collectors, I woke on a Saturday morning to a full stomach, even though I hadn't eaten. Throughout the morning, the fullness increased, as did the pain, like barbed wire wrapping my insides. When I moved, I could hear acid swish inside me. I started puking in the afternoon, and when I hadn't stopped by early evening, I walked to Lennox Hill hospital, where I spent the night. I cried when a nurse held my hand, asking me to swallow the cool medication that would allow her to see inside of me. I didn't tell anyone I was sick because, at the time, I was estranged from both my parents, and there was no one to tell.

Debt was still a promise held by my body, and absent of the money, my body paid in other ways. I learned from the endoscopy that I had an ulcer and had developed gastritis. The cystoscopy was inconclusive, but years later, in my early thirties, I'd begin to notice pressure on my left side—the feeling of a tiny fist punching softly outward just below my rib cage. After doctors told me it was nothing for several years, I'd find the right doctors who gave the right tests, and I'd learn that my kidney had died. Perhaps, my doctor said, it had died when I was young, having lost its blood supply through a misfire in design, or it might have died later as a result of the many escalating UTI infections. *A stomach for AES, to which I owed $51K; a kidney for JPMorgan Chase, to which I owed $30K.*

Debt's impact on our health is well-documented. Good debt—a manageable mortgage, for example—corresponds with positive health outcomes. It's also indicative of a higher household income. But bad debt—debt that is or feels unpayable, debt incurred through unjust systems, predatory debt, debt that makes it hard to live—corresponds with high blood pressure, stress, depression, and overall worse health. Chronic stress can be especially dangerous because it continually triggers the body's fight or flight response without allowing the body to recover when the stress has passed. The body's attempt to protect itself impacts all of its systems. It leads to hypertension, heart attacks, and strokes. It gives us stomachaches, bloating, heartburn, and acid reflux, and it weakens our intestines, making us vulnerable to bacterial infection. Professor Elizabeth Sweet, the author of a study on the relationship between debt and health in *Social Science & Medicine,* reminds us that, in addition to all of that, chronic stress associated with debt can also suppress the immune system, impairing the body's ability to fight infection.[3]

⁜⁜⁜

As a market economy emerged in the 1700s, according to Jill Lepore in a *New Yorker* essay on the historical treatment of debtors, debt punishments shifted away from imprisonment—which also meant that

---

3 Elizabeth Sweet, Arijit Nandi, Emma K. Adam, and Thomas W. McDade, "The High Price of Debt: Household Financial Debt and Its Impact on Mental and Physical Health," *Social Science & Medicine* 91 (August 2013): 94–100.

punishments shifted away from the body.[4] Individuals, she explains, *had* to take on debt to acquire the things they needed, a relationship that necessitated debt relief, which came in the form of bankruptcy.

However, that relief has come with limitations, especially in the field of student loans. Until 1978, students facing unmanageable debt could petition for bankruptcy—though it's worth noting that in 1978 the semester tuition for a four-year public university was $777, so fewer students took on debt in the first place. Through the combination of the Education Amendment Act of 1976 and additional legislation in 1978, 1984, 1990, and 1998, students gradually lost more and more protections, a loss that coincided with a precipitous increase in tuition fees. First, students could have their federal debts discharged after they had made payments on them for five years, then that time period was extended to seven years, and then extended to the lifetime of the borrower. Finally, the lifetime sentence was extended to private student loans as well as federal.

What that means is that people are paying off their student debts into old age. People are dying with this debt based on decisions they or their families made when they were eighteen. Sometimes these decisions were made with counsel from for-profit colleges that promised salaries and degrees they couldn't produce. Sometimes these decisions were made with counsel from private lenders, who offer predatory interest rates that make it nearly impossible to pay loans down. Other times, racial or structural inequality or even just bad luck forced students out of school, funneling them into jobs that would never yield the salaries necessary to pay off even relatively small amounts of debt. In other instances, students graduated and found employment, but because the cost of tuition has ballooned and wages have flattened, they are still stuck with this debt sentence, even after falling on the right side of luck, the right side of privilege, and even after they did everything right.

Those who suffer the most from the current student-lending structure are the same people who suffer because of historical and structural

---

4 Jill Lepore, "I.O.U.: How We Used to Treat Debtors," *The New Yorker,* April 6, 2009, https://www.newyorker.com/magazine/2009/04/13/i-o-u.

inequity: descendants of enslaved people, people of color, women, and poor people. Black women hold the highest levels of student debt, and, because they make sixty-one cents for every dollar that a white man makes, Black women struggle to pay this debt down, even as they work multiple jobs, even as debt extracts their health and their labor.

✦✦✦

The decision to enter into my loan agreements was not mine, of course, but my mother's, a fact that I communicated to the debt collectors with whom I tried to negotiate in my early twenties. In one of the many calls I remember, I'm standing at the corner of 78th Street in the early evening, just as day tips into night.

"You don't understand," I tell the debt collector. "This debt isn't mine. I didn't take it out. My mother did."

"That's not our problem," he says. "You should take it up with the police." He sounds young.

At the time, I didn't know that collectors are required to verify contested debts. However, this requirement is widely ignored by debt collectors, one of the many abuses—along with harassment, threats, and the disclosure of debts to family and colleagues—that the Federal Trade Commission documents.[5]

I cup my hand around the phone, to muffle not the wind but my own voice. I don't want the couples leaning against the railing or the people running with their dogs to hear me. "Why would I need this much money in private loans to attend a school with an in-state tuition of $13,000 a year?"

Occasionally I did this, said things that required the collectors to imagine a human from the numbers listed in front of them: a one, a two, a five, and so many zeroes unwound into legs and arms. Sometimes, the collectors sounded sad for me. At least a few times, they said they were sorry. But, still, they recorded what they were required to, the distillation of which was that I couldn't or wouldn't pay. And then my

---

5 "Debt Collection," Federal Trade Commission, accessed February 14, 2023, https://www.ftc.gov/news-events/topics/consumer-finance/debt-collection.

name was added to the next escalation in collection efforts: another letter, another call, and, eventually, a court order and wage garnishment.

The collectors' emotional disengagement is a necessity of a cruel industry. To respond to me humanely would make the task nearly impossible. While debt cleaves to bodies, its collection requires severance from them. To them, I'm not a terrified twenty-one-year-old too ashamed to take the call in her apartment, but rather I am a name, an interest rate, a monthly payment, a total debt paid, a number yet to collect.

✤ ✤ ✤

I call AES a couple of weeks after Thanksgiving. It's been years since I've last spoken with someone representing the lenders, and I'm haunted by all the conversations that I've already had. When I speak, my voice sounds distant and caffeinated.

"This can't be right," I say to her, the same thing I said sitting on my college bed thirteen years earlier, holding the credit report printed for me by the bank. No longer an incantation, but an elegy.

My disbelief is an evolution of the original, a shared origin with a new context. At the nadir of my indebtedness, unable to save enough, unable to pay enough, I met with several lawyers who said they couldn't help me. They first told me that to file a criminal charge and potentially transfer the debt would endanger my grandparents—my mother's immigrant parents—who, unclear on the US lending system, had co-signed on many of the fraudulent loans. "The banks will go after them and they will likely lose their house," he said, mapping an elaborate spider-like diagram of the debt. He called in several colleagues to consult with, explaining the complexities of my case. At the center of the drawing was me, alone in a thick, black circle. The second lawyer, whom I met with a few years later, said criminal charges couldn't work even if I wanted to pursue them because the statute of limitations had passed. Later, a lawyer friend recommended a bankruptcy attorney. I met the attorney, Todd, in his office in the middle of a late fall blizzard. I was buoyed by his fancy brass lamps and sprawling Persian carpet. I needed him to help me and he did.

While my loans were protected through the bankruptcy codes, we'd use my bankruptcy petition to pause collection while I could pay down the credit card debt my mother had also taken out through the Chapter 13 bankruptcy plan—a plan traditionally used to help people keep their homes. I'd also pay off the federal debt, which I had taken on knowingly. We'd use the legal framework to force a conversation with the lenders that refused to communicate with me otherwise. These conversations were logistical hurdles because locating all my lenders required piecing together credit reports, old statements my mother had sent me, and statements the lenders pulled. No one database records all private loan debt. At least once, we thought we'd found it all only to realize we'd missed $50,000 from a loan servicer I'd never heard of.

Our strategy was bifurcated: I moved through the traditional bankruptcy process, taking the required financial management classes, showing up to court dates, and sending monthly checks to my trustee, and Todd ushered me through fraud proceedings according to the requirements of the lenders, proceedings which mostly relied on handwriting analysis. I signed my name a hundred times. I wrote addresses and numbers in cursive and print, or random men's names, seemingly taken from a list of Dickens characters. When the lenders rejected my fraud claims on the basis of my handwriting, we hired our own expert. Eventually, my mother, shielded by the seven-year statute of limitations on criminal convictions, signed an affidavit that the debt was hers, and after a settlement with the lenders, the loans were moved from my body back to hers, though the lenders have never reached out to her. They're likely aware that her economic position, as a minimum wage worker, makes the debt uncollectible.

"I have a legal agreement with the loan companies," I tell the woman. My voice is thin and wet. "It's from several years ago. I have the signature of someone representing AES. It's a legal document," I say again.

"I have you paused for bankruptcy, but now you're done and there is nothing about any settlement," she says.

I catch my partner's eye as he walks into the room, alerted by my rising voice that something is wrong. I'm self-conscious of how

I sound, the way I'm escalating the conversation, begging her to put someone else on the phone, which she doesn't do. When I ask her if I can email her the settlement, she says it's impossible: they'll only accept faxes and snail mail. Eventually, she suggests a convoluted form I might fill out that will put someone in touch with me over email.

"This isn't fair," I say to her before we hang up, a sentiment that startles me in its naivete and desperation. Of course it isn't.

In my early twenties, I took a free poetry class through my teaching program, and when we practiced writing exercises for imagery and metaphor, I wrote about my debt. A red balloon for each dollar: 125,000 balloons, enough to fill a city block. They follow me as I walk around the city, west on 77th to the train station or east on 77th to the river. Cloud-like, but alive, each bobbing and swaying separately. The balloons cast a long shadow. Sometimes, I stand beneath them looking up. No more sunshine. They've ushered in a new world, a red sky.

⊹⊹⊹

After I speak to the collector, I ignore the new set of emails, the mail correspondence, the alarming language of delinquency. Already the last three years—the years without large monthly loan payments, without collectors—seem far away. A shadow gathers above.

My lawyer thinks this new debt is a forgotten one, a lost one now found. When I call him, he's surprised to hear my voice.

"This can't be right. We settled all of this," he tells me. But we haven't. After cross-checking the settlement details and the loan, I discover it's not listed on the settlement. It's also not on the list of all the private loans that we painstakingly gathered piecemeal to guide our strategy. When I explain this to my lawyer he says, "But that list came directly from AES. So, if there is an error, it's theirs. Or they didn't have the loan at the time."

This new loan, this zombie loan as I've taken to calling it, belongs to the National Collegiate Student Loan Trust (CSLT), which is neither a lender nor a servicer but an investment opportunity. It's essentially a bucket of private loans, which are sold off as bonds to investors. Right now, the National Collegiate Student Loan Trusts—which includes fifteen trusts—"holds nearly $12 billion in student debt, more than all the stars in the milky way."[6]

When I learn that CSLT owns the loan, I imagine the people who have benefited from the events that upended my life. These investors are likely the same people that escaped to second homes during each of the pandemic's sharp peaks. As ICUs filled up, as lungs broke down, as the poorest in the country struggled to breathe, they ordered in their groceries, worked from home offices with ergonomic chairs and stand-up desks, their isolation tethered to the exposure of others. One body in exchange for another.

Those who've been most at risk in the pandemic are the same people with shifting red skies above their own heads. They are working class; they are Black people, Indigenous people, Latinx people. They are people whose race or economic position has forced them into frontline jobs. They are people whose debt makes their bodies more vulnerable to the virus in the first place.

"We'll get this figured out," Todd says to me before we hang up. His belief in justice encourages me, even though this time, he might be wrong.

⊹ ⊹ ⊹

These days, my mother and I see one another twice a year. Once, in mid-summer for a three-day weekend when we take walks along Lake Michigan, comment on how high the water is, how small the stretch of beach that guards the housing along the bluff. My mother is always tanned from the hours she spends walking along the lakeshore, collecting rocks that she'll glue to picture frames, lamps, candleholders, and doormats. In the years following her incarceration, my sister moved away, and my father and she moved into a rental across town, after losing their home to bankruptcy. Then he died of cancer, and so did one of her cats. Another disappeared into the purple-blue of the early

---

6 "National Collegiate Student Loan Trust Guide," Student Loan Solved, accessed December 27, 2022, https://studentloansolved.com/national-collegiate-student-loan-trust/.

evening, never to return. Now, on summer weekends, my mother sells these rock items at art fairs where mostly out-of-town rich people buy them to commemorate their vacations on the lake. To supplement her small art fair income, she cleans homes for other rich people, scrubbing away the memories of family BBQs and beach days to make room for the next. I wonder if the homes and her art are painful and constant reminders of a domestic life that's been altered.

I see her a second time at Christmas, driving ten snowy hours from Minnesota to a house remade into a memory—each wall, shelf, and furniture decorated with a Christmas-something from my youth. As we prepare the deviled eggs for the family dinner, I compliment her on the Nativity scene or tree lights, and she always says, "It's just not the same putting them out by myself. Next year, maybe I won't." My cousins, uncle, and sister join us for dinner, and we swap stories of our distant lives across the Midwest. At some point in the evening, when I'm telling a funny or detailed story, I look up to find my mother watching me, hungrily taking in these narrative threads. For this has been the true cost of what she stole from me: she doesn't really know me.

We talk on the phone once a month or so. When people ask me why we still talk at all, I give them a constellation of incomplete but honest answers: I can't bear her loneliness; she's suffered enough; she, too, was a victim—of addiction and a predatory lending system; I love her. When she and I talk it's not about much. Mostly, I ask her questions about her art or my grandmother who has Alzheimer's and for whom she cares. We don't talk about the debt that is all around us, trapping us, shouting at us so loudly we can hardly hear. Despite trying my best to kill it so that we can escape, it lives, and though it was born from us—her decision acted upon my body—it seems to live beyond us now, dwelling in the data systems of lenders and banks and credit reports. Sometimes, I want to yell to my mother above its roar: I am so, so sorry. An apology big enough to hold it all, big enough for both of us. But I don't.

✦ ✦ ✦

Historically, there were ways to free us. The introduction of debt in Mesopotamia, in the form of interest-bearing loans, led to social fragmentation, according to David Graeber in *Debt: The First Five Thousand Years*. In years when the harvest collapsed, for example, farmers witnessed the seizure of their land by wealthy merchants who had lent them money. Unable to pay back what they owed, the farmers were forced to enlist their family members in debt bondage. These loved ones lived in exile, working to pay off their debts. Sometimes, exile was self-inflicted when people fled their homes before they could be sold off to debt peonage.

Families forced apart, scattered, ripped from their intimate bonds threatened to destabilize society, so it was tradition for kings to periodically issue massive "declarations of debt freedom," called jubilees. Graeber reminds us that the earliest word for freedom came from the Sumerian word *amargi,* which means "return to mother." It was only when debts were canceled that debt peons could drop their sickles, pack their small bags, and return to the place where they were not an engine of labor, of repayment, but a daughter.

✦✦✦

COVID-19 has exposed and exacerbated existing crises—brought about by our economic, political, and healthcare systems, our inability to contend with and repair our history as a slave-state, and debt. Any ongoing relief efforts that don't address the complex relationship between disease, vulnerability, and indebtedness don't go far enough. Canceling student debt would be a start. As I type this, the total federal student loan debt is $1,811,629,805,092, but in a few seconds, that number will be inaccurate, and in a week or month even more so. The debt grows rapidly. Unable to exchange those numbers for narratives, all I can say is that those loans are owned by people who want to go to school, who want very badly to have agency, to lead meaningful lives.

Under the Higher Education Act, the president could issue an executive order to cancel all federal student debt, at any moment of any day. This declaration won't impact my private debt, but it could change the lives of millions of others. Though lenders, servicers, and trusts make students into investments, into delinquents, into lists of interest and payment, a jubilee can do the opposite: see us as humans.

Heal us, free us, give us back our bodies.

Debt Demands a Body: The Conversation

DAVID   Do you remember Channel Nine back in the day? They'd have these advertisements for Globe College and basically guaranteed people employment to just do this program. But then they didn't really? I don't think they delivered.

WARREN   I mean, hiring numbers were all fudged.

JEN   Kennedy, why are you nodding?

KENNEDY   No, I'm just surprised at how long that thing took before people discovered it. Yeah, I mean, like you're learning. When you go to college, you're around smart people that know stuff. Local governments can always tell if that school is delivering quality human beings, and it's like . . .

DAVID   I mean their goal is not [to] develop quality human beings; it's about delivering jobs.

JEN   I like that distinction.

KENNEDY   You have to be a quality human being to get a job.

WILL   I think that's kind of important too, that the people who are typically exploited by the for-profit institutions at that level, are people who might be on the fringes or on the bubble, you know; they don't have an experience with institutions of higher education.

CHRIS   And they're trying to do something about that.

WILL   And you're trying to do something about that you know, I'm working as a dishwasher or a bricklayer. You know, basically pushing carts around and doing some basic labor stuff, and no one had an opportunity to be at school.

WARREN   It goes with the hype too. Community colleges have been around forever; they do work in the community for what that community needs. But people believe in the hype. You need this education, you need to go to this higher ed, you know, you get this great fancy schmancy program, and we'll guarantee you work. Sure, you will.

CHRIS   Speaks to our idea of college being necessary for success.

WILL   This conversation circles back to the American dream. The idea that a certain standard quality of life [is possible and that] the current generation [was] the last one to get a good dose of, "Well you gotta get good grades so that you can get into the advanced placement. So that you can score well on your standardized tests." You know, some prominent universities aren't using the ACT or SATs any longer to evaluate. But the whole idea was that you can get into a good school so that you can get a good education so that you can get out and you can get a good job. But now, [people realize] "Wait a second, my liberal arts education from a prominent institution of higher learning is about as effective at getting me a high paying job as a community college, state college C-average liberal arts education." Which isn't to say that the value of experiencing the education is diminished somehow. It's more the way that it's packaged to us as we grow up, that it's a necessity to get a certain kind of job to acquire a certain dimension of success in society. That's the part that's the lie.

CHRIS   Okay, Kennedy, what are your thoughts on the economics of it all? I mean, from your perspective, and obviously, it excludes class, people that can afford to go to college from their parents saving up. I don't know much about the lending act that [Collier] talks about. And being from Kenya too, how do they deal with higher ed? And what's your perspective on that whole thing?

KENNEDY   Now, I think the problem [is that], people are training people, you know, for jobs. I mean how many English teachers can you train? How many MBAS can you train? You know, if people are not starting enough businesses to acquire those guys, then that education is not very valuable.

JEN   That sounds so Republican, Kennedy.

WILL   Why is that Republican?

KENNEDY   That's Democratic.

JEN   That makes it sound like the job is the be-all end-all. This nexus of success and growth and the necessity for education, and it negates, from of all people, *you*—this poet-philosopher-educator, it negates the value of an English degree.

KENNEDY   No, no, no. I think, if you get an English degree, and you're able to create a lot of value through it, say you become a writer, you know, you go to school, and after they help kids learn to read and write better than that, that really works. But to get an English degree means you also have to do some more work to be an accredited teacher before you can teach. And that costs time. So, there are all these hurdles that you have to jump through. But the biggest problem is that the school fees that the colleges demand, they are not worth that. They're not worth what they're providing. I don't think that an English major needs to spend hundreds of thousands of dollars to read books and sit at a desk for three years for that cost. [The costs] are over-bloated. You know, they're basically overcharging these poor kids, maybe because their own companies are powerful enough and they make [loans] available, like Collier mentions. But the product really doesn't justify that. You know, I mean, my daughters graduated from engineering school from Cambridge and they don't owe as much money as an American.

WILL   Yeah, but there the government also pays more of it.

KENNEDY   Well, you can talk about education policies, but that seems to be a fair market value for that kind of money.

DAVID   I think, whenever I have talked to Europeans, from my understanding, people will go on a path early on; they'll take the test, test their skills or aptitudes, and then the government looks at what the economy needs. And that's how many people get into these programs.

KENNEDY   Yeah, they do check that. But even over here, that should be the criteria. The university is supposed to produce what society needs, you know. And that goes back to my earlier point, that you gotta graduate people for jobs that are there, but I think universities are basically graduating anybody.

DAVID   But I think that's why, when I look at education, I think that there's two different roads, or two different purposes. Like one is for a job and another is for enrichment. In that way, an English degree I think is incredibly valuable, and other liberal arts degrees. I once read this article about bus drivers, and it asked the question, "Should bus drivers have a liberal arts degree?" And [my answer] was, "Absolutely, always." I just think we need to redefine what the purpose of education is. I don't think education should be linked to the job market.

KENNEDY   I wasn't denigrating education.

WILL   A bus driver can't afford $100,000 in the hole just to be more enlightened.

DAVID   Okay. I think I'm going to slightly disagree with Kennedy here. I think high school is not enough education. But I think people shouldn't go to college until they're twenty-two, twenty-three.

CHRIS   That's not debatable, of course. We're talking about how do they do that? And how do they pay? That's what the whole thing is about, right?

WILL   It's not a question of "Do we have too many English majors?" It's [about] your average kid coming out of high school, who goes to college and says, "Well, I'm passionate about English, this is what I want to do." Or, "It's a liberal arts education that enriches me as a human being." And this kid in particular goes into college, believing that, "Well, if I go get a degree, then I'm going to be successful in the world. So, it's okay to spend all this money on it, or to borrow all this money to go and get this education."

WARREN   Well, even on that point, from my first parole hearing . . . I did this psych eval with this state guy, and got my bachelor's in inter-disciplinary business theory. And this whole time, he was under the impression that I was going to go into business as a manager. I said, "No, I'm going to start my own business, you know, at the farm level." And he looked at me and he said, "Why would you want to waste an education on that?" The first thing I thought was, "How can you not apply what you learn in a business theory [degree] to the epitome of the American Dream, which is owning your own freaking business?"

CHRIS   I think this is why we're in such shit shape right now, because people think that that's what they want, but they just want to be a boss. They don't give a fuck about it. They don't get furniture or, you know, cars. They just want to be a boss.

WILL   But then we've got this whole class of bureaucracy that has justified it. So, you get all these administrators and all these CEOs and all these people that paid [who knows] how much for these educations and now they have to justify it. [You paid] $200,000 for this business degree and it has to be justified by an $80,000 starting salary. So, it's just like a fucking repeating cycle, isn't it?

JEN   Totally.

KENNEDY   In terms of debt, David, in terms of debt, just think of an English major or business major. You know, all we need is a pen, and notebook, and textbooks, and a teacher like Jennifer in front of us, you know, and maybe a TA like Chris. Now, for a year, you know, for a year of that training, you know, it's gonna cost these kids sixty- to one-hundred-thousand dollars.

DAVID   I didn't mean to simplify that statement. You're absolutely right. I just wish that people, when [they] grow up, like in a society, they'd just be more into education just for education's sake.

KENNEDY   Education is valuable. I've been an English major. I love English majors.

DAVID   But I'm saying people growing up, because of the economic system that we live in, how it's consumer based, and all that. People . . .

JEN   Capitalism.

DAVID   You can't really talk about education without talking about capitalism. And you can't even talk about that till you're talking about the values people have, and how people just like to buy stuff. And that's what makes them happy.

JEN   Well, okay, how different would this very book we're making look if education were free in the US?

CHRIS   You just blew our minds.

JEN   I mean, if we're not just looking at business majors versus lit majors and asking, "What's your tuition?" And quantifying rates of return for a major versus what job you can get divided by people's values, because [if it were free], education would be education for the sake of it. Then what would happen?

WILL   At this table, I think, half of us have read Ishiguro's new book, *Klara and the Sun*. So, there's an artificial friend, that is, an artificial intelligence (AI) that is purchased to just say—not spoiling anything—but to engage another teenage human. But one of the background things that's happening in the novel is that automation and AI [have] advanced to the point that most people don't need to work. And so there's a brief cultural discussion in the subtext, a subplot of it, where the father in question had an education and was a genius in his field, but they just didn't need him anymore. Which I think circles back to the point of, why are we doing education in the first place, and what is its value apart from commercial value? But also, it's the idea that if [I] look, the thing that launched the United States into the forefront of economic dominance was in part because, at the time, its free education system was equal and accessible to everyone.

JEN   So, [are you saying in] *Klara and the Sun,* they're moving more toward a communist model?

WILL   Not effectively.

JEN   Okay, Kennedy, what economic model would support a society that educates themselves for the sake of it? Education is free, and people are doing it not because their job depends on it, but because they value knowledge.

KENNEDY   I don't think it exists. And I don't think it will ever exist, because I think when it comes to education or knowledge, [there is] somebody who goes to school to train to be a good waiter, and some countries do have [such programs], like tourist hubs, my country, Kenya—that is an education [in those places]. A bus driver does actually go to train to be a bus driver. That's an education. I think when people talk about education, they're always just thinking about higher education or college education. You know, but I don't think everybody deserves that.

JEN   You don't think everyone deserves it, or everyone wants it?

KENNEDY   The only thing people deserve, as far as education is concerned, as far as I'm concerned, is free access to it, if they need it. If you feel like you need to get your PhD in education, there shouldn't be those high fees that are gonna dissuade poor kids from going there. As long as access is free, that increases our choices of deciding what kind of knowledge we want.

CHRIS   Yeah, you're saying that you don't believe that can ever happen?

KENNEDY   It's not even practical, you know, because joining the army, that is actually a school, you know, and we may despise it, we may not, but there are people that want to go there. And as long as that is open to everybody, [it is good].

CHRIS   So, you're saying free access not necessarily . . .

KENNEDY   There's no free access, just affordable access.

JEN   That might have meant the bus driver decided they wanted to get their PhD instead of go[ing] to bus training.

KENNEDY   The cost is unnecessary. There's nothing in capitalism that justifies regularly charging the kids.

CHRIS   Kennedy, you're talking about regulation here!

WILL   Institutions are already regulated because . . .

CHRIS   They're poorly regulated.

WILL   I didn't say they were regulated well, but they're definitely all regulated.

CHRIS   Look at the predatory lending.

WILL   That's not the college though; the college isn't lending money. There's a financial system that exists to finance education, that the college helps to facilitate through the financial aid, because there's federal Pell Grants, there's state subsidies. Depending on where you are, all of that goes to the financial aid department. But when you fill out that Free Application for Federal Student Aid, the FAFSA, it's that information that is then shared with lenders. So, the system in place to determine your eligibility for federal student aid is also the system that then gets passed on to lenders. The part that has gotten so much worse is those lenders coming in and responding to the rising costs of education.

CHRIS   But that's what we're talking about. The precarity in America is because people control shit, so it's not right. I don't care how many institutions or names that you have. It's not regulated fairly. So, we're talking about systems, and how would we change the system? All I'm saying is, I'm not speaking about law right now; I'm speaking as a citizen, in the context of this system that was supposed to look out for people, to take care of people, and which has completely failed people. [Collier's] mother took advantage of the system, and then [Collier] had to pay for it. Because why? Because the debtors needed to be compensated. They said, "Unless you take your mom to court or unless you call the police on your mom, we're not going to believe you." They couldn't send somebody out to assess it. They failed [Collier] completely. And she didn't want to send her mother to the cops.

JEN   Police State rules.

WILL   And who is it protecting?

JEN   Wealth, of course.

CHRIS   It's the financial institution that needed that two-hundred-thousand dollars? "Oh, sorry, we can't let you slide here, your mom's a gambler."

DAVID   But even then it's a matter of the quality of education because I believe that if people are really educated, they won't be predatory.

CHRIS   Do you?

DAVID   I think the purpose is to be truly liberated. I think that education is liberating.

WILL   Education without empathy is pointless. So how do you teach empathy? We're talking about an intellectual system.

JEN   What's liberatory education to you, David?

DAVID   Yeah, I mean empathy is probably part of it. I mean, that's why, when people take liberal arts courses, they examine the history so much. I think a lot of it is to create a sense of empathy. What I mean when I say "educated" is this idea that people learn to seek out and desire community more than possessions.

KENNEDY   It doesn't always happen like that. If you look all over the world, the people who write most of the propaganda that is fucking up the world, they are super educated. To have an enlightened human being is [to have one] based on the total experience of their life. In prison, we see precarity in a totally different way than maybe somebody [who has] gone to the University of Minnesota or Harvard. You know, we've survived. We've lived the experience, so we identify easily with other fellow human beings who have suffered.

DAVID   I think maybe incarceration is its own education.

JEN   Do you think it was a good education?

DAVID   For me, it was and continues to be. When I was first starting out, I was in Oak Park Heights. There was a lifer who was in his sixties and was Black. And I was a skinny white guy. He kind of became a mentor. I worked out with him every day and listened to what at the time seemed like impromptu monologues, but now I see as knowledge from decades of reflection. And we talked about the University of Minnesota, because I had recently graduated from there. I naïvely believed it was the only type of learning in the world and that I'd probably never be able to access it again and wouldn't shut up about it. And he would just say, "Well, now your education begins." I never really talked about this story because I thought it might come off as corny. But it was so true. And I don't mean because of the crises you have to work through, but rather the day-to-day years of just serving a prison sentence is its own education. It is the rhythm of monotony that steadily and slowly shapes your mind in ways you wouldn't have imagined. It was prison, not college, that gave me everything that had lasting value. But then again, I had things that many prisoners don't: like the art room, like the writing classes, and the discussions that take place in those settings.

JEN   So, it wasn't prison that gave it to you. It was the arts.

DAVID   For me, personally, I can't divorce prison from the arts, and it's the monotony of prison that made the experience of the arts, especially of literature, really stand out in my mind. It became a more vivid, virtual reality that would explain the world I was no longer living in.

WILL   I think all of us to some extent, we were all out in an environment where arts existed, where education existed. And it's not to say the arts weren't a catalyst to making a transformational experience while incarcerated. But if any of us were prepared to hear it in the first place, we weren't listening before that. Coming to prison gives the bird's-eye view of what's actually happening in our culture and in our society now. I mean, there are things that I think we all just take for granted about how society functions. There are open-minded, well-meaning people who have no clue about, not just what it's like in prison, but what is the role that prison plays in our society, not just the literal concrete role. But as long as that exists, as long as there's a place for me to put "others," then I can continue to function under the illusion that everything is peachy.

JEN   When I think of this environment, I think it's a cruel training ground. But because of it, you all probably know more about politics than politicians, more about human psychology than most psychologists. I could go on and on and on.

KENNEDY   Let's talk about debt in prison, because one of the things I've really liked about Collier's essay is the way of doing business out there actually transfers in here. Take the way we do business with each other in prison. You know, if I want to buy a pen from you and it's costing $1, I have to pay back $1 and $1.50 [totaling $2.50]. And when the guys are playing cards, they're gambling, and somebody also mentions they can't pay, one of the ways that that debt is going to be cleared if somebody really doesn't have a way of paying it back is hey, they move into [the others'] cells and beat each other up, and that for some men actually clears the debt.

DAVID   Debt demands a body.

KENNEDY   Exactly. You know, it's okay to talk about the way precarity is created by systems out there. But we do create our own sense of precarity around here through the debt system or the way we do business with each other. You know, that is America.

CHRIS   There's this fucking stereotype, it's been around forever, like loan sharks and shit—"Oh, we got to break your leg now." That's not necessarily what pays the debt. It's that you have the audacity to rip me off and I gotta hurt you and [you] motherfuckers still gonna have to pay that back, which is kind of what Kristin's talking about, too. We're gonna put you through the wringer. And then the layered emotional suffering, of just the weight of the debt and the inability to pay, you're going to suffer, and we're going to make you suffer

[more]. By your intractability. And for the stigma you're going to carry around with you, your own credit situation, and then you're still going to have to pay. But see, in our culture it's valid because it's based on your word. It's based on respect. It's based on circumstances. But for predatory lenders? It's bullshit.

Saskatoons

by Angela Pelster

1. Michael walks upstairs from the basement and into the damp heat of the living room. He flops onto the couch like a boneless slab of meat and lies there as if paralyzed. The basement is cooler than this, but it smells like cum. And shit. A pile of shit covered in cum. David shit beside the toilet again, and the staff haven't found it yet. Or maybe they have and don't want to deal with it. David will whine about having to pick it up. And then he'll get mad. "Fucking bitch," he'll say, and the staff will add a swear chore to the cleaning up the shit chore, and he'll raise his soft pale hands and swipe at the air, wanting to swipe at a face, his plump boy boobs jiggling under his T-shirt. Michael wonders what it would be like to take those in his mouth, if they'd feel like a girl's or like pouches of pudding. Probably like pudding. Is he a fag? Does wanting to suck David's boy titties make him a fag?

2. The fan flips the air around but doesn't make it any cooler. One of the staff walks into the kitchen and opens the fridge. She takes out ground beef, dripping a trail of blood on the floor to the stove, and drops it into a frying pan. In a minute, the smell rides on the hot air, dark and moist like old mushrooms. David follows the smell up the stairs from the basement and shuffles into the kitchen to stand at the side of the staff.

"What's for dinner?"

"Tacos."

"Make a lot."

"Yeah. You need to change your shirt before you eat."

"No. Why?"

"There are boogers all over it."

"So."

"It's gross. I don't want to eat looking at your bloody boogers."

"Fuck you."

"You can't eat until you change your shirt. And you can add a swear chore to your regular chores after dinner."

"Stupid bitch," David says, and goes downstairs to change his shirt.

3. When Michael was six, his foster mom made him eat Spring Breeze scented laundry soap for swearing. Spoonfuls of it burning his stomach until he threw it up all over his shoes, sudsy and fresh. She had stood there with the box of soap and smacked at his head with the metal soup spoon for messing his shoes. She was wearing a bright red shirt; he should have known better. The red shirt or the blue one with the bows on it meant she had woken up with a violence in her. She would squint at him like he was a stranger when he asked her something, or she would keep her head down and swing her hand against his face without looking.

He started paying closer attention after he noticed her shirts. It didn't take long before he could tell just by the sounds of her coming down the stairs what she would be wearing, how she would feel, or what she would do when he asked her to sign the field trip permission note from school. He thought it meant he had special mind-reading powers, like a gift to make up for the other things. When someone noticed his bruises and he was sent to another foster home, it was like his eyes had been plucked from his head or his ears cut off. He couldn't read minds at all.

4. Someone new starts every three or four months at the group home. Once, a woman came and stayed only a few weeks. She was fat and loud with huge tits and wore shirts that stretched thin over her belly rolls. She made fun of the other workers when they weren't around. She told Michael about her boyfriend, what he did to her with ropes once. He could tell she was saying these things because she wanted him to like her. "You don't need to fight with me like the other staff," she'd say. "Just tell me what you want. I'm reasonable." So, he asked to see his case report. He had said it all cool and casual like, as if he had seen it before, as if he hadn't been wanting for years to look at its pages, and she had given it to him, as if she didn't know she wasn't allowed.

5. It was thinner than he had imagined it would be—a half-filled, three-inch binder with doctors' reports, court orders, and school assessments hole-punched into it. His name written in black Sharpie marker on the spine. The first page was his intake report:

Circle one
- Head lice: Y / N
- Sexually active: Y / N
- Sexually abused: Y / N

A listing of clothes brought with him:
- T-shirts: 2
- Jeans: 1
- Socks: 3
- Underwear: 3
- Sweaters: 0
- Winter coat: 0
- Boots: 0
- Shoes: 1 pair (too small)

A tally of bruises, scars, wounds.

The psychiatric assessments: violent tendencies, ADHD, fetal alcohol, below-average intelligence. No one had taken him away from his mother. She had given him up. No other family had wanted him.

Most of the pages were copies of copies, the handwriting a ghost spider skittering off the page. It was good that he saw them now, before it was too late to read them at all. David hadn't wanted to see his. "My mother is a bitch who used to tie me to the toilet," he said. "I'll kill her if I ever see her again." There is a note written on the whiteboard in the staff office that says David is not to take calls from his mother. His mother has never called.

6. Michael saw his mom yesterday. Sometimes she phones after having not talked to him for months, and his pits start sweating as soon as he picks up the phone. He forces himself to speak slowly though she giggles and teases. "Hey, Mikey," she'll say. "I miss you. Want to

come stay for a few days? Get away from those whores?" And then they'll both laugh and he'll forget to keep his words slow.

7. Last Christmas, Michael's mom asked him to come for two weeks. He hadn't lived with her for that long since she'd gotten rid of him. He didn't want the staff to help him pack. He knew they'd say he didn't need to take every single thing, but he'd shoved it all in the bag anyway, sides bulging, zipper gaping open. When he carried it up the stairs, the worker on shift just looked at the bag and raised her eyebrows. It was Christmas holidays. No one wanted to fight about anything. When he was dropped off at his mom's, the staff handed Michael a plastic garbage bag full of wrapped presents they had bought for him with his "Celebrations" fund from the government. "Merry Christmas," she'd said, and hugged him before she left.

8. His mom put on lipstick and did her hair his second night at her house. "There's a Christmas party downtown," she said. "I'll be back in a bit." But she wasn't. She'd left Michael's baby sister with him, and for a while he did all right. But when the macaroni and the crackers and the cereal and all the frozen ends of bread shoved into the back of the freezer were gone and there was no money to buy anything and his sister wouldn't stop crying and he hadn't remembered to take any of his meds and he was so fucking tired, he cried into the cushions on the couch until the blood vessels burst at the corners of his eyes, and then he called the group home. He yelled at the staff; said he needed a ride back. His hockey duffle was still half-packed; it only took him a minute. Someone came for the baby. The bag full of presents went back to the car, to the group home, spread under the tree there. All the other boys had been sent out to spend the holidays with some family. Michael unwrapped the presents Christmas morning by himself. The staff who had been called in last minute sat in the kitchen texting on her phone.

9. Yesterday, when his mom had called, she had asked him if he wanted to come over for the afternoon. "I got lasagna," she said. "You can stay for dinner." Michael's pits were sweating. "Yeah, I guess," he said.

They ate on the couch watching *The Price Is Right* and scraping burnt noodles off the bottom of the tin. "Stouffer's is better," his mom had said during the commercials. "I should of got Stouffer's."

"It's good," he said. "I like it."

"What do they feed you there?" she asked, not turning from the TV.

"I don't know. Spaghetti and chili and stuff."

"They make you eat vegetables?"

"Yeah, but I hate it."

"You eat your fucking vegetables." But she wasn't angry, she was putting on her motherhood like putting on a coat. "It's better than those other places you were."

"Yeah."

"Remember that woman who gave you instant porridge for every meal? And macaroni for a treat?"

"I hate that shit."

"Bitch had it right. No cleaning. No cooking. Just making money off of you." Bob Barker was on the TV again, but his mom kept talking. "That must piss you off. You think about that stuff and get pissed off?"

"I don't know. Maybe."

"Maybe? You just take that shitty food from them and you don't care?"

"I got good stuff now."

She turned and looked at him, looked at his plate scraped clean and smiled, pleased. "Yeah, you do."

10. Michael went to the museum with his grade six class once, to learn about the shit white people did to the Indians. "Is that your mom?" they asked him at the tepee display. There was a red mannequin with black braids, a deerskin dress, and a baby strapped to her back. She held a wooden bowl full of wrinkled saskatoon berries that she was grinding for pemmican. "Look, it's Michael camping with his mom," one of the girls giggled. "It can't be," Michael said loudly, sweating. "She isn't drunk." Everyone laughed until the teacher shushed them.

They washed their hands in a line at the sink in another room, and mixed flour and shortening and currants in a bowl for bannock. It was lunchtime and the class was hungry. When the pans of bread were pulled from the oven hot and puffy, every hand shot out for a taste. "This is so great," one of his friends said with his mouth full. "I'm not even kidding. You should bring this for lunch every day." Michael nodded back. He had never tasted bannock before. It was good. He hadn't expected to like it. He folded up a copy of the recipe and put it in his pocket.

11. When the staff picked him up from eating lasagna at his mom's house, it was dark but still warm. His mom had fallen asleep on the couch when the lasagna was gone, and he didn't want to wake her, so he left without saying good-bye. They drove home in silence; he was so tired. He stood in the basement outside his bedroom, and the staff told him to hurry up and brush his teeth before bed. "Don't be such a fucking whore," he yelled at her, without wanting to, hardly thinking about it. She moved back slightly, and then gave him a swear chore, turned and climbed the stairs away from him in her ugly dress. He came up behind her then, reached out his hand, and hit her on the calf with the back of his fingers. Smack. Hard enough to sting but not to bruise. She had stopped and stiffened, and Michael felt a hot rush of blood through his throat and into his chest. She turned and looked at him and her eyes were already wet. Her neck flushed. She opened her mouth and closed it.

12. A little bird, he thought.

13. "You bastard," she said.

14. She was new and she was going to cry. She walked up the stairs without saying anything else, into the office and shut the door.

15. He was grounded for the week. The incident would be recorded on his chart, hole-punched, and placed in his case book, now one page thicker. He had told her he was sorry later, and he had meant it. He liked her good enough. She had nodded back at him after his apology. "It's all right," she had said. "I'm sorry I called you a bastard."

"Maybe you should get a swear chore, too."

"This entire job is a swear chore," she said back, and went into the office to write the report.

16. He wonders if she is afraid of being alone with him now. The others were going to a movie after dinner, and she was staying behind to supervise him. Once, he heard the staff talking about some woman who was killed at a home. She had been working alone and one of the kids had beaten in her face with a bat. He can imagine it happening. Two years ago, when girls used to live at the home with them, one of them had grabbed a butcher's knife from the dishwasher and chased the staff around the house with it, screaming that she was going to push it into their eyes. The staff yelled at the boys to go into lockdown and then they barricaded themselves in the office until the cops came.

He's way stronger than her. He can tell from her skinny arms. She can hardly carry all the plates to the table at once. And she only comes up to his chest.

17. "What do you want to do?" she asks, when the dishes are clean and the house is empty except for them.

"I don't know."

"The saskatoons are ripe in the backyard. Want to pick some with me?"

He's never picked berries before. He doesn't really want to.

"Come on. They're so good and it's hot in here."

18. The only thing she can find for a bucket is a plastic box that used to hold mail. She rinses it out and they put on their shoes and go around the house to the back. The ground is soft and spongy around the trees because of the sump pump drainage, and the grass a brighter shade of green than the rest of the yard. He bounces a little in his runners. "Look at them," she says, and pulls a cluster of berries into her hand. "They fall right off." She has long dark hair in a braid down her back.

19. The mosquitoes are thick by the saskatoon trees, and the repellent makes Michael's lips tingle when he licks his fingers from the first berries

he tries. "This is like camping with my mom," he says to her. He tells her all about their summers in the woods, about the hikes they took, about the time they even stayed in one of those tepee campsites.

"We fried bannock over the fire, and I picked some berries to go with it. I can hardly wait until we go this summer."

He tells her about his baby sister, about how much he loves her, how smart she is—she's already talking and she's only a year old—and about his uncles and aunts and how they always come over to visit when he goes to his mom's and how he wishes he was old enough to live on his own, do what he wants, see his mom all the time. It's the heat. The sweet berries. The soft ground. It's her smiling nicely, nodding, and staying quiet. It's that she's new and doesn't know anything. It's the thickness of the air, the sun caught in the trees, like little pieces of foil hung in the branches.

He opens his mouth and all the stories fall out.

20. Michael's box is half full of berries by the time he's done. He stopped picking awhile back and has been holding the high branches down low for her to reach. They will go inside soon. She'll mix flour and shortening and teach him to roll out a crust. They'll put in sugar with the berries and dot the filling with pats of butter. She'll show him how to pinch the edges of the pie closed with his finger and thumb, and then he'll take a knife and slash his initials across the face of it, sprinkling it with sugar again. When the pie is done baking, he will hold it while she takes his picture, while he tries to look tough in oven mitts. She will stay three years and imagine she loves these boys. She will leave them one month before Michael runs away to live with his uncle, and then to run away from his uncle, to nowhere, disappearing into the cracks of the city forever.

All names are changed to protect the innocent.

The guilty are protected accidentally, since guilt and innocence have not yet been determined.

Saskatoons: The Conversation

KENNEDY   I think the thing that intrigued me the most about "Saskatoons" was the role that food plays in it. That is something I haven't seen in Western literature. I could relate to their story very much because the role the food played in the story is the healing part. It just kind of took me back to where I am from. In Africa, to the Bantu-speaking people, to us, food is healing. When you feed me, you're actually healing me. But the other intriguing part of food is that our word for eating food, *Kula,* is the same word for having sex, or for making love.

DAVID   What is the word again?

KENNEDY   *[Kennedy laughs.]* Don't make me say more, I'm too shy for that.

[Room laughs.]

The thing I liked about this story is that this woman comes in, she just invites the kid to go and pick the stuff up. And then they go in and make food. Among the Bantu in Africa, you don't ask anybody if they're gonna eat. You know, if you come to my house, I'm just going to cook for you.

JEN   No matter what time of day it is?

KENNEDY   Yeah, no matter what time of day it is. And it doesn't matter if you already just ate before you came into my house. You know, if I cook for you, you gotta eat. Otherwise, we consider that as being rude. If I ask you if you're hungry, that is very rude. It means I'm not being kind. Because it's basically inviting you to say no. And if you're not eating, you're not healing.

DAVID   That's beautiful.

KENNEDY   And that is the thing that really attracted me to this. When these children are put in this place, everybody's just thinking, "What is wrong with them? You know, let us medicate them. We can't have them on the road. Let's punish them for being rude." You know, this story gave us more. If the people in these foster homes could just be kind. Kids are complicated little human beings. You know, there are other things you can do with them other than talking to them or throw them around like prisoners. Do something better—something they can learn from, you know? And basically, that is what made this story. I've never seen anybody write, or use food in such a beautiful way. It has so much meaning that we always forget. Like around here, we eat and disappear. It's like that food we just ate doesn't have any meaning. I was wondering if, maybe if food had meaning, it could change a few hearts.

DAVID   [In the chow hall] we don't even have time to talk when we eat. We eat it so quickly, it's not healing. Unless you cook with your friends [in your cell]. And then that's something different. But eating meal after meal after meal where there's no conversation, you're just going in, and it's like . . .

KENNEDY   Absolutely, absolutely.

WARREN   And you can't wait to get out.

WILL   I was actually just thinking about that too. There are a lot of guys I've seen [who] will cook together, like they'll all throw in on a meal. But then they won't eat together. But they all take the bowls and then just retreat to their cages. But if I'm going to take the time to actually make something that we're all going to eat, we're going to sit and eat it together. Otherwise, what's the point? I could just make it for myself, or you would pay me and I would make it for you. But also, lately, there's a friend of mine, who's getting out, he's been down for almost thirty years and did all of his time up in the wasteland and Siberia [another prison] for the last three and a half years. And it just so happens that his switch out for chow is immediately after ours. When he leaves in October, I'm not going to see him again for a few years. So, I'm sort of pushing the boundaries of what's allowed by waiting as late as I possibly can to switch out so that we still go to chow together. And oftentimes Warren's with us. We don't cover any grand philosophical notions. But, you know, even over the garbage food that they serve us here, it's still something that we do as an expression of our love for each other.

WARREN   Country folks have just an open invite for half a cup. "Got time for half a cup?" And that's half a cup of coffee, or a cup of coffee and whatever else is there, cookies or snacks or whatever. And that's the excuse for conversations. A lot of ruffled feathers have been settled over half a cup.

DAVID   How often do the two neighbors do that with each other, in the country?

WARREN   Whenever they see each other. I mean, whenever they're in the same place at the same time or have business one way or the other. It can be stopping in the local café, which there are so few of; all four that I worked at in high school are all closed now because nobody goes there anymore. And it's kind of a lost art.

WILL   One of the things in the discussion so far, we're sort of leaning into the softness of the lovely things that are in the essay. But there's this line: "The soft ground. It's her smiling nicely, nodding, and staying quiet. It's that she's new and doesn't know anything." And then at the end of the essay, "She will leave them one month before Michael runs away to live with his uncle, and then to run away from his uncle, to nowhere, disappearing into the cracks of the city forever." It's not happy, for as lovely as some moments are, and as generous the new girl is with them.

I'm grateful for the uplifting perspectives, because that's not what I got from this at all. It's hard. It's heartbreaking. That's how I felt.

Every time there's an exposure to [Michael's] past, or dysfunction, or the inability to just control himself just because he's not capable, it's heartbreaking. There's a lot of guys like that in here. That's one of the things I thought about: these guys, they're all on their way here because they'll age out of care, end up on the streets.

I got in trouble a lot as a kid, as you might imagine. Quite frequently I got community service and so I found a good spot working in a place called Lake Owasso Residents. It was in Shoreview, Minnesota. It used to be like a big old hospital facility, like they used to operate, but [by then] it was a home for developmentally disabled adults. I spent lots of time with those guys when I was in my early teens. And when the funding ran out, they tore the building down. They're in these pods that looked like some of the classroom pods they used to put outside of our high school. They're outbuildings. And that's where they moved a couple dozen adults who aren't capable of caring for themselves. So, it's not even a group home environment. It's super institutional. This just reminds me of that.

CHRIS   Whose responsibility is it, though? Whose responsibility is another's precarity? We have all these essays about the people in systems that are failing them, for the most part. How are we going to fix this stuff? But at the same time, I don't know, is it a sad ending? I thought it was pretty happy. He's finally on his own. He's finally out there. I know plenty of Michaels. They're fine.

Can We Move Our Forests in Time to Save Them?

by Lauren Markham

I drove to Oregon because I wanted to see the future. Our rapidly changing climate vexes me, keeps me up at night—perhaps you've felt this, too—and recently I'd become particularly preoccupied with trees. In California, where I live, climate change helped kill nearly 62 million trees in 2020 alone, and that same year, 4.2 million acres of our state burned.[1] I wanted to know what was in store for our forests and, because we humans rely on them for so much—for clean air, for carbon sequestration, for biodiversity, for habitat, for lumber and money, for joy—what was in store for us.

I'd read about a group of scientists who were not only studying the calamities befalling our forests but also working to help the trees migrate in advance of the coming doom. So, in May, I headed to a three-and-a-half-acre stand of roughly one thousand Douglas firs at a US Forest Service nursery outside of Medford. The grove was situated in a wide valley in the southwestern corner of the state, nestled between the Cascades to the east and the Coast Range to the west. Brad St. Clair, a Forest Service scientist who has studied the genetic adaptation of trees for more than two decades, met me by the road. He's short and rugged, as if built for adventuring and tending to the lives of trees, and he arrived in a souped-up Sprinter van loaded with an armory of outdoor gear. In 2009, he and his team planted this and eight other stands of firs after they'd gathered seeds from sixty tree populations all over Washington, Oregon, and California. The team had grown them into seedlings in a greenhouse. The seeds were sourced from as high as 5,400 feet in the Sierras and as low as sea level at the coast, and from as south as Mendocino County, California, all the way north to central Washington, and were planted in intermixed clusters at each of the nine sites to see how they would fare in a hotter,

---

1 "Stats and Events," CAL FIRE, State of California, accessed December 16, 2022, https://www.fire.ca.gov/stats-events/.

drier climate than the ones from which they'd come. In other words, to see if they'd make it in the future.

Douglas fir, a tall, narrow-trunked evergreen often dragged indoors for Christmas, is a favorite of foresters and logging companies because of its combination of strength, fast growth, and pliability. It can also withstand a change in climate of about four degrees Fahrenheit without much trouble. But global average temperatures have already risen by almost three degrees since the 1900s, and all models predict average temperatures to blow through the four-degree threshold in the next several decades, perhaps rising more than seven degrees by the end of the century.

In the wide, flat expanse of the nursery, the firs were rimmed by fallow land on all sides. St. Clair instructed me to put on safety glasses, and then he ducked down, pushed aside the outermost branches, and slipped into the trees. I followed him. Within two steps, we were in a veritable, dense forest, as if an enchanted wardrobe had been pulled open to reveal a world transformed. On the periphery it had been hot, but here, as we moved through the dapple, it was cool and fragrant with pine.

A sign mounted on a PVC pipe marked the provenance of the cluster of trees we stood beneath. They came, St. Clair explained, from the Oregon Siskiyou, a dry zone at only slightly higher elevation than where we were today. This is why they were doing so well: their native climate wasn't so different from Medford's. As we moved on, the trees, while still lush and full, grew shorter. This next batch was from up in the Cascades, he pointed out, at an elevation far higher than where we stood, and, because of that, the trees were somewhat stunted in this new habitat and couldn't grow as tall. We kept walking, and after a while the trees grew taller again, looming three times my height before breaking into sky. These trees also came from climates that were dry like Medford, and so found here a happy home—at least for now.

We ducked and trudged through the lower thickets of the healthy trees until we suddenly emerged from the woods onto what I can only describe as an arboreal apocalypse—an open tangle of dead branches, brown and brittle, like an upright graveyard. These ill-fated trees, St. Clair said, had come from the Oregon coast, where it is far wetter. While they'd done okay in the first three years of the study, they just couldn't make it in the long term. "As the climate warms," St. Clair said, looking around and pointing up to a dead fir with his walking stick, "you're going to see more of this."

The future of forests is a grim one—too grim for some of us to bear. By 2030, 75 percent of redwoods will disappear from some of their coastal California habitats. In some climate scenarios, almost none of the namesake species in Joshua Tree National Park will exist. Sea level change is creating ghost forests all along the Eastern Seaboard— already, less than a third of New Jersey's Atlantic white cedar habitat remains.[2]

Like humans, forests have always migrated for their survival, with new trees growing in more hospitable directions and older trees dying where they are no longer best suited to live. The problem now is that they simply can't move fast enough. The average forest migrates at a rate of roughly 1,640 feet each year, but to outrun climate change, it must move approximately 9,800 to 16,000 feet annually—up to ten times as fast.[3] Moreover, in most habitats, the impact of highways, suburban sprawl, and megafarms prevents forests from expanding much at all. Forests simply cannot escape climate change by themselves.

Back in 1992, forest geneticists F. Thomas Ledig and J. H. Kitzmiller coined the term "assisted species migration" in a seminal study in the

---

2 Chrissy Sexton, "Suitable Redwood Habitats Are Changing with the Climate," Earth. com, last updated June 23, 2020, https://www.earth.com/news/suitable-redwood -habitats-are-changing-with-the-climate/; Hilary Clark, "Joshua Trees: An Uncertain Future for a Mojave Desert Icon," National Parks Traveler, accessed December 16, 2022, https://www.nationalparktraveler.org/2021/03/joshua-trees-uncertain-future -mojave-desert-icon; Frank Kummer, "Rising Seas Could Be Turning Jersey's Coastal Cedars into Ghost Forests," *The Philadelphia Inquirer,* May 21, 2017, https://www .inquirer.com/philly/health/environment/new-jerseys-atlantic-white-cedar-ghost -forests-harbingers-of-sea-level-rise-rutgers-20170521.html#loaded.

3 Mary I. Williams and R. Kasten Dumroese, "Preparing for Climate Change: Forestry and Assisted Migration," *Journal of Forestry* 111, no. 4 (July 2013): 287–297.

journal *Forest Ecology and Management.*[4] Since then, hundreds of biologists and geneticists like St. Clair have been studying how best to move forests in advance of their looming destruction. To do so requires a complex set of mapping and experiments—understanding, for instance, which climate trees are best suited to grow in, which region will most closely resemble that same climate in, say, fifty years, and which adaptations best ensure that a tree will take root and flourish, build symbiosis with the soil fungi, and not end up a mere matchstick awaiting the next megafire.

St. Clair is something of an assisted migration evangelist, a firm believer that we need to move tree populations, and fast, if we want to keep apace of climate change. But due to bureaucratic logjams and a fervent commitment to planting native species, there's very little assisted migration in the United States—unlike in Canada, where the practice has been adopted with more urgency in recent years. St. Clair and other Forest Service scientists are working to transform assisted migration from a mere research subject to a standard management strategy in our vast, imperiled public lands.

We finished our walk through St. Clair's baby forest, making our way back to the cars along its outer edges. "The future is terrifying," I told him. He understood what I meant, he said.

During the talks he gives about his research, he likes to show an image from Lewis Carroll's *Through the Looking-Glass,* in which the Red Queen charges forward with her crown and sturdy scepter, pulling frenzied Alice along in her wake. He had the slide printed out and handed it to me as we walked. "Now, here, you see," the Red Queen says to Alice, "it takes all the running you can do, to keep in the same place."

"So that's what we gotta do," he told me, pointing to the Red Queen. "We gotta run."

While assisted migration is a relatively new concept, the movement of forests is as old as trees themselves. Since they first evolved, trees

---

4 F. Thomas Ledig and J.H. Kitzmiller, "Genetic Strategies for Reforestation in the Face of Global Climate Change," *Forest Ecology and Management* 50 (1992): 153–169.

have been shifting north and south, east and west, up and down in elevation as the climate has changed. Forests outran the frost as an ice age set in, and as the ice began melting, they darted back the other way, traversing mountain ranges and unfurling themselves across continents—moving, sentiently, toward climatic conditions that suited their ability to grow and produce the trees of the future.

Of course, while forests move, individual trees can't. "They are stuck where they are," explained Jessica Wright, a senior Forest Service scientist based in Davis, California, who studies conservation genetics. Trees must try to survive whatever environment they land in, and yet, as Peter Wohlleben writes in *The Hidden Life of Trees,* while every tree has to stay put, "it can reproduce, and in that brief moment when the tree embryos are still packed into seeds, they are free."[5] The seed sets forth, as Zach St. George chronicles in *The Journeys of Trees,* carried by the wind or in the belly of a blue jay or stuffed in the cheek of a squirrel, toward its destiny. If it is among the luckiest, the seed will find a hospitable home and carry the forest forward.[6] Because seeds will only take root in areas suited to their growth, forests tend to move in the direction of their future survival.

Unlike humans, most trees are long-life species, ranging from the yellow birch, which lives roughly 150 years, to the bristlecone pine, the oldest known of which is nearly 5,000 years old. Forests are the trees' complex civilization, functioning not unlike human cities: a community of beings that talk to one another, organize, defend themselves, create offspring, and bid farewell to their dead. In this way, and many others, recent research has revealed that trees are spellbinding, rife for anthropomorphism. They tend to live in interdependent networks, like families, where, with the help of symbiotic fungi, scientists like Suzanne Simard have discovered, they care for their sick, feed one another, and, like a mutual aid society, share resources

5 Peter Wohlleben, *The Hidden Life of Trees: What They Feel, How They Communicate,* trans. Jane Billinghurst (Vancouver: Greystone Books, 2016), 6–13.
6 Zach St. George, *The Journey of Trees: A Story about Forests, People, and the Future* (New York: W.W. Norton, 2020).

with those in need.[7] Trees of the same species—and sometimes even those across species—tend to respect one another's personal space, shifting their growth patterns so that everyone gets enough sunlight. Trees are also adept community organizers who know how to band together to crowd out competitor trees as well as guard against other threats. When a pest comes, trees can issue chemical warnings to one another so they can launch their defenses. Trees can also register pain. Scientists have found that their root networks, which work with the underworld organisms of fungal mycelia, seem to hold intergenerational knowledge, like a collective brain. Read enough about the mesmerizing science of trees and one begins to feel certain that, if humans behaved like a healthy forest, we'd be far better off—and that we wouldn't have gotten into our current climate mess in the first place.

Left to their own devices, forests migrate on a near-geologic scale. But people have been moving trees for our own purposes for thousands of years. We've done this in small doses, such as planting trees in city gardens or backyards for shade and aesthetic delight, or planting a wall of cypress along a tract of farmland to block the wind. We've also moved trees on a far more substantial scale, with a range of outcomes. While apple trees originated in Central Asia, early settlers brought seeds to the Americas and famously scattered them throughout what is now the United States, where apple pie is now both a signature dessert and a cultural symbol.

Such interventions haven't always panned out so well. In 1895, the emperor of Ethiopia ordered the planting of fast-growing eucalyptus trees imported from Australia so people would have abundant firewood.[8] But the thirsty eucalyptus crowded out existing trees and parched once-fertile farmlands. (Eucalyptus trees are also invasive transplants in California, though they have become critical nesting habitat for the threatened monarch butterfly—the web of interconnectivity is a tangled one.) And in 1904, US foresters began planting Japanese

---

7 Wohlleben, *The Hidden Life of Trees*.
8 Ronald Horvath, "Addis Ababa's Eucalyptus Forest," *Journal of Ethiopian Studies* 6, no. 1 (January 1968): 13–19.

chestnuts to cultivate for wood, which brought chestnut blight to their North American cousins ill-equipped to fight the fungus; by 1940, most adult chestnuts were gone. The movement of trees, scientists caution, must be done with extreme care—and based on history, many are hesitant to do it for fear of throwing off the delicate balance of an existing landscape.

Proponents of assisted migration claim that this balance has already been upended by climate change. They also stress that assisted migration is an umbrella term for a range of activities, some way more far-reaching than others. The most drastic intervention is known as *assisted species migration,* which transplants species of trees from places where they naturally occur to faraway places where they do not. Then there's *assisted range expansion,* which plants trees slightly outside their naturally occurring territory. The strategy involving the least human intervention is known as *assisted population migration,* which, like St. Clair's studies of Douglas fir, plants trees of a single species with certain adaptations to a new location where other members of that same species already live. Most scientists advocate the latter two strategies and consider the first one too extreme.

So how to safely move a population to a new habitat—and to know how far to do it, and how fast? "If I knew the answer to that," Forest Service scientist Kas Dumroese told me, "I'd have the Nobel Prize." To find out which plants are best suited to which environments, scientists tend to use something called the Common Garden Study, which, like the artificial forest I visited in Oregon, plants flora from a wide range of locations—and thus adapted to a range of conditions—on a single plot to study their response and growth patterns. What scientists have found in most assisted migration garden studies is that the trees that do the best are those whose parents and ancestors thrived in similar terrain.

If you move a population of trees adapted to a particular climate too slowly, it's bound to succumb to the hotter, drier conditions brought on by climate change. But move it too fast to a colder, wetter climate, and the trees might fall victim to too much frost, or to root rot in damp conditions that make them vulnerable to pests. Shifting trees that can handle mid-century climate projections—so new forests are adapted to the temperatures of roughly 2040 to 2070—seems to be the Goldilocks balance that will ensure a population's survival.

But there are other important considerations, including the symbiotic relationship between soil fungi and trees. Simard, the author of the recent bestselling book *Finding the Mother Tree*, explains that, while trees will likely find some symbiotic mycelium as long as they are moved within their species' existing range, that mycelium might not be the best adapted for their needs.[9] Trees can't be seen as growing in isolation, but instead need to be considered in terms of the overall health and relationships of a larger ecosystem. "There's a lot we don't know," Simard told me. Assisted migration "is risky, but, you know, we also have no choice. We have to start experimenting with this. We have to start moving things around and watching and seeing how they do."

The Forest Service scientists who study assisted migration couldn't agree more, and they hope that the agency's forest managers will start using this strategy in actual forests. Despite decades of research, the Forest Service has rarely put assisted migration into practice, in part due to some foresters' and scientists' resistance to moving trees outside their agreed-upon range. In the 1930s, the Forest Service created the idea of seed zones—mapping the landscape into areas "within which plant materials can be transferred with little risk of being poorly adapted to their new location," as the agency states on its website.[10] Ever since, forest managers have stayed loyal to these zones when selecting seeds for planting.

While assisted migration isn't strictly prohibited by the *Forest Service Manual* and its accompanying handbooks—the official policy documents that, as Forest Service land manager Andy Bower explains, guide "every aspect" of how the agency operates—it isn't

9 Suzanne Simard, *Finding the Mother Tree: Discovering the Wisdom of the Forest* (New York: Knopf, 2021).

10 "Seed Zone WebMap," United States Department of Agriculture, accessed February 14, 2023, https://www.fs.usda.gov/wwetac/Seedzonemapping.php.

encouraged, either. Last fall, Bower, St. Clair, and five other forest geneticists in the Forest Service proposed changes to the manual that include assisted population migration and, in some cases, slight range expansion as forestry strategies. If their recommendations are accepted, it could drastically accelerate the use of assisted migration nationwide.

The Forest Service doesn't have to look far for an example of a country taking a more aggressive tack. Canada is substantially ahead of the United States in research and implementation of assisted migration. This is, in part, a result of urgency. In the early aughts, aided by worsening climate change, lodgepole pine forests were devastated by invasive bark beetles and massive wildfires. This was also true in the United States, but when it happened in Canada, the country acted far more aggressively. "It was huge," Greg O'Neill, a scientist working for the Canadian Forest Service, told me, "like they got hit by a sledgehammer. It really woke up the forestry community." The Forest Service of British Columbia launched the Assisted Migration Adaptation Trial, or AMAT, in 2009, planting roughly 153,000 trees to see how each would fare in different climates. With more than a decade of results, they have begun to use this data to reforest areas that have been logged or burned.[11]

This is not to say that the method should become the land management strategy in all, or even most, scenarios. Moving species across a landscape in response to climate change, Dumroese argued, should be undertaken according to the Hippocratic Oath. "We're talking about making some decisions that have some implications that we may not understand or even be recognized for one hundred years," he said, "or even longer."

One of the troubles with assisted migration is that it's difficult to know what future climate to anticipate. Human choices are hard to predict. The adoption of a Green New Deal, for instance, would significantly affect climate modeling, as would the reelection of Donald Trump in 2024 or the return to power of Amazon-destroying Jair Bolsonaro in Brazil.

But even in the most optimistic of climate scenarios, the forests need to get moving—from south to north, from lowlands to highlands—so that our landscapes remain populated with trees.

"It's almost like we have this temporal centric view of nature," O'Neill said. "A lot of people view climate change as something that's going to happen, not something that has already happened." And though all trees can generally survive a change of 4 degrees Fahrenheit in either direction, O'Neill reminds me that 2.7 degrees—the amount that the climate has already warmed in the past century—is a cataclysmic change of circumstances from a tree's perspective. Seen this way, he said, "These trees are already a long way from home." If all we do is help them get back to the kinds of habitats they'd lived in before the climate began to change so rapidly, he added, "I think we'll be doing a great service."

In May, a few weeks before driving to Oregon, I accompanied Forest Service scientist Jessica Wright from her research station in the Sierra Nevada foothills up Route 50 and into the mountains of the Eldorado National Forest, one of the most ecologically diverse tracts of land in California, spanning nearly one million acres. The road wound us upward into the rolling expanse of the Sierras, where towering green pines spread in all directions. Such sights always reminded me of the state's largesse, and I used to find them transcendental: the sanctity of open space, the vastness of the landscape a mirror for the vastness of the human spirit. But now, this feeling is accompanied by a twin coil of fear. *Fire.* Those trees are exquisite fuel, and it all feels doomed to burn.

We turned onto a dirt road and knocked our way through the forest. After a few minutes, the trees thinned. The lowest branches of ponderosa pines and Douglas firs were charred, and the blackened sticks of former trees pointed skyward like bayonets. The road took us to an open clearing, bare and treeless like a wound. This was the site of the King Fire, which destroyed roughly 250 square miles of the central Sierra foothills in 2014,[12] and it was only now, seven years later, starting to look green again.

A few years back, Wright started talking to a Forest Service program manager named Dana Walsh about the prospect of an assisted migration research trial on a tract of land that Walsh oversaw—and they decided to plant along this twelve-acre patch that had burned. In the winter of 2019, they sowed their 1,200 trees sourced from twenty-four different, original populations. Their hope is to convince other forest managers that assisted migration can be used to replant burned forests in the future, instead of reforesting strictly with local seeds. Additionally, several Forest Service scientists, including Wright and St. Clair, are building new seed selection databases that map climate predictions with seed source adaptations, should assisted migration finally be put into practice in the US.

Wright, who has hip-length hair and seems equally at home sporting a hard hat and presenting at a conference, is particularly optimistic about the prospects of planting in burn zones. If a forest will be replanted anyway, why plant what was already there and burned, when we can reforest these burn sites—which have grown all the more common, and so much bigger—with trees that will be better suited to that future in thirty to fifty years? A stressed forest brings diseases and pests, which kill trees, offering more kindling to burn. The healthier a forest, the less likely it is to catch fire.

Along twelve acres of the King Fire site, Wright and her team had planted two kinds of pine: ponderosa—which grow up to 200 feet tall with thick, striated bark—and a type of sugar pine resistant to white pine blister rust, a fungus then decimating western sugar pines. To mimic nature, the trees had been planted somewhat willy-nilly along the hillside, as they would grow in the wild. We walked along the planting site, where I tried to spot the trees; at only two years old, the saplings were not much higher than my ankle. Some hadn't made it

---

12 "King Fire Facts," US Department of Agriculture, accessed February 14, 2023, https://www.fs.usda.gov/Internet/FSE_DOCUMENTS/fseprd566026.pdf.

at all, and some were still slight wisps of life, while others were growing strong and burly.

I asked Wright what she made of the differences in growth. She laughed.

"It's too early to say," Wright told me.

But weren't they impatient, I wanted to know? I was. Why was this tree, on the lower slope, doing so beautifully, its tiny trunk much thicker than the rest, its needles skewering outward like porcupine quills, its yellow-green buds promising new growth?

Wright countered that it's not until about ten years into a study that the data starts to be meaningful. "That's when I start to believe it," she said. So many things could happen between now and then, and early growth might not end up meaning much. After all, those dead Douglas firs that had so rattled me in Oregon had done great the first few years of the study.

We found some shade under the trees that had survived the 2014 fire, and sat down for lunch. To consider the future of forests is to slip into a timeline so abstract that it's hard to conceive, but scientists like Wright are in it for the long haul, imagining a lifespan far beyond their own.

"I won't see this big tall forest we're planting now," she said. Her kid might see it, or perhaps her grandkids. Tending to any kind of future is a gesture of optimism, she conceded, particularly such a distant one. "But I'm good with that."

As a member of the living, it can be difficult to understand how unlikely it is, statistically speaking, to become alive. A healthy beech tree, explains Wohlleben in *The Hidden Life of Trees,* will produce roughly 1.8 million beechnuts in its lifetime. "From these, exactly one will develop into a full-grown tree," he writes, "and in forest terms, that is a high rate of success, similar to winning the lottery."[13]

For Joshua trees, the odds of successful reproduction are even longer. For a Joshua tree to be born—a tree that lives in far starker conditions than the beech—its mother has to flower and seed when it

---

13 Wohlleben, *The Hidden Life of Trees,* 29.

reaches sexual maturity. The seed, which resembles a flat puck of black putty smaller than a dime, has to find a home conducive to its germination and bloom. That's hard enough in the dry expanse of the desert, and harder still as the landscape warms. The seed's best-case scenario is to find its way to a spot beneath a nurse shrub or blackbrush, where it can germinate protected from the chomp of roving jackrabbits. It would particularly benefit from finding a spot atop a symbiotic soil fungus that lurks beneath the sandy loam and can help the baby Joshua tree grow. If the tree makes it past the perils of early life, it needs another thirty to sixty years before it's ready to reproduce. Then it would rely on the yucca moth to pollinate it; otherwise, it won't bear fruit. Then and only then, after this confounding and unlikely gauntlet has been run, will a Joshua tree be able to seed, the whole tenuous cycle repeating itself.

Scientists have mapped Joshua tree survival against the direst climatic conditions—that is, if humans continue at our current rate of consumption and emission—and found that by the year 2100, essentially zero Joshua tree habitat will remain in California's Joshua Tree National Park, even for trees that are already among the most drought tolerant.

Lynn Sweet, a plant ecologist who studies Joshua trees at the University of California, Riverside, told me that her team calculated that, under more mitigated scenarios in which carbon emissions were reduced, "we could preserve up to 20 percent or so of habitat in the park and the surroundings," assuming the moth and mycelium make it in this scenario, too.

When it comes to conservation efforts, humans most often think of the forests most dear to them—the places they grew up visiting, the places where they got married or take their beloved weekend hikes, the national parks known for their iconic trees. These places—Sequoia National Park, Muir Woods, the Everglades—loom large in our collective consciousness. "I often joke with reporters," Sweet told me, "that no one is coming out to do a climate change article on the blackbrush bush," an equally imperiled species in the desert.

Joshua Tree National Park is central on my personal map of sacred places. It was the first place I went backpacking as a kid, the first place I slept under the stars, and a place I've returned to again and again to reattune with the world. The Joshua tree's silhouette is imprinted on many significant memories throughout my life—these are trees I really, really, *really* want to survive.

After getting vaccinated last spring, I headed down for a few days in search of desert light and those fabled trees. I drove from the south end of Joshua Tree to the north, moving through a low, flat valley where Joshua trees and cholla clustered in mighty, baffling stands. The Joshua trees here in the valley looked healthy enough, but botanists know better. Look closely, they told me, and you'll see there are no young sprouting among the noble elders. This was a forest of childless parents, living their final days as the last of their kind to call that spot their home.

Sweet had directed me to visit Black Rock Canyon, where the healthiest of Joshua trees were now finding space to grow. Here we were at higher elevation than the park's sweeping flatlands, meaning it was cooler and slightly wetter. "They're essentially running uphill," she told me, on an intergenerational march toward higher ground. I took a long solo hike through these highlands where hundreds of Joshua trees stood. The trees were lovely to behold from all angles, like benevolent apparitions from some absurdist underworld. But the best view was from above: beholding all those Joshua trees across the valley floor that were thriving, surrounded by their young, with room still to move upward. The problem with up is there's only so far to go before it's just sky.

The living will do whatever they need to survive. In the apocalyptic grove near Medford, I had seen one desiccated former tree whose branches were covered in hundreds of cones still affixed to it like Christmas ornaments. St. Clair explained that this behavior was normal enough for a tree in distress. Sensing it will die, the tree bursts forth into cones in a frantic final act of hope: not so much for itself, but for its species.

I left the desert, like I'd left Oregon, having seen what I'd come to see: the future. There wasn't a single version of it, but many. Another quote St. Clair likes to share is by the late forester and politician Gifford Pinchot: "The vast possibilities of our great future will become realities only if we make ourselves responsible for that future." If we look into the crystal ball, we see ourselves peering back at us in search of answers to the same questions.

Can We Move Our Forests in Time to Save Them?: The Conversation

WILL   Go ahead, David. Tell us all about trees. *[laughter]*

DAVID   Well, I actually have like a fifteen-minute monologue I want to share, and that's not going to work.

JEN   We can try throwing a monologue in.

DAVID   Okay, so Chris brought up *The Overstory,* and how the book brings up things in nature that have rights. I would hope that that sort of thinking—that something like a tree could ever have rights—is going to make it to the classroom. And if it hasn't made it to classrooms, I really predict that it will. You have the fires that are happening out in California, but something hasn't triggered—there aren't mass protests out there.

CHRIS   Isn't Greta Thunberg a thing?

WILL   If you talk to literally anybody in Canberra, in Australia, there's a pretty acute sense of the damage that climate change is causing and the rights of their natural space. Because it was easily the most lush, beautiful, invigorating natural experience in the country, by all accounts, and it just burned.

DAVID   So, in your mind, it's reached that level? Like this is something that people are actively having discourses about?

RUBY   I think a lot of people are talking about climate change and the effects climate change has on humans. But I'm not sure if, in the mainstream, people are talking on the micro level about whether or not natural things, such as trees, would deserve the same rights as the people who benefit from those trees.

DAVID   OK, here's the monologue. There are at least three reasons why trees should have rights. And one is kind of really obvious and would probably be the easiest argument to sell. But in my mind, it's not the strongest argument. And that is that the health of trees affects the health of humans, so therefore, they should have rights. And I think that's pretty obvious. But I think the sentient argument, when you look at all the things that trees can do, like a tree can literally recognize its offspring and give that offspring its resources. And they take care of their old, like when you see a trunk, a stump in the woods, other trees around the area, through the fungal networks, the mycelium, are sending that stump nutrients and that's costly to them. And it makes you wonder, why are they doing this? But here at Faribault, I had an experience that made me think about another awareness of trees. When I got here five years ago, it had been a while since I had been around trees. I got here in the winter, and in the spring, I experienced the spring with trees. And you know, spending most of my life in Minnesota, it was always the fall that was a big deal, because you'd see the leaves change and all that. But anyways, in the springtime, you had the flowering trees. And to me, to see those trees in full bloom was just incredible. I started to pay attention. Like every year for about three or four days, you could really smell the bloom of those flowering trees. It was kind of like lilac, but there was something more perfumy, and it only lasted for three or four days. And that was it! And then I noticed in the last couple of years, slowly one of the trees had some disease, and it was losing its branches. And then one was almost completely dying. And so, I thought, "Okay, this is the year I'm going to really pay attention to it, because it's probably going to be very faint. I probably won't be able to smell it at all." But just the opposite happened. It was the most heavily scented that I ever experienced. And my theory is that the tree knew that distress was coming, that it was going to die and it did whatever it could do to reproduce. And so, it made those scents that much stronger to attract the pollinators. Anyway, so that's just the complexity of trees that we don't normally think about, and the complexity of trees is one of the reasons why I think, you know, trees should have rights. But there's also a third reason I haven't really come across. And that is that things are beautiful in nature, and if we don't give those things rights, then we lose part of what it means to be a human, because they transcend our daily concerns. And if we're not willing to protect that, then we're losing something of ourselves. The whole thing with nature rights, [they have] to exist completely independent from humans.

WILL   It goes back to the question of the rights the river bears. The only way that we can currently perceive the rights of natural systems and natural individual beings to exist, is in their utility for us. Every means that we'll concoct and construct and try to apply in order to save and rescue the systems from us are ultimately doomed to fail, because we're only ever saving them for our sakes, as opposed to saving them for their own sakes, which is a fundamental concept in order to establish the rights of a thing, a being, a person, or a plant. Or anything.

WARREN   Even though we would also ultimately benefit from the preservation of the resources, you know, just the preservation for the future of us should be enough to incentivize it.

WILL   I've heard this sentiment echoed from people in our community outside of prison—one of the things that was really apparent when, in the early phases of COVID, various federal agencies struggled to respond to a problem they did not understand, when people were still dying and we didn't know anything about what was going to happen or how long it was going to last. Even then it was apparent that, with all due respect to some well-intentioned individuals, the system was never really concerned about whether we lived or died. In particular, the joint CDC press conferences were always aimed at the consequences of deaths, and never the death or the dead themselves. Everything that was coming out of the NIH and CDC was concerned with the wrong thing because they weren't concerned with our lives. They were concerned with consequences to themselves. And that's the same thing as—if I only preserve the river so that I can irrigate my crop, or dump my crop, rather than preserve the river for the sake of the river, then that river's screwed, because I have the power, but with misguided concern.

KENNEDY   The name in Swahili for traditional healers is *Miti shamba*. If you translate that into English, it just means a garden of trees. So, it wasn't very hard for us in Kenya, when we saw the Sahara Desert constantly approaching, for us to create a national tree planting day. You know, once a year, the government actually gives us a mix of tree seedlings for everybody to plant around. And you've never seen the joy of a kid for adding a tree. And as we grow, we protect those trees. *They were ours,* and I could protect my own brothers and sisters. We started seeing the loss of trees earlier than most people in Europe or in America, and we took it very seriously. You know, we can tell them that if you plant a garden of trees, you're healing the earth. You're healing the place where you live. [And that convinced] the government that [had been] jailing tree lovers—as you guys in America could say—[instead of encouraging them] to start growing seeds, which they [the government] give to everybody. Every school kid, you know, plants a tree. Businessmen have to go to the countryside and plant a tree. And that has actually saved a lot of Kenyan soil, of which we have very little; only like an eighth of the country is suitable for agriculture. The rest is sandstorms, basically useless. So, it can be done, it can be done. It just takes everybody to understand. If teachers, kids, parents, hotel workers, and dancers understood the value of trees the way we do in Kenya, it couldn't be so hard for the United States to plant and to have some really great trees growing everywhere.

CHRIS   I think that's the problem with this whole thing, because I think, when you come up, you have your environmental science class. And then you start recycling, you start getting excited about the earth. And then you go into the real world, and then you adapt to the system. I don't think knowledge is the problem. I think people don't give a shit. I think a lot of people are doing good stuff and moving forward. But [some] don't value trees. I think they just value their own economy more.

JEN   Let's give Ruby the last word, because hers is the generation stuck with the planet that we've left them.

RUBY   Well, I do come from Oregon, and we have been suffering from increasingly worse forest fires every August. And it's gotten to the point where we have had the worst air quality index in the world on some days. And you know, [when] you see ash from the sky, it does feel like the end of the world at times. And I think that the idea of trees deserving rights outside of our own human use or utility is something that I hadn't ever thought about before. Because I wasn't the one burning; I just had to breathe in the smoke.

Shape of the Wound

by Lacy M. Johnson

Before the storm, my children and I carried the potted plants indoors. We emptied the linen closet onto the floor and hauled the contents to the yard, where we wrapped the citrus trees in sheets and covered the cactus with a thin blanket. My husband wrapped the trunk of the peach tree in a sleeping bag. That evening, we played a board game and ate stew. My children went to bed excited that—for only the third time in their lives—they might wake up to a little snow.

In the morning we indeed had a little snow on the ground, a "skiff" as we would have called it back home in Missouri. The light was thin and gray, the sky a little overcast, and, because the power had gone out during the night, the house was already cold. The cell phone towers were also out of commission, so we had no cell service and very little information. The children went outside to throw snowballs. I lit a fire in the fireplace, and all day the house grew colder and colder. That evening, I turned on the car radio while I cooked dinner over the propane camp stove in the garage and heard that we might have days of rolling blackouts, and then that maybe the blackouts wouldn't roll. We dragged a mattress to the living room, piled the couches with blankets and pillows. That night, when it was twenty-three degrees in Juneau and forty-three in Reykjavík, the temperature in Houston plunged to twelve. It was thirty-five inside my home.

At one point, the power came on long enough for us to discover that our pipes had frozen, and for them to thaw just enough to burst. The power went off again just as water began pouring from light fixtures, and it stayed off while drywall and insulation sloughed from the ceiling. At the hardware store, lines of people looking for water went out the door. Cars extended for blocks from the only open fast-food restaurant. With burst pipes all over the city, water pressure dropped enough to trigger a mandatory boil order. In a city where most people have electric stoves, how would we boil water without electricity? Some of us dragged burning charcoal grills into our living rooms; others left their homes to get warm in cars, which were left running in garages. An elderly man died of hypothermia in his recliner. A child, just hours after playing in snow for the first time in his life, died of carbon monoxide poisoning in his own bed. It felt, if only briefly, as if we were living in a collapsing civilization.

It took two weeks to learn what had happened. The storm had brought snow, ice, and freezing rain deep into Texas, coating not only streets, trees, and power lines with a thin layer of ice but also gas lines, coal transformers, and wind turbines (none of which had been winterized). When the equipment froze, producers lost their ability to transform the energy in coal, wind, and gas into power, and the grid lost its supply of electricity. Operators forced outages to avoid catastrophic failure, telling reporters later that they were "seconds and minutes" away from a total uncontrolled blackout that would have taken weeks or months to repair. The whole disaster could have been avoided, the Federal Energy Regulatory Commission concluded, if only operators had been required to winterize after the last power failure a decade earlier. Their negligence left us all vulnerable, but our vulnerability wasn't distributed equally.

At my home in west Houston, for instance, we lost power for sixty hours over three days, but an acquaintance who lives in one of the city's wealthiest neighborhoods reported she never lost power at all. Near the Houston Ship Channel—a massive industrial corridor of refineries, chemical plants, storage tanks, and pipeline terminals that form the second largest petrochemical complex in the world—communities were exposed not only to freezing temperatures and longer outages but also to harmful carcinogens when refineries illegally burned off millions of pounds of toxic chemicals to prevent damage to their equipment. Because of lax regulations and enforcement, these emissions didn't amount to crimes, even if they were tantamount to poisoning.

The freeze made these communities vulnerable to emissions this time, but refineries near the ship channel emit toxic pollutants regularly—when there is a winter storm, or a flood, or a hurricane, or for reasons that are never explained. The accident is a matter of routine. Two tankers collide and an oil sheen spreads across the surface of Galveston Bay. A chemical storage tank near the ship channel burns uncontrollably for days and days, sending a plume of black smoke over the entire city and beyond, extending halfway across the state, visible from space. The violence these disasters inflict isn't accidental; it's a feature of the toxic petrochemical infrastructure on which our society is based.

What makes people more or less vulnerable to this violence is structural, a relationship we have been told is inevitable and necessary to protect the comfort of those who are already living comfortably. It's not only a history of decisions about where to concentrate our most toxic chemical operations, but also of prioritizing prosperity at the expense of people's health and safety, or sometimes at the expense of entire ecosystems. Vulnerability, as a social structure, makes it possible for companies to force chemicals into the earth in order to squeeze out more oil, triggering earthquakes and poisoning aquifers, spilling forever chemicals along any of the hundreds of thousands of miles of pipelines that span the entire state and sprawl across the continent. When the next freeze or fire or pandemic or hurricane hits us, vulnerability will determine who gets to live, and who will die—and how. The disaster won't be the weather, but the shape of the wound that structural violence has already made.

Officially, the freeze claimed the lives of 246 people, though some analysts have suggested the casualties are more than triple that. It was deadlier and costlier even than Hurricane Harvey, which was already the second costliest disaster in US history, after only Hurricane Katrina. The freeze came after an already disastrous year: a year of the most active hurricane season on record, the worst wildfire season on record, the driest year on record in the Southwest, one of the wettest in the Southeast, after the hottest ever temperature was recorded in Death Valley (130 degrees), after the warmest year ever on record for Europe and Asia, a year that ended the warmest decade on record for the globe and saw a new record for the highest daily carbon dioxide concentration at the Mauna Loa Observatory. (In the year since the freeze, that record has been broken again, twice.)

This August, the latest Intergovernmental Panel on Climate Change report predicted that our worst disasters are ahead of us, not behind.

As I write this, in November 2021, Congress has just passed a massive infrastructure bill, with $35 billion designated for Texas, meant to repair the crumbling highways and airports and bridges we've built in the past, as well as to winterize our pipelines and power plants. None of this will prepare us for the disasters of the present moment, much less the ones of the future—a failure as much of preparedness as of imagination. I have an excellent imagination for the catastrophic—storm surges, super hurricanes, an act of stupid human negligence that might plunge us forever into darkness—but the freeze helped me to understand, with a little more clarity, that what most needs our attention and repair isn't the infrastructure our society has built, but rather the structure of its vulnerabilities.

Despite my best efforts, the citrus trees did not survive the freeze. The leaves turned brown and fell; the bark changed from brown to gray. Even after we cut them down, I watched the stumps for signs of green shoots sprouting. None came. We cut down the peach tree and shoveled the liquefied pads of the cactus into a paper bag. Today, outside my window, the sun is shining. There isn't a cloud in the sky. But I can't help feeling as though, at any moment, everything will collapse from under us. Or that maybe it already has, and we just haven't yet realized it's gone.

Shape of the Wound: The Conversation

CHRIS   My friend had been in Texas for twenty years. So, she knew what to expect, knew that things weren't winterized. So, when they talked about wrapping the trees and shit, she wrapped her pipes. So, like those noodles, the noodles open wrap the pipes and all that shit. And they lost power for a little bit, but then she went to a hotel, too, because she could afford it.

WILL   Who fucking winterizes Texas?

CHRIS   Well, yeah, but I mean, I think it's one of those things. At a manager level when somebody's like, we can save a couple million if we don't, yeah.

WILL   Well, you can't get flood insurance in the Lower Ninth in New Orleans, you just can't 'cause it's cost prohibitive for that whole space, but you still know the flood is coming.

WARREN   The biggest irony about the whole winterizing thing, [is that] when you run machinery at a consistent temperature, it's cheaper in the long run. So, winterizing all their equipment, not only would it protect it against the cold, but it also would protect it against the heat. You know, the rolling blackouts they have for all the heat and all the stall ups and undue stress they have on equipment generating [electricity]. [Winterizing would have] saved them millions, and probably by now billions, if they invested in the beginning.

CHRIS   It goes back to capitalism, colonialism, you know, this manifest destiny and this whole idea of, "Is it my responsibility to take care of poor people?"

WILL   This is what we were talking about earlier about agency. The idea that if you do things the way you were taught and programmed by the larger culture, and participate without making the most of an opportunity to question or actually decide things for yourself, then you're an algorithm, you're a fixed variable in a spreadsheet that people are exploiting in order to monetize your existence. Meaning, by virtue of our [prison] ID numbers, we're all trapped in that in ways that a lot of people don't ever actually get to get plugged into. I mean, we're conditioned to believe this by a system that was designed to benefit the people who are on the profit side of the equation.

CHRIS   I don't understand why this book is not about revolution. Is the revolution real? Is that happening?

JEN   Why do you think this book is *not* about revolution?

DAVID   As long as plants are in this revolution.

CHRIS   I feel like, and maybe you can dovetail on this, Jen, I believe that the next generation understands cosmic energy. And I think they understand spirituality more and better than ever, you know, without biblical bullshit.

JEN   They're a much better generation than us, than mine, [or] y'all's, our generations. I feel really grateful that Ruby is here. I want to hear Ruby's thoughts.

CHRIS   I think that there's a moral and spiritual reckoning coming with the energies that we've been putting out on this planet, on each other.

RUBY   I think, well, hopefully, with a reckoning would come something that's actionable. I do think that we are in a pretty intense reckoning in terms of like, a lot of folks are being introduced to concepts that have been around for years but are just now resurfacing into a common consciousness. I think with people in my generation, it's very easy to feel very cynical. There's very little trust in higher leadership. And you know, a lot of people my age are taking action and initiating their own movements. I think it's really hard though, when things are so stratified within the movement. There is a lot of division because people are purists, and they want things to go exactly their way. And so, in terms of revolution, it really requires, it requires collective movement that gets shattered when people are not using the right rhetoric, or when people are not, you know, acting on like, I don't know, on grounds that appease everyone, which is impossible to do. And so that is why I currently feel disheartened. But I also think that anger is really resurfacing. And I think that, like I've said in past discussions, anger's really actionable. The hardest thing, though, is to sustain it because people get tired and exhausted by it. I think the number one thing that we have to figure out before real change can take place is how do we get everyone on board and stay on board until things actually happen?

KENNEDY   Nowadays, Americans always talk on the Internet. In my time, you know, we met in class, we met in the cafeteria. We talked after school. When we sat at the president's office, we were *there*. And we could say, "Now who else do we need?" So, it was easier to build a revolution from that standpoint than [it is] nowadays.

The View from Mount Failure

by Steve Almond

"If you want to really hurt your parents," Kurt Vonnegut once pro-claimed, "and you don't have the nerve to be gay, the least you can do is go into the arts."[1]

Vonnegut was my favorite writer growing up. I read his novels incessantly in high school and wrote a lengthy and tiresome thesis about him in college. But this quotation in particular has stuck with me, no doubt because my twin brother is gay, which meant I was left with option B: the arts.

To be clear, neither of us were particularly rebellious kids. On the contrary, we were good Jewish boys from the suburbs who did our best to honor our parents and the ambitions into which we were born. Both of us stayed in the closet as long as we could.

Mike knew he was gay from an early age, but he dated girls all through high school. He was so handsome I assumed every one of my girlfriends really wanted to be with him. I was certain, for instance, that Jessica Vitkus, whom I saw the summer after my first year in col-lege, was secretly sleeping with Mike.

I carried this hunch around like a hot stone until the evening Mike mentioned to me, quite off-handedly, that he was gay. He never actu-ally used that word. He made reference to the person he was seeing using a male pronoun. It would take years before we talked about any of this.

❖ ❖ ❖

In this sense, Vonnegut's quote is full of shit. Mike wasn't trying to make our parents angry. He was trying to figure out, from the time he was maybe five years old, how to give himself permission to be gay. He resisted doing so, in part, to protect our parents, who were enlight-ened people, but were also as full of homophobic garbage as the world

---

1 Kurt Vonnegut, *A Man Without a Country* (New York: Seven Stories Press, 2005).

around them. Gay people don't "come out" to enrage their parents. They do so because they can no longer live a lie.

It's okay, by the way, to call out a literary hero for saying something full of shit. We are all, to some extent, full of shit, which is to say: blind to our bigotries, lazy in our self-expression, eager to confuse wit and wisdom.

The Vonnegut quotation assumes that young people make wrenching personal decisions to punish their elders when just the opposite is true: they make those decisions as a means of forgiving themselves.

✦✦✦

I wasn't so quick to forgive. It took me till my late twenties to come out of the closet as an artist. Even now, I can feel myself cringing a little bit at that word: *artist*. It's like I'm drawing a little halo of misery and self-importance above my head. I'm even leery about the word *writer*. It implies expertise, like I know something the rest of the world doesn't.

I don't.

In my experience, every human being is capable of writing beautiful prose or poetry. You don't have to have a fancy degree, or a pedigree. You just have to tell the truth about the stuff that matters to you most deeply. Simple, direct language works better than fancy, metaphorical language. But granting ourselves permission to do this turns out to be a lot harder than it sounds.

Why?

For one thing, we're living in an age where the capacity to concentrate for long periods of time has been ceding ground to the shiny, frantic distractions of capitalism.

For another thing, telling the truth is an act of tremendous vulnerability. This is why we spend so much time bullshitting ourselves and those around us. It's hard enough to be a human, to be conscious of our failings and disappointments. Now add to that the burden of baring your inner life (with its continual buzz of doubt and fear and shame) to the outside world.

It's much easier to sit back and lose yourself in a ballgame or a sitcom or some reality TV nightmare. Why transcribe your internal ruin when you can passively consume someone else's?

❖❖❖

It took me three decades to admit that I wanted to write, and years more to start telling the truth. Even now, I fail most of the time. Which is to say: I get distracted. Just now, in the midst of writing this paragraph, I went on the internet and found a video of a cat attempting to leap onto a nearby roof. The maker of this video has cleverly drawn all these thought bubbles above the cat's head, so that he appears to be doing the complicated math required to figure out his precise acceleration and trajectory. Then he jumps and misses the roof by, like, five feet, and plummets out of the frame. I watched this video three times. Then I returned to this essay, strangely refreshed.

As a writer, I feel like that cat *all the time.* I'm continually hoping that my prose will have precision and the power to reach the reader. I'm continually doing the math in my head. And I continually fall short and plummet out of the frame.

That's true of every writer. Whatever magic sauce you think they possess, you're only seeing their published work, their most polished decisions. You're not seeing the mountain of failures they had to amass on the way to those decisions. That, in fact, is how you reach the roof: you leap from atop a mountain of failures.

I strongly recommend that writers (budding artists of any kind, really) take a look at the archives of their heroes. I did. I traveled out to the Lilly Library at Indiana University to check out Kurt Vonnegut's papers. Amid those stacks of documents were dozens upon dozens of unpublished short stories, all competently written but lifeless and mannered. Like my early stories, they were imitations of other writers, nothing like the Vonnegut I would come to worship, whose narrative voice was so wise and funny and merciful.

Reading over these early stories in a quiet room in Bloomington, Indiana, I had two thoughts.

1. Kurt Vonnegut once sucked.
2. There's hope for me yet.

❖❖❖

I've just been informed by the editors of this anthology that, while they appreciate the foregoing material, they expected a treatise of some sort about the "creative class." Let me assure the editors (and the rest of you) that I am getting to that part and that I have many thoughts.

But, I'd like to quarrel with the term a bit first.

It seems to want to draw a border of some kind around those who are creative, or creative enough to make money off their talents, and thus to compose a class of their own. Fine. But let's acknowledge what we all know to be true: that this class is largely defined not by the inherent creativity of its membership but by the socioeconomic class into which they were born.

The extent to which people indulge in creative endeavor (and the forms that creativity takes) depends almost entirely on the material wealth they inherit, as well as the opportunity and ambition they have. That's what class defines: how much privilege you were born into or acquired.

Wealthy Americans don't like to talk about privilege in such overt terms. They consider it "class warfare," the standard propaganda term deployed when the masses start agitating about economic justice, rather than, say, racial grievance. The rich also resent the implication that their wealth is a function of luck rather than merit. They prefer a system of thought in which the rich are rich because they are inherently virtuous, and the poor are poor because they are morally defective.

✤ ✤ ✤

As for me, I was born insanely lucky. Sure, my grandparents struggled, especially during the Great Depression. Two of them became members of the Communist Party. But by the time I showed up, our family was firmly upper middle-class, which is the term enlightened people use instead of rich. My parents dabbled in the counterculture, but eventually became prosperous doctors. They expected us to excel academically. In this sense, my decision to leave journalism and pursue creative writing was not a heroic leap so much as an unorthodox lateral move.

My wife, on the other hand, was born into a family in which her obedience was valued more than her ambition. Her early childhood was ruled by the dogma of the Catholic Church, and when she rebelled, her parents flipped out. (This is putting it gently.) She left home at sixteen.

She eventually made it to junior college, then on to an elite university, where she walked around feeling like an imposter. She was the first member of her family to graduate from college, and later graduate school. But she has struggled to feel at home in the creative class, because she never internalized the idea that she could be creative for a living. Work was something you did to pay off your debts, not to express yourself.

The fact that I am writing this piece—that I am in a position to hold forth on any of this—is a function of my birthright.

⁜⁜⁜

Weirdly, this brings me back to Vonnegut, and what I loved—and continue to love—about his work, which is his refusal to keep his trap shut when it comes to class.

Eliot Rosewater, the obscenely rich hero of one early novel, speaks of "the Money River, where the wealth of the nation flows. We were born on the banks of it—and so were most of the mediocre people we grew up with, went to private schools with, sailed and played tennis with. We can slurp from that mighty river to our hearts' content. And we can even take slurping lessons, so we can slurp more efficiently."[2]

What's more important, as Rosewater notes, is the manner in which our culture vilifies those born into economic struggle, a self-hatred that is deeply felt but almost never spoken of—"Those who have no money blame and blame and blame themselves. This inward blame has been a treasure for the rich and powerful, who have had to do less for their poor, publicly and privately, than any other ruling class since, say, Napoleonic times."[3]

---

2 Kurt Vonnegut, *God Bless You, Mr. Rosewater* (New York: Holt, Rinehart and Winston, 1965).

3 Vonnegut, *God Bless You, Mr. Rosewater.*

Vonnegut wrote these words in 1964, back when the marginal tax rate on America's millionaires was 75 percent.

✢ ✢ ✢

The point I'm trying to make here is that most people who occupy the creative class—who get to create things for a living, in particular writing—were born within shouting distance of the Money River, if not on its banks. We got a lot of help along the way.

To put that another way: there are barriers—both internal and external—to joining the creative class, especially for people who are born into economic struggle. You can multiply those barriers by a hundred when it comes to people who have been incarcerated.

If you're working a job, or two, or three, just to pay off your debts, there's not a lot of gas left in the tank at the end of the day, or in the wee hours, and there's not a lot of mental or emotional space left to wander and imagine and doubt and confess, which are all essential to creative work.

And there's something more here that almost never gets talked about, and which bears directly on the relationship between creativity and class. Remember when I talked about how much failure factors into literary success? Successful writers are the ones who outlast their doubt. But that kind of emotional resilience is nearly impossible to sustain when you live in a world that makes you feel like a failure.

The self-belief I've developed over the years isn't some testament to my inherent psychic fortitude. It's a function of my class advantages.

✢ ✢ ✢

All of us are endowed with a creative impulse. It's part of the human arrangement. We daydream. We whistle. We sing. We cook. We doodle. We crack jokes. We imagine.

Working people, vulnerable people, formerly incarcerated people, those stressed by legacies of deprivation and abuse, simply have less time and energy to create. They suffer more persistently from what the poet Wallace Stevens called "the pressure of the real."

Stevens was referring to the incessant drumbeat of terrible events and realities in the world around us. But there is also a "pressure of the real" that arises from the world within us, a voice of doubt and catastrophe that undermines our capacity to believe in ourselves, and to believe we can produce creative work that others will value.

How does an oppressed person scale a mountain of failure, let alone leap from it, when the gravity of self-doubt presses down upon them? It's not impossible. But it's also not as possible.

Not only do marginalized people struggle to monetize their creativity, they also have to keep others from skimming off the top of their talent. This is why Aretha Franklin, to her dying day, refused to set foot on stage until she'd been paid in cash. The money went straight into her purse, which she brought with her onstage. When the show was over, she walked backstage and opened her purse and paid her staff in cash.

✢ ✢ ✢

As a female African American artist, Aretha was up against a culture shaped by racism, patriarchal abuse, and commercial exploitation. But she at least could count on her immense talents to put butts in the seats. Most writers—particularly literary writers—cannot.

This is why I urge young writers to uncouple artistic creation from financial expectation. In more candid moods, I tell them to consider writing a bad habit, one they'll have to support. I say this not to be an asshole (though I am often an asshole) but because I know how hard it is to sit down and write without expecting your imagination to yield a dividend.

So, find a way to underwrite your creative work. And don't feel a lick of shame about it. Lord Byron could write his immortal verse because he was born atop a mountain of money. The rest of us have to take a patron, whether that means bartending or data entry or marrying well.

We have this myth in our heads that "true artists" exist on the astral plane, that they don't have to worry about the rent or the price of bread. But even the most insanely gifted artists—the Mozarts and

Coltranes and Morrisons—had to live in the material world, too. They all needed patrons to survive: aristocrats, club owners, universities.

Nearly twenty-five years after securing my MFA, I make a living by patching together dozens of gigs. I teach. I host storytelling events. I edit manuscripts. I write service journalism. I speak at libraries and conferences. I do radio gigs and sell books out of my trunk and earn a pittance in royalties. I have forty bosses. None of them return my emails in a timely fashion, and I'm lucky for every one of them.

I enjoy most of this work. But the work I find most fulfilling—the writing of short stories and novels—earns me next to nothing. That's precisely as it should be. The moment you start expecting the market to reward you for your creative work is the moment you stop heeding your own instincts.

❖❖❖

A demonstrative story:

Back at the turn of the last century, I stalled out on a novel, something I do every few years. As noted above, this failure is a central feature of creative endeavor, at least in my case.

The point is that I had some time on my hands. The American body politic—spurred on by the terrorist attacks of 2001—was undergoing one of its regular moral regressions, seeking vengeance against a nation that had nothing to do with the attacks, led by the usual cast of for-profit demagogues. Citizens were chanting for blood, tracking on television the delivery of glowing bombs that would blow up actual human beings, some of them innocent women and children. All this had me thinking about old Vonnegut again.

He was quite near the end of his life, though I didn't know that yet. I returned to his novels, which were remarkably prescient. Vonnegut, I decided, was the great lost prophet of our age. I set out to write a book that would remind our fallen world of his vision. I had no illusions about the commercial reach of such a project. It would be a short, intensely personal effort.

The literary agent who represented me at the time had a more mercenary vision, and, to his credit, he managed to convince a publisher to pay me an obscene advance. But there was a catch. The publisher didn't want a book about Vonnegut. He wanted an essay collection. My wife, with whom I had just eloped, was pregnant with our first kid and we were looking to buy a house, so I didn't argue. But I had a bad feeling about the whole arrangement.

Sure enough, my essay collection tanked—at least relative to its exorbitant advance—which meant I got to walk around for two years feeling like a dumb bet. Capitalism has this way of colonizing our egos, convincing us that making money for the home office is more important than making art.

✛✛✛

Then came the day I found myself sitting in the office of my New York editor, high above Manhattan, trying to sell her on my next project: a book that could be read in two directions. One direction would be one-page essays about the technical and emotional challenges of writing. The other would be tiny short stories. My editor had no idea what I was talking about; her eyes glazed over.

It suddenly occurred to me that I had no business asking her to invest more money in my talents, and that I would be happier if I just published the damn thing myself. So, I wrote the book I actually wanted to write and got in touch with my pal, the graphic artist Brian Stauffer, and begged him to design a cover. We printed up a bound copy at my local indie bookstore.

I've since made several books this way. One is composed of the hate mail I've received over the years. Another is full of my worst poems, with brief essays about why they suck. I sell them for five bucks a pop, mostly in person, out of my yellow courier bag. The transactions look a lot like drug deals.

This, too, is part of what it means to be in the creative class. You have to be adaptable and you have to recognize your scale. In my case, I had no business working with giant corporations who thought I could earn them money. It made much more sense for me to put books into the world myself, niche products I could hand deliver to a few dozen customers at a time.

Then again, I'd already published a few books with traditional publishers, so I had teaching and speaking gigs where I could sell my little weirdo DIY books. Most aspiring writers don't have that option. So please don't run out and print up little weirdo DIY books, unless that's truly what you feel called to do.

A better course of action would be to step back and figure out who you are as an artist, and what role you want writing to play in your life. That means doing a self inventory. Ask yourself what success means to you. Is it writing every day? Getting a short story or a poem accepted for publication? Publishing a book?

My own sense is that the people who decide to write in order to get rich and famous burn out pretty quickly. Those who stick with it are the ones who have gone in search of themselves, who desire what MFK Fisher described as the right to be precise about their own lives.

※※※

Ultimately, I'm not sure there's even such a thing as the creative class. It's a squishy (perhaps wishful) term meant to describe the emergent population—as distinct from agricultural and industrial laborers—who are "creative" for a living. But this demands we accept only certain human pursuits as inherently creative.

Anyone who works on an assembly line, or as a home health-care aide, or at a fast-food restaurant isn't "creative." They are service economy drones, soft robots who trudge through their days just waiting to get home and consume "content" produced by brilliant creatives.

But anyone who's ever watched a home health-care aide try to convince a dying cancer patient to drink their protein shake knows what a load of crap that is. Home health-care aides have to be unbelievably creative. They have to create a language—verbal and gestural—that allows them to minister to people who are frightened and in pain, people like my mother who, at the end of her life, exhausted and ashamed by the ravages of her illness, no longer wished to eat.

And what of the social workers? And the ICU nurses? And the kindergarten teachers? My God, the kindergarten teachers! Do you have any idea how much creativity is required to teach two dozen five-year-olds? I'm not trying to downgrade the folks (like me) who create articles and illustrations and computer code and curricula for a living. I'm simply pointing out how absurd it is to limit our definition of creativity.

Are the prisoners who edited this anthology now part of the creative class? What are we to make of the creativity they used in navigating the criminal justice system, and their own incarceration? Or the creativity they will have to summon to reintegrate themselves into a world that regards them with suspicion and fear?

✤✤✤

My own experience tells me that people are happiest when they find a way to make money at something they love. But there are plenty of people—Wallace Stevens, for instance, or Anton Chekhov—who find paid work elsewhere and write purely because they felt called to do so.

"The arts are not a way to make a living," Vonnegut concludes, quite sensibly. "They are a very human way of making life more bearable."[4]

Maybe a more honest way of looking at all this would be to admit that capitalism creates an incentive system wherein citizens agree to place their imaginations in the service of profit. When we ask "what somebody makes" in the United States we mean how much money they earn, not what they create.

✤✤✤

It's important to recognize the fundamental irony embedded in all this talk of the creative class. Which is this: the sorts of people whose stories most need to be told and heard are not the ones, by and large, who populate the creative class.

This is why the rich and powerful have such an easy time demonizing vulnerable populations, flattening them into caricatures—because so few stories in our culture are told by poor people and people of color and incarcerated people and disabled people and gay people and

---

4 Vonnegut, *A Man Without a Country*.

neurodivergent people. Instead, stories are told *about* them. Most of those stories are pernicious or naïve myths. But even the most well-intentioned of these stories cannot hope to fully represent the truth; such stories must come from the people who have lived them.

If enough of these stories get told, they will start to pierce the dream in which guys like me float along through our lucky lives. They'll stop pretending that the American experiment is going just swell, when so many have suffered its cruelty and greed. So perhaps the time has come to call for an end to the creative class altogether, with its expensive lunch salads and its easy bigotries. Perhaps it's time to call for an uprising of the creative underclass.

If that puts me out of a job, well then, we'll be even. And I can return to the work I'm supposed to be doing anyway, which is not chasing paychecks or seeking regard from the world, but paying attention to my own life.

The View from Mount Failure: The Conversation

DAVID   The more I think about this essay, especially in this stage of my life, with the work I'm doing—because I'm doing factory work [in prison], and I'm trying to write on the side—I judge myself. But after reading this essay, after thinking about it, I believe life itself is a creative act. And this goes back to what we were saying: there are so many different ways to find meaning in this world. There are so many different ways to create, and I think about the guys I work with, you know, they don't write, they don't paint pictures. They work and they consume television. But then I look at their conversations sometimes, and the jokes they make, and they are creative. In my mind, they're doing creative work. And one thing about this essay is that "hey, look, if you're going to assign monetary value to what you create, you're going about it the wrong way." And especially when you look at the market. The market wants certain types of stories that are gonna sell. I think what's important, though, is to have something in your life that you do create, whether it's baking, or making something out of wood. And I think that people [who] don't have that, [who] don't have a creative avenue, I think they suffer more because they start identifying with their job, or they identify with their political beliefs.

JEN   What I love about the idea of a creative class, as somebody who grew up with class self-consciousness—

WILL   Personally, or your environment was self-conscious?

JEN   Both.
  I love the possibility of an alternate class, right? It doesn't have to be upper class or upper middle class, or, you know, it doesn't have to fit into any of the class systems, really. It feels like this other realm where you could do anything you want. You can drive a crappy car. You can drive a really sweet car. You can share an apartment with three buddies. If you're part of the creative class, you're writers. No one says, "Oh, look at those five grown adults that live together." It's

an entirely different perception. They're poets, they all live together, so that they can devote their time to their art and get by on, you know, very little. It's admirable, right? I think I love that about the idea of the creative class.

CHRIS   Starving artist.

JEN   I know it's overly romanticized. I'm not saying it's easy or glamorous. I just liked the idea that you can kind of step outside of the expectations of capitalist class structure, and that feels really liberating to me. But I'm not sure I know where that line is.

DAVID   What do you think it means to live as a member of the creative class? It's not an accountant who comes home and does Legos, right?

WILL   What is art versus what is play?

JEN   Maybe what we're talking about is how you decide you're gonna live your life. Like, are you willing to have an old car or not put your kids through college because you're going to devote your days to building the Legos? Even if no one thinks the Legos are art?

CHRIS   I think, in this capitalist society, look at all the artistic jobs out there—marketing, for instance. The fucking best commercials on the TV are GEICO insurance commercials. So, you got these people that are sitting in marketing rooms coming up with these fucking great, iconic commercials.

JEN   Marketing employs a lot of people. But I would think of that as a corporate class, not the creative class.

DAVID   But there's creativity in the corporate class.

WILL   My understanding is some people end up in those corporate positions—or in teaching positions or whatever to pay the bills—

because they consider their art to be their primary focus. But there have to be people who love writing jingles. And I'm sure that the person who is in charge of the creative team that produces GEICO commercials is intensely proud, or at least proud of the paycheck.

DAVID   But many novelists, they actually know, or care, what people who read books are looking for.

JEN   A great contract for a novelist might be $100,000. That's *rare.* And then, that novelist might not get paid again for another six years. Thus, the gig at a college or a coffee shop, etc.

WILL   The job at the ad agency might not be the thing that qualifies them for the creative class.

JEN   Correct. I think they made an economic decision.

DAVID   My reading of [Su Hwang's poetry book] *Bodega* was different after working on this anthology.

JEN   Oh, interesting.

CHRIS   Do you feel like your eyes are open now to precarity in different avenues? Is that what you're saying?

DAVID   Yes. And also Steve Almond's novel. Because when I got done reading Steve's *All the Secrets of the World,* I realized it's explaining systems in America during the Reagan administration that are still in place now.

WILL   Isn't that the job of the creative class? I think it's paramount because we already have all the data. The economists have this responsibility of bringing all the data together: "This is what the numbers say." The numbers don't lie unless you make lies of them. But to explain them in ways that connect with human beings, that motivate and engage us to do things differently than the way we've done them up until now?

JEN   Yeah, sometimes I believe narrative is the only thing that's going to save us. Kennedy, we were going to ask you your thoughts about the creative class from somebody who has a more economic perspective.

KENNEDY   To me, the creative class has always been defined by people who give up something important.

DAVID   Opportunity cost.

KENNEDY   The creative class, to me, is people, you know, like my grandmother—she used to make really beautiful pots for cooling water or for cooking. And she also was a very good basket weaver. And until I read this essay, I always thought my grandmother was somebody who built tools. That was the first time I thought of her as really being an artist.

JEN   Pots with fitting lids?

KENNEDY   Exactly. And people always looked down upon her, like, "Why is she doing that? She should just go to the market and buy them." But she never did that. And, to me, that is that love of art, to sacrifice standing in society to do what she loves best. And, to me, that is the creative class. It would be nicer if society was set up in such a way where you didn't have to give up something in order to create art. I think eventually society could be set up like that. I don't understand how we make all these advances in technology, you know, with robotics, or AI, or all that stuff. And human beings are still working the same amount that we worked twenty years ago, or thirty years ago.

JEN   More.

WILL   Specialty manufacturing still remains in Western Europe and in the United States. But a lot of entry-level, high school-educated, union, full-time manufacturing that used to be in textiles and auto manufacturing in this country has been replaced by robots. It's just that—some of this is gonna sound red—the means of production still belong to, you know, capitalist overlords. And so average people who could benefit in a more egalitarian sense from the increase in productivity and expansion of the economy don't because the wealth still remains constrained, because the rules are set against them. All that being said, one thing that I was thinking about is that I think there are more people now who are saying, "You know, what? I like the life I have. I need to have enough to survive, but I don't need to generate wealth for future generations. I don't need to leave an economic legacy that sustains my grandchildren's children." Whereas historically, at least for us, I think we all kind of came up with a different sense of the "American Dream," which we realize now is prevaricated and perhaps nonsensical. But, you know, people want to live in communal housing. It is conceptually plausible. People choose to live that life because it's the life they want to live. They're not, strictly speaking, impoverished in the same way that we—not we as [in] this group, but other people from the outside—might look and say, "Oh, look at those poor people, look at those people who are disadvantaged and sacrificing themselves for their art."

CHRIS   Almond [in this essay] speaks about his literary agent and his publisher and who gets a literary agent. There's all these gatekeepers even in the creative class, right?

JEN   It's the way the game is set up, for the most part.

CHRIS   Right, and it's the structure. But I also see growth in that because, like, in terms of movies, you look at the streaming platforms, look how many different stories are being told. You look at Facebook and social media, like, people are hella creative on there. I mean, TikTok, these things are beneficial now to the creative classes. When

I came to the joint, you taught me a lot about producing art for the sake of art and having something to say. Whereas in the beginning, it was a hustle too, so like doing cards, portraits, and then tattooing—art as a hustle to get by. So, it was an economic decision.

JEN   And you'd be making the designs they wanted from you?

CHRIS   In tattooing, I got this redundancy of requests. It was always money, women, drugs, you know. And so many skulls and roses. But after a while, I started to challenge the cliché of it by finding originality in these things, you know, so you could tell like, that was *my* rose.

DAVID   It's different as long as someone values what you're doing besides just yourself. And I'll tell you in terms of with me, you know, back when I started writing in prison, just for the exercise of it, just to keep the mind sharp and this sense that, "Okay, I want to be my best self." I needed to exercise the mind, exercise the creativity. But now I noticed that writing lets me have conversations with other people that are also creating, and that has a whole other dimension that I didn't see—the *communal* aspect of creative class. And I think people that aren't part of the creative class, they don't see that; they don't know what they're missing. It's like, the dudes that don't take writing classes. They have no idea how cool these spaces actually are.

CHRIS   Picasso said good art is borrowed, great art is stolen. And that goes back to what creativity is. There's nothing that appears from a vacuum. Everything can be traced to something else. There's always influences in everything right? That's part of the thing that's so beautiful about art, because you're not this genius in a cave that pops up and just does these things. You're part of a system. Basquiat was just a kid roaming the streets in the world and then became an artist. And he's no different than [our friend] Haji. I look at Haji and think, "Haji's Basquiat."

JEN   I love the idea that community, maybe, partly defines the creative class.

DAVID   Which community?

JEN   You guys are all helping me understand that when art is shared or borrowed or thieved or when you're in community like we are—and I'm thinking about my own life specifically—I identify as someone in the creative class, most of my friends are . . . We share a community based on creative pursuits, but I think that's different from other class categories. And I think that's really something that hadn't occurred to me until we were sitting in this discussion.

DAVID   Let me ask you this. Is someone always part of the creative class? Like let's say someone created art when they were in their twenties? Or thirties?

JEN   Class is fluid.

DAVID   The community is valued because of the connections, not just the final artistic product.

JEN   Yeah. Just wondering if we would agree—and we don't have to—but this idea, [would we agree] that the creative class is defined by a different sort of community than, say, a neighborhood of working class folks? Or doctors and lawyers in the suburbs? Do they feel community in the same way?

KENNEDY   I think what you're saying is true because when a writer in China gets oppressed, I suffer with that individual. If an Arab journalist or writer gets arrested, I empathize with them. And I don't think it's the same with a blue-collar worker. I don't think that the blue-collar workers in Minnesota are really gonna feel the same kind of depth if a plumber is getting shot in Chile. I think there's more connection that would cause identity within the creative class than some of the other classes that may be existing out there.

DAVID   Writers, especially, are reading about different life situations. Reading causes you to have empathy toward other people. When you're part of the creative class, there's certain habits that you acquire, like feel[ing] empathy, that allow you to look for other people's perspective.

JEN   I have a question that maybe is a step before David's question. *Why* do we feel a sense of community? Is it because we read that we experience empathy? I would wonder if it's worth asking, who enters the creative class? Who are the sorts of folks that come to be writers? I've heard people say all writers are outsiders, or were outsiders. I don't know if that's accurate.

WILL   I think the nature of observation, being observers, puts us on the outside.

KENNEDY   I think there's a kind of honesty in what we do. You know, for example, when we create a character, that character isn't gonna change tomorrow, you know, when we, when our characters are set, they remain the same all throughout their entire life. Take a *Mona Lisa*, for example. She's still as mysterious today as she was when she was created a few hundred years ago. In most of the other classes, meaning changes, like every second, you know, given whatever pressures that are . . .

DAVID   Outside pressures.

KENNEDY   I think that is what kind of sets creatives apart from the other classes out there. You know, it's kind of a unique thing that all [such people] seem to possess, wherever we are. It doesn't matter whether you're in Africa or Asia, or in America, you know, when we're writing about the human condition, we just present it exactly the way we know it best.

JEN   When we're at our best we do.

KENNEDY   And I think that matters, you know. I think that is what brings us closer as a group in this room, and as a social class.

There Are No Bars in Rush City

by TM "Redd" Warren

At Rush City Correctional Facility, you find your rush where you can. It's nearly 2:00 p.m., so that means second watch is in a hurry to finish their final security round, punch the clock, and peel out of the staff parking lot as quickly as they can. Eager, I can only imagine, to do the things civilians do after their work day is done. Meanwhile, third watch has already parked their vehicles, locked them, double-checked them, and slogged in from the lot to the prison. In the span between their vehicle and the entrance to the facility, they have donned their canisters of pepper spray and their prison guard personas in order to get through another perfunctory eight hours. Monotony is motion. Welcome to Rush City close-custody pen. Population: 1,000 incarcerated men, more or less.

Meanwhile, back in the cell, I'm sitting at my desk, taking a break from painting. Not a still life, but a portrait from the shoulders up. "Just an old bald white guy," was how my former cellie Scott used to describe himself. It might look like I'm watching paint dry, but I'm really gauging what I've put down so far and planning my next moves. I pour a cup of coffee and dig out some cookies I smuggled from chow. They're chocolate with those fake M&Ms baked in. I don't like eating sweets alone. So, I offer some cookies to my new cellie who is perched up on the top bunk watching his TV. He declines. He claims that sweets mess with his 18-karat gold teeth. More cookies for me then. Why do these cookies seem to taste better, here in the cell, than if I ate them in the chow hall? Is it because I have my hot coffee and relative peace and quiet? Or is it because I made it through customs with the illicit chocolate treats?

I take another bite of cookie as I look at the head and shoulders portrait in progress. The composition may be simple, but the subject is not. The man contains multitudes, and it's a tricky thing to recapture a life on canvas. It's more than mere talent. Talent is like tap water, and it's more than endless hours of honing the craft. But that is a big part of the process. Consistency beats the occasional flash of brilliance. Hard work beats talent when talent won't work. I've spent enough time around my friend Scott to learn these little mind morsels.

For hours each day, Scott and I would do artwork. He would work in pen and brush on paper. The pieces were done in a technique using tools at hand, by opening up a Bic pen and blowing out some of the ink into the bottom of the plastic sewing kit (without scissors). He would load one of his customized bristle brushes with ink and lose himself in another world, creating beauty in grayscale, rendered with subtlety and nuance. He would sometimes ask me to stop painting and chime in, looking to the "more experienced" artist for affirmation and direction. I am fifteen years younger than Scott, and there are few things I am more experienced in, so I enjoyed the role reversal. He was an open vessel. He was deliberate and efficient. When he wanted to learn things, to understand things, anything, he would be all-in. He was a man of many talents and curiosities.

One time, Scott wrote a paper on bulldog ants. It wasn't for a college class. He was just interested in bulldog ants. The paper was close to ten pages—typed. He read it to me over coffee and snacks. I believe I may have forgotten more than most have known about bulldog ants. But I do remember my friend Scott reading it with enthusiasm and panache, pausing at all the appropriate moments, using the gruff voice of a prison thespian. The paper would've been an "A." The audiobook would have been rated MA/SLV (for strong language and violence).

Scott and I would get our workouts in every day: gym, courtyard, or in the cell. We'd also run stairs for thirty minutes a few times a week. "The heart's a muscle too, Redd." Before I met him, nearing twenty years ago now, I thought I knew what "in shape" meant. He had a level of fitness honed over decades. His workouts were grueling and effective. They burned copious calories and casual workout partners. "Most guys can't hang, Redd." He called these torture sessions "Bailey Workouts." He had a lot of salt in his ass.

Scott was over six foot, with muscles like braided bridge cable under his tattooed hide. I remember being in the cell with him, kicked back on our bunks, staring at our 13-inch SecureView television, watching some nature program, where a giant constrictor put the squeeze on some poor, pitiable prey. Breathtaking, this beautiful horror. An apex predator. Nature does nothing in vain, or so it would seem.

Before Scott relinquished being "the best" at handball. Before his legs would occasionally betray him when he ran stairs. Before he had to strap his hands to the pull-up bar while I pretended not to notice. Before he shook out his hands like they were frozen or on fire. Before Scott signed up to see the physical therapist because it was "just some tendonitis, Redd." Before he alarmed the PT enough to order more tests. Before Scott or I had ever heard the medico invoke the possibility of "global nerve damage."

Scott and I would work on our art pieces until shift change—the guards on second watch would clock out, and third watch would clock in. During this time, we would take a break and have coffee and snacks. Many times, it would be vanilla wafers or store-bought pastry—a Mega Honey Bun, or a Bearclaw. But sometimes, if occasion called for it, it would be Scott's "Bailey Bars." He'd make them in his exclusive "Bailey Bowl," one he brought with him from out west. His special bowl was the size of one of those 450-page best-selling hardcover books. A rectangular Tupperware deal with a foggy bottom and crisp denim-blue lid, into which Scott had carved his name and inmate number. The bowl was one of his prized possessions. Scott had done some hard time in harder places. His Tupperware may have been warped, but it still kept its seal.

Before Scott signed up for health services. Before they tested his blood and urine. Before they put a scope up his ass and looked inside his shit chute. Before they took a muscle biopsy—a small chunk of Bailey—out of his calf and sent it off to the lab where the report came back suggesting a neurological problem. Before Scott sat in a special seat—"an electric chair, Redd"—where they zapped him with electrical current and studied his neurological responses and noticed his "times were slow, Redd." Before all this diagnosis-before-prognosis horseshit. The Bailey Bars were an alchemical mixture of peanut butter, honey, dry oatmeal, and crushed graham crackers. The bottom crust was kneaded, tamped, and perfectly massaged into a one-and-a-half-inch foundation. The middle layer, a grout of burnished liquid bronze, was hand-whipped caramel rendered to a just right, gooey Goldilocks consistency. The top layer was a bowl of M&Ms (real ones) cradled, slow heated, and intermittently drizzled with a splish and then a splash of milk—stirred over low heat, in order to make the chocolate agreeably shake hands with the caramel. This chocolatey final layer—the Coupe Deville—once cooled, would settle into a firm-yet-soft, fudge-like frosting, as cool and cushy as mocha-colored Cadillac seats.

Before he kept dropping his toothbrush in the toilet. Before it was the same for his mustache comb. Before Scott took an extra ten minutes shaving his head in the shower only to have more battle damage on his dome than if he tussled with a tomcat. Before plastic forks, spoons, and knives were shattered frustrations. Before ink pens and brushes were sent screaming from the art table. Before turning pages broke book bindings. Before health services finally gave him a roll of Coban in which to wrap all his utensils.

Scott would invest a lot of time and care in making these Bailey Bars just so. The process couldn't be rushed, the contents mixed and mingled artfully—deftly handcrafted, intuitively applying the right amount of heat and pressure and time to sculpt his bars. He would then sequester his creation under the bottom bunk, cloistered among our gray property bins. He would give it time, time to meditate and achieve enlightenment—or at least time to cool to room temperature. Scott would occasionally stop his pen work, sneak a peek, pop the lid on the Bailey Bowl, test and probe the convivial contents with a connoisseur's finger. The aroma of baked goods, a vestige of "home" permeating our cell. He would then put the lid back on and say, "Almost ready, Redd."

"You can't rush Bailey Bars, Redd." It takes as long as it takes, before we give. More agonizing minutes would pass. Scott would put down his Bic pen or brush, and pop the bowl lid again, test and probe and tease his bars with his contented finger. The blue bowl lid may go back on, the process may repeat—lid up, lid down—a few more pernicious rounds. Inevitably, the torture turns, the savory ballet ends with Scott speaking the words, "Bailey Bars are ready, Redd."

Before Scott lost his grip. Before Scott had to wrap his every uten-
sil in Coban as if it were a burial shroud—he might have picked up
any plastic fork and knife and expertly cut out a perfect two-inch
square piece of Bailey Bar and balanced it on the knife as he held it
out to you. He might have waited for you to lift it from the knife, and
you had better be quick and sure about it, lest it fall and hit the floor.
There is no "five-second rule" with Bailey Bars. If you let it hit the
floor, odds were you'd hit the flagstones as well.

I once saw Scott hit a man with his open hand square in the ear-
hole. The guy dropped like a sack of spuds and was out for a spell.
Scott picked him up and set him in his chair, revived him, and asked
the guy if he had anything else smart to say. Now he knows what PTSD
feels like. Scott didn't suffer fools, but he didn't hold grudges either.
He was deliberate and efficient.

Grab the bar. Take a taste. Smile and say, "Mmmmmmmmm, Big
Scott, best bar ever."

You didn't have to say thank you. His giving you a piece of his bar
was his way of saying you're cool with him, that you were in the car. The
car could only hold maybe six people at a time, and sometimes that was
more than he was comfortable with. If he deemed you unworthy—for
whatever reason—he wouldn't pull over and politely drop you off somewhere. Instead, he'd kick you out like he was running 'shine after dark,
hightailing it, boot to the floorboards, lights out, with a trunk full of
hooch, mason jars clattering together like ghost chimes.

Before they made Scott a revenant. Before the Department of
Corrections banished him. Before Minnesota, Wyoming, and Iowa
juggled Scott's afflicted and expensive not-quite-fatal-fast-enough car-
cass. Before Scott was viewed as a plague of medical bills and extra
staff scheduling in order to shuttle him from one cut-rate horse doctor to another. Before the bean-counters stepped in and collectively
wished for a Corrections version of "terminal velocity"—where Scott
would crash into the earth and spare them all the headache and high
costs and just die already. Before they would dream of paroling him.
Before they would ask him to debrief. Before he told them to "pound
sand" and that "they can kill me, but they can't eat me, Redd."

"Stop gawping at the bar, or I'll clither you in the gob!" "Quit holding it in your clumsy mitts; it'll start to melt, you daft bastard." "What's it going to be? The bar or the pavement?" "Be quick or be dead." All this running through your head, while he might float there like a phantom, a phantom with a plastic knife pointed at your throat, waiting for you to bite down on this spectral hunk of Bailey Bar. "Best bars ever, right, Redd?"

There are days that ask, and years that answer, Scott.

I remember when Scott gave voice to his oblivion. It was during shift change, and therefore coffee and snack time. I remember breaking open a bag of pink frosted animal cookies. We were lucky to get them. They were on special from the prison commissary—for a limited time only. I can't recall if Scott bought the cookies, or if I did. I do remember spilling them out, onto his blue bowl lid. The cookies were coated on top in bubble gum-pink frost—camels and elephants, monkeys and bears, giraffes and hippos, but no sharks.

Scott relayed it to me like he was reading from a teleprompter. He told me he had ALS, and that he was a dead man walking. He delivered the grim news and I provided the weather. I sat there and sipped my insipid coffee and looked at Scott's blurry bowl lid with a three-ring circus's worth of animals in miniature. I noticed some of the animal cookies were missing their legs and tails and trunks and heads. Like an ineluctable circus, you come from nothing and you leave from nothing.

Before I read up on amyotrophic lateral sclerosis (ALS), a brutal, unforgiving illness of the neurological system with no known cure that usually kills you within five years of contracting the disease. Before I learned that Lou Gehrig was a man before a disease, a New York Yankee who batted fourth in the order ("clean-up") right behind Babe Ruth. And after Lou's final game he gave his fans his "Luckiest man in the world" farewell speech. Before I understood why Stephen Hawking, the brilliant physicist who wrote *A Brief History of Time,* was stuck in a motorized wheelchair and why he sounded like a robot. Before I took comfort in knowing the mind is like a rubber band—it remembers where to return to after having been stretched. Before I read Jim Harrison's novel *Returning to Earth* and understood why Scott stopped corresponding. Before I realized that sometimes you have to leave the world in order to understand it. Before I discovered there is sadness in sweets and that I will always miss my friend. . . . I sip the dregs and take a final bite of cookie as I look at the portrait of Scott that I've been trying to animate. There's a blue shirt buttoned all the way up in order to cover his prison ink. His angular skull cones to a bit of a peak. Reminds me of the moment before the shark fin breaks the ocean surface. Supposedly he's got shark eyes, an attribute pointed out to me by a former art teacher. He said that when he looked into his eyes—he saw nothing. No soul, just inky blackness with a couple million years of predatory evolution behind them. I've looked into his eyes and seen humanity. I see my friend. Scott also had an "operator's" mustache, the type of mustache I've seen on those Special Forces snapshots, on Navy SEALs, on the military channel, or maybe on a particular group of fellas doing hard time with the harshest of consequences.

"Right, Big Scott, best bars ever."

My coffee cup is cold, and chow hall contraband is stowed, lonely, in my belly. Meager cookie crumbs brushed off the stainless table. The canvas is dry, unlike my memories. So, I pick up the paint brush, because my body allows it, because I can and I must. There are no bars in Rush City. Not on the front of any cell. No bars, just a two-inch-thick steel door with a five-inch-by-three-foot security window with a multibillion-dollar view of an incarcerated future. Ensconced in that impassible door is a fourteen-by-seven-inch cuff port used to pass through meals—or when occasion calls, to cuff up an ignoramus in the throes of existential crisis.

The cell door is gray, solid, and indifferent. I suppose it could be core-filled with broken lives and shattered dreams, mixed with the aggregate of time wasted and talent squandered. The door is secured with bank-vault precision on blast-furnace hinges. Within, I feel close to the specter of whole years lost. Life is short, shorter than we ever gave thought to. There are no two-inch hunks of chocolate bar nestled within a blue-lidded bowl. Not anymore. There are no bars in Rush City.

There Are No Bars in Rush City: The Conversation

JEN   In the first or second year that I was teaching [in prison], or—
I'm embarrassed to say it might have been as late as the third year—I
was facilitating a forum at Lino Lakes. We were doing this forum,
and the students were talking about so-and-so calling from the outside after returning home. And I was like, "Oh, you guys still talk
after you get out?" And they were so offended. They were like, "Um,
yeah, because we're friends." I realized what an incredibly ignorant
assumption that was, as if your friendships aren't deep or real, or like
family. I know better now, and I think that that aspect of this essay
is really moving.

DAVID   But I had the same assumption [before coming to prison].
And I remember how happy I was the first time I called someone who
I knew in prison who had been released. I never thought I'd be in
touch with some of these people once I got out. And I think in prison,
[if] you spend enough time with someone, you're naturally going to
get close to them, no matter what environment you're in.

WARREN   The choice for who you can and who you must spend time
with is so limited and arbitrary. Maybe of the hundred or so people
in the units I live in, there's probably fifteen guys that I will talk with
casually that I don't go out of my way to be an asshole to. And there's
maybe four or five that I can actually have meaningful conversations
with. Some of the connections that we form in here do get fairly intimate with people, especially [in] the double cell, so you're with somebody a lot. Your cellie learns about your family and outside traumas
and stuff like that. Being in society out in the world is not that much
different except that it's more distilled in here.

CHRIS   I have a very personal relationship with this essay. I was with
[the author] when he wrote it, plus, [his cellie, Scott], I knew them
really, really well. He did my side piece on my ribs. He stepped up
and did me a solid. And then he brought that whole ink style from

Rush City [Prison] to Stillwater [Prison]. And so, he inspired me to start working with that style a little bit. I remember knowing about Stillwater when I was six and being in the visiting room. Prison was just a part of our culture, even though I was in the suburbs. I don't see this shit as like, as such a big deal. I feel, I think it's a nice idea that we have, [the idea that] we think we have control over things. And then we think that we can really, like, decide shit on a grand level. It's fun to talk about it and have opinions. In the grand scheme of things, focusing on the relationships and focusing on the moments, I think, is the real value. I'm a poet, not a novelist, so I just love the moments. I don't believe in happiness. I don't believe that's a thing. So, yeah, so this [essay] just encapsulates those little small moments that are just great and that are central to individual relationships and the way you go about your time.

And then like the craft of [his] bars and you know, people could do shit with microwaves. Rush City [Prison] had a rich culture like that. Like [if] my homeboy from Colorado were to cook, it'd be the best food I've ever had in life and *from a fucking microwave*—prison shit.

JEN   What'd he make?

CHRIS   I don't even know what the shit was called. He'd make this fish stick or something. We simplified it—it was a fish dish.

WILL   There's this observation that stands out when you're talking about the illusion of control. It's significant that we're not in control. The vast majority go back to the inexorability of the past tense. We're all here, so we were all definitely going to come here. But the fact that most everyone in prison who was in prison was going to come here from the moment they were born or shortly thereafter, because the factors in this social arrangement were set up in such a way that there's a—we would call it an epistemic possibility—there's a nonzero chance that they would do something different or get to go somewhere else or get to be someone else than who they are. But this is who we are. And this is where we're at. And this is our community. And these are our people. And it was the way that things are designed and structured in this country and in this society.

CHRIS   Go ahead, Jen. Tell me, tell me why you're shaking your head.

JEN   I'm not saying it wasn't stacked against you, but there's no way you were all born destined for prison. Look at all the other people who are on the outside that aren't here that were *this* close. That were *this* close. I just don't believe that's the way the universe works.

WILL   I agree. I don't think that's how the universe works, either. I think that's how our society works. I think that's how our culture works. Because late-stage capitalism requires a permanent underclass to grind into grist and feed into the machine in order to exploit.

JEN   Absolutely. But they didn't put your name on a name tag like Santa's naughty list.

WILL   No, no, I agree. But that's an individualistic specificity that I agree is not the case. Is my name written on a parchment in the ether? No. There's a kid who has been in foster care. He didn't do anything to get put in foster care. He didn't do anything to be abused. Not every kid who has been through that comes to prison. But nobody in prison doesn't have a story that connects with something almost identical to that experience. So, it's not a matter of, you know, we've been selected. I think we can make a difference for the people who aren't here now. I think we can make a difference for the forests that aren't on fire today, maybe. But there are vast tracts of old-growth forest with an overwhelming amount of tinderbox fuel on the floor, and nobody with the resources or the inclination to pay attention to them. Is it absolutely certain? Are they destined to go up in flames and burn entire sections of the country to the ground? No. Are they going to go up and burn vast swaths to the ground? Absolutely they are.

CHRIS   So, I think you hold like an optimistic perspective of maybe the existential idea of purpose and all that, and I understand what you're saying. And that can bleed into the belief in the multiverse and different decisions along the way. Or, you know, whether intelligent design is a thing, whether somebody's up there rooting for you, or trying to intercede. But I would argue that that's exactly why I felt like [I was destined to go to prison], because so many people were *this* close, and didn't. And it just took, like, whatever it was to nudge left or right. Like, if I didn't go out that night. There's so many little things. But then, I don't know, maybe this is a little creepy to share, or you don't believe it, but I remember I had this vision of always knowing that my life was gonna be hard. And I remember it just happened one day. And I don't know if it was a dream, something I saw. You know, it's just a memory I have. But I just remember sitting on a cliff and this presence was like, behind us. It wasn't God or anything, but it was just like, "Are you sure you want to go down there?" I'm like, "Yeah, I'm good." It's like, "It's gonna be hard. This one's gonna be hard." And I just remember signing up for this shit. And I remember at a certain point in Stillwater, I had to decide what I was going to do with my life and where I was going to do it, and I had to accept the fact that this is what it looks like. I don't believe I was *destined* to come here. I don't believe I suck. But I think I'm a stoic in the sense that I believe that pain and suffering was a definite necessity for me. It broke me open, and it made me who I am today, and I'm finally proud of the man I am. And I wouldn't trade it for the world. I wouldn't trade it to get out.

WILL   Speaking to the deterministic quality, the durability of incarceration, they built the buildings, somebody's going in them. The cells are here, somebody's going in them, so you know who it is. I respect the argument that we're not predestined. But you have a whole philosophical position of—and it's the conservative, grounded in sort of religious ethos of individual choices [and of] an individualistic consequence, and personal responsibility—this whole neoliberal concept of how it's all on you, and your choices and your ability to be healthy, to be educated, to pull yourself up by the bootstraps, and to participate in the world in a different set of circumstances, regardless of all the things that you have going against you versus the massive structural weight that rests on so many people.

JEN   I'm not denying that the structure as it is makes it inevitable for people to be here, even wants it to be so. That's as true as anything I know.

WILL   The first time I came to prison I was a kid, and then there were twenty years in the interim before coming back to prison. And looking at that whole run, [it was one] where the idea of having an identity that was defined by incarceration was something that I was running from. I mean, not *running, running,* but deliberately moving away from by design with everything else that I was working on in my life. But now, if you look at me on paper, from the first transaction that's made after my birth, all the way to where I am now, I was definitely always coming to prison. I mean, statistically, and that doesn't mean that I wipe myself of individual agency because you know that I'm not for that either.

CHRIS   During [incarceration at] Rush City I would look at the prison and think, in fucking one hundred years, this place is gonna be beautiful. I would love to see this place, I would love to be the warden of this place, because I could see like, "This is how corrections could be." Me and Zeke were in the yard a while back and he said something that always stuck with me about, you know, [how] in one hundred years, you're gonna look back at this shit, and it's gonna be such a different perspective. And I always kept that in mind, like, how this is just temporary. This is a temporary thing. This is just a place to really get your shit together. Correction could be beautiful. I think that's what abolitionists talk about. Angela Davis said that on CBS Sunday Morning. They asked her, "What does prison look like?" And she said she's not talking about prisons, or that she's not focused on prison. She's focusing on the culture around prison, and how things would change. That's how you abolish prisons. I think our trajectory is going where it needs to go and we're all playing a part. You just got to decide what you're willing to sacrifice for it, right?

WARREN   The things that we do, the approaches we take, the relationships we have, and the rest of the relationships we choose to foster in here, and the relationships that are foisted upon us—I mean, that's the basis of our agency. And, you know, I feel really bad for the Scott character because my uncle died from ALS. But the grace, that is in this friendship already, and toward the end when he said he knew why [Scott] didn't contact him [Redd] anymore, because it was just too frickin' hard to talk about it, or too hard to even communicate. And that's something that so many people on the outside just totally miss—the humanity that we show even to each other, even the people we don't like in here.

DAVID   Yeah, there's random acts of kindness in prison every day that people don't see.

JEN   Like what, David?

DAVID   I think a random act of kindness, now that I think about it, is just the way people give advice to each other, and sometimes just giving people attention. I mean, just the fact that if someone's having a bad day, where someone's not understanding how a situation is going down, whether it's something that's happening in prison or something that's happening outside of prison, the person might give that [other] person a significant amount of time to voice their concerns, and that person might not have anywhere else to go—to offer "half a cup," as Warren would say. I mean, that's just one small thing, but I think it's a pretty big thing.

CHRIS   Kennedy, can you speak on your experience tutoring?

KENNEDY   I teach because one of the biggest problems, I think, for people that come into prison, is that they didn't have a parent that could help them with school. Most of the people that are in here didn't have a parent, you know? By that, I mean [a parent] that could help them with their homework. So, for me, I realized a very long time ago that if the guys in prison could read and write, these guys had the potential of actually raising a kid who had the potential of being an Obama—"bosses." Parents who teach their kids, I think, actually make the biggest difference. So, for me, I enjoy cooking more than I enjoy teaching, but cooking [for a job] wasn't contributing, I think, to a better world. If you're a good observer of humanity, prison is like this huge mountain that just sits on a lot of human potential. And you could say that MPWW opens a hole into the mountain. But, in my view, MPWW is like Ali Baba's cave. For us writers, we're gonna get the treasure, or [we'll get the] art class for us artists. You can create a masterpiece and you can put it in a museum. The best way I found to give all [younger] inmates the potential of being great, if they have a chance of getting out of here, is really through education. My father used to say that if you know how to read, you've actually cracked the code of knowledge. And the only question I asked myself about this essay is, "What if Scott just wasn't in here?" With his talent for sweets, he could probably be the Muhammad Ali of baking, wedding cakes, birthday cakes. [Scott and Redd have] created a system like any professional on the outside: they have a schedule, they work, they have a time when they rest, and they don't break it. I mean, if you want to see how big the prison mountain is, you could just see it through these two guys—too much time just wastes a lot of human potential. And that is the sad thing about the precarity that we're experiencing in every prison.

Kuv Niam Zoo Nkauj: My Mother Is Beautiful

by Kao Kalia Yang

It is rations day in Ban Vinai Refugee Camp. I'm five years old; it is 1985. The rations yard is full of people, men, women, and children all clamoring for a look at what the United Nations people are handing out.

On a slab of cement, I see a pile of whole chickens. They are dead. They are plucked haphazardly, a few butt and wing feathers still standing. Their skin is beginning to gray. Their long necks twist around each other. Their feet stick up. Their toes point in every direction. Their eyes are only partially closed. I hide behind my mother's legs.

The men and women jostle toward the pile of chickens. My view is blocked by the backs of men and women. Everyone is hungry. The last time the ration trucks came was two days ago. There are families who've not eaten since. Each time the wave of people moves, my mother's body moves too. Her body is slender. She is like a blade of grass in turbulent water. Her right hand reaches back to hold me tight.

The man beside my mother stops all of a sudden. He looks at her. He pushes a hand out. He's a thin man, but not yet old, no wrinkles on his face, his thick black hair is parted to the side, his hollowed eyes are clear and bright. He does not see me, only my mother. He says to the people around us, "Let the young woman go through."

My mother is grateful. Her stiff body softens. A guard in uniform grabs a chicken from the top of the pile and hands it between several bodies to my mother. My mother lets go of my hand to accept the dead bird. I make a noise.

I'm a wisp of a child, pale skin, bangs cut straight across my brows, a frightened child. The man who spoke up for my mother sees me for the first time. The guard who has just handed the chicken to my mother sees me for the first time. I see the surprise on their faces as they look from me to her. They blink and blink again. How can someone so young, so fresh, so beautiful be a mother?

My mother, skin dewy now from the push and pull of the tight crowd, blows the few strands of loose hair from her face. She has smooth, pale skin, and dark eyes. Her face is small, fine-boned. Her lips are full, but they are not smiling. They are parted in the heat.

My beautiful mother slips out of the crowd before the men can say anything. Her long, thick hair, gathered at her nape, looks heavy to me. Her one hand is still holding me close as we walk away from the pile of dead chicken, from the people waiting to get dinner. I can feel the wet of the chicken's body against my arm. It's cold despite the dry heat of the day.

My mother is walking slowly in front of me in a church basement in St. Paul, Minnesota. I'm ten years old; it is 1990. On either side of us there are tables of folded clothes. They are dusty. The basement smells like mildew and dust. I scrunch my nose up and try not to breathe too deeply. My mother's hands linger on the soft, shiny fabrics, the blouses that women who work in offices wear with skirts and slacks. She touches a white one again and again. I can see the flounces at its neck, the buttons that look like pearls going down the front.

I say to my mother, "If you like it, take it, Niam."

She turns at the sound of my voice.

She smiles at me.

She shakes her head and says, "I have no reason to wear such a pretty shirt."

By way of an explanation, she adds, "At the factory, we are required to wear jeans and shirts that don't go past our elbows."

My mother is an assembler in a factory. She works on the night shift along a line sorting through coolant parts.

The white woman with the round glasses who carries a legal pad and a pen, the woman in charge of the church basement's inventory of donated clothes, walks toward us.

Her voice is louder than it needs to be when she says, "We're closing in five minutes. Hurry up. A bag per family."

I interpret the announcement for my mother. My mother quickly chooses a pair of jeans for herself. She chooses a pair of jeans and a T-shirt for my father. She gets me a dress with lace along the seams of the bottom. She gets my sister a pair of dusty dress shoes that she'll wipe clean with a warm towel when we get home. The bag in her hand is full; there is no more room for other things.

My mother looks wistfully back at the table with the nice blouses. A tall woman with painted nails walks to the table and picks up the white shirt with the pearl buttons my mother was touching. My mother averts her gaze.

In the car, I tell her, "Niam, I think that shirt would have looked really pretty on you."

She smiles at me, "When you grow up, you can get a shirt like that. If you study hard and do well in school, you can have a job where you can wear shirts like that."

I tell her that I'll try harder at school. She reaches out a hand to smooth my bangs, now past my eyes, away from my face.

We're celebrating the Hmong New Year at the old Civic Center in downtown St. Paul, Minnesota. I'm fifteen; it is 1995. My mother is pregnant. She's wearing wide-legged pants and a white shirt that is loose and flows around her belly. She's wearing two-inch heels so she looks taller than usual. Her hair, cut in a bob, is combed away from her face. There are a few white streaks in her hair. They catch the fluorescent light when she turns her head. She's thirty-four this year.

My mother is walking with my older sister and me around the open arena where lines of young men and women are standing. The young, in their finery, toss beautiful homemade balls covered with sequins and the less decorative but equally glaring neon tennis balls in the air between them. Older people stand behind the groups of young men and women talking, commenting on the looks of the young, reminiscing about their own days of youth—now long gone. Other people are taking photos. A lot of the people, old and young, are chewing gum. My mother is not chewing gum. Her full lips rest on her face, no smile, no frown, a cool face in the crowd.

I'm wearing Hmong clothes for the first time to the New Year celebrations. I'm wearing one of my mother's two heavy silver necklaces. It rests on my collarbones and they ache. The red and green sashes tied tight around my middle make my breathing shallow. The turban on my head forces my neck to stand straight and tall. I feel stiff in the clothes of the women of my clan.

My mother had insisted that my older sister and I wear our traditional outfits. She asked an auntie to make them especially for us from the heaviest velvet she could afford at the fabric store. She asked our father to drill tiny holes into a pile of thin French coins she'd bought with her Christmas bonus from the factory. Beneath the bright light, at our kitchen table, she'd sat the weekends through sewing tiny beads to the coins and then connecting them to the embroidered bags she made for us when we were just girls. She sewed and sewed until the dry skin of her hands cracked and droplets of blood seeped from her fingertips. She bandaged her fingers and sewed some more. We had to honor her work by wearing the Hmong clothes.

There is a plethora of scents in the air, perfume and cologne and chewing gum flavored with mint and cinnamon, all mixing with the familiar smell of mothballs. The blue turban my mother has carefully wrapped around my head has stretched my skin. My eyes feel tight and my smile even tighter. Instead of the high heels that many of the young women around me wear, I have on heeled combat boots. My sister said they set me apart. There is a growing pressure on my chest and I'm not sure if it is from the weight of the necklace or my discomfort in being a young Hmong woman at a Hmong New Year in Hmong clothes for the first time in my life. I remember years past when I could run between the lines of the young men and women playing hide-n-go-seek among my cousins. I try not to let the discomfort of my body show on my face, a face that has on more makeup than I've ever worn before: pink lipstick, black eyeliner, pink blush, black mascara. My nose tickles because of the many smells, but I don't scratch because I'm afraid the makeup will streak.

A group of young men approach me. My sister and my mother are talking quietly, walking several feet behind me. The men are older than I am, but not by much. There are six or seven of them. Two have on traditional Hmong vests with French coins swaying along the bottom seams. The rest have on a variety of American formal wear: jackets too large for their small frames, pants tapered and bunched around the ankles. These are the good boys, the ones who carry roses in their hands and give them to the girls they admire. In their pockets, they carry notepads and pens, prepared to collect the phone numbers of willing girls. I pretend not to see them. I look really high at the lights shining down. I am too new at this growing up stuff and not at all ready to meet men at the Hmong New Year.

A short guy, just a few inches taller than I am, in a red shirt and black jacket, a small gold chain hanging from his neck, is the bravest of the bunch. The rest are as nervous as I am, looking up and around, not making eye contact.

He says, "Excuse me, Girl, what's your name?"

I say, "What?"

He repeats himself, word for word.

I say, "Kalia."

I'm not smiling. I have a feeling I'm scowling.

He says, "Uhm. My friend here thinks you're really pretty."

The friend is a head taller than he is, one of the men in the traditional vests. His thick hair is left a little long, parted in the middle, a sign of the times. His lips form a thin line. His Adam's apple bobs in his neck. At least now, his gaze is on me, no longer at the wall in the far distance.

I look for my mother and older sister. They've stopped about five feet away. The group of men follow my gaze.

They look at my mother.

Several of them say, all at once, "Your mother is so young. She is so beautiful."

Yes, my mother is beautiful. I'm glad the men see her beauty. It softens my feelings toward them. Very few people see her beauty anymore. Not the people at the clinic, to them she is sick. Not the people at work, to them she is a worker. Not even the everyday people in my life, to them she is my mother. My father, who I'm sure thinks she is beautiful, doesn't even say it—at least not around us. These strangers, these young Hmong men, are seeing what I've always known to be true.

The young man who thinks I'm pretty speaks very quietly, "Kalia, can I have your number?"

I say, "Are you going to call?"

He responds looking at my mother, "I don't know. Your mother is so beautiful."

I laugh.

He's intimidated to call because of my mother's beauty. Beauty as a shield—this is an idea I had never explored before.

I'm graduating from Carleton College. I'm twenty-two years old; it is 2003. My big family is coming to the ceremony. For many of them, it will be their first time on campus.

My favorite uncle and his wife and his children all get to campus first. They come out from their cars bearing flowers and something I've never seen before. It is the shape of a heart. It is like the flowers we see on stands at the Hmong funerals. It is made up entirely of orange roses. Real flowers, on a real base, filled with wet foam bricks to keep the flowers moist and happy. It takes two cousins to put the heart-shaped wreath around my neck. It's heavier than a traditional Hmong necklace. The other graduates around me and their families are beginning to notice, but I smile and smile and smile.

My mother, father, and siblings arrive within minutes of my wearing the rose wreath. They can't believe it either. My cousins have really gone all out. My mother is so happy she's laughing out loud, her mouth open. Her front teeth are white and bigger than the rest. Her bottom teeth show in the bright sun. Her eyes wrinkle up at the corners. Her eye dimple beams at me.

All throughout the graduation ceremony, I can see my mother in the crowd. Her hair is now short, like a boy's. She wears it parted and to the side, clean, nonsensical. Her skin is now wrinkled—even when she's not smiling or frowning or stretching the muscles in her face.

After the ceremony, one of my American Studies professors wants to meet my family. He's never met my family before and is eager to shake hands. Few of the professors at Carleton have ever met a family like mine, new refugees, poor, uneducated in the ways that the institutions value. I introduce my large gathering of family to my professor and they shake hands in return and nod their greetings.

He tells my parents and my aunt and uncle how good of a student I have been.

My aunt and uncle and mother and father all say, "Thank you for teaching Kalia."

My professor says, "She is a joy to teach."

My family has nothing else to say to my professor so they look at the trees and the grass, point out the squirrels that linger close by to each other, call to the younger children to stay close, admire the architecture—from the old English hall with its ornate steps leading up to the double doors to the math building with it shiny metals and glass—but most especially, they look at the other parents.

My professor says to my mom, "Your daughter is so pretty because she looks like you."

My mother says, in halting English, "No, I'm old."

The professor says, "No, you are not old. Look at me."

My mother nods, but says, "I'm old."

The professor excuses himself and walks away to meet another student's family.

I watch the whole of the gathering, with my heavy wreath around my neck, and I see how my family is not like the other families and how I'm not like the other students. The other fathers have on college caps, shorts and polo shirts, or dress shirts and khakis. The mothers are particularly interesting. Some of them have on shorts and t-shirts and sandals like it is a regular summer day. Others are dressed up in nice outfits that make them look like they don't live in Minnesota or shop here. My own father is wearing a purple Vikings cap. He's wearing a suit but no tie. My mother is wearing capri pants that show her ankles. She's wearing padded flip flops because her feet hurt from her work at the factory. She's wearing a polyester shirt from the Hmong market with a black and white design that is not a zebra or leopard print. Everybody is so much taller than all of us. I feel in my heart that no other student is wearing as much love as I am.

I've met the man I'm going to marry, only I don't know it yet. I'm twenty-eight years old; it is 2008. I'm taking him home to meet my parents. My family is not home though; they are all at my aunt and uncle's house. My future husband has to take me there in order to meet my parents.

He's white. He's only ever known white people and a few people of color because of academic work with refugees and immigrants. I'm the first person of color he is really getting to know. He's nervous and sweaty.

I've never taken any man home before, friend or boyfriend.

It's summertime and day has disappeared. Around, the night sounds, frogs croaking, crickets chirping, are loud beneath a sky strewn with stars. The moths and mosquitos gather around my aunt and uncle's front door light. The scent of barbeque lingers in the air, pork fat and hot charcoal. My aunt and uncle's doorbell is broken. I knock on the door.

No one hears us.

We hear them. There's a baby crying. Someone is yelling. Lots of people are talking. One of my aunts is laughing, her signature laugh, husky and loud. I can feel the tension in the body next to mine.

I knock louder but it isn't producing anything, so I call out, "Open the door!"

There's movement. The door opens. My uncle pokes his head out.

When he sees me, he's not surprised. When he sees the man beside me, he is because he pauses before he spreads his lips wide and flashes the deep dimples on either side of his cheeks.

He says, "Kalia, invite your friend in. Come in. Come in."

I say, "Go in. Go in."

Inside the front door, there are small hills of shoes. I take off my sandals and throw them on top of a pile at the corner. The man beside me proceeds to do the same but all the adults tell him, "No need, no need. Just come in."

There are two banquet tables set side by side, full of food. There are many chairs indicating that many people had been at the table.

There are many different voices telling us, "Eat. Eat."

We've already eaten but I make my way to the table. He makes his way to the table. No one else is coming to the table. My father, my uncles, my aunts, my cousins, my brothers and sisters, they all say they've already eaten. One cousin from France is the only one who sits and eats with us.

My cousin points to the boiled fatty pork and sour bamboo shoots.

He says, "It's sour bamboo and pork."

He points to the chili sauce, "Very spicy."

He points to the rice, "Can I serve you?"

He serves the man beside me a first spoon, then a second spoon, then a third spoon, until the man puts up his hands and says, "Oh, that's plenty."

There's more pork, boiled with greens.

There's barbeque pork with black pepper and salt.

My cousin says, "Also MSG."

He shrugs. "Some white people don't like MSG."

Then he points to the plates full of cut up boiled chicken and says, "Best thing on the table. Fresh from the butchering house. Not like Golden Plump."

The man beside me reaches with his fork for a drumstick, specked with black pepper and bits of cilantro.

I eat. I love my aunt's cooking. I love Hmong food. The boiled chicken, for me, is a sign of love, of home. Sitting beside the white man, I'm hungrier for my family's food than I have ever been.

The whole time, I see my mother looking at me, looking at him, looking at us.

My mother sits in a chair. The chair is so high that her feet can't reach the floor. Her bare feet are crossed at the ankles. She's swinging her legs back and forth underneath her. Her hands are gripping the sides of the chair like a kid about to embark on a scary ride, or a mother looking as her daughter gets on a scary ride. My mother isn't talking to anyone.

After dinner, I'm thankful to the French cousin who talked and talked through dinner, trying to make the man beside me comfortable.

At the door to my uncle's house, I tell the man I don't know I'm going to marry, "Good-bye."

He asks if I could step outside for a minute.

I agree.

Outside, the bugs fly around us. I swat at them. I take my hands and clap at the fluttering wings that fly about my face. I can hear my family behind us, getting normal again, getting loud again, laughing and talking. Outside, a small breeze blows, and I take a big breath.

He says, "Was that your mother, the one swinging her feet on the chair?"

I say, "Yes."

He says, "I like that."

I say, "I do too."

He says, "There is something young about her, something beautiful, something time cannot take."

We stand in the dark looking not at the splendor of the stars above us, but toward the line of houses across my uncle's street. I can hear sounds of the highway, cars going by, wheels turning over pavement, the evening air, cut through again and again. I see myself in my mother for the first time, living a different life far from the refugee camps, reaching for the blouses with the soft, silvery fabric, one day walking slowly behind my growing daughter, another day, swinging my legs on a chair that is too high, watching the man she would marry look at her over steaming bowls of pork and greens, servings of rice, platters of whole boiled chickens.

Kuv Niam Zoo Nkauj: The Conversation

KENNEDY   I can't remember my mom cooking, or ever eating anything that my mom made. So, when I read the essay, about a mother in a refugee camp who actually did much more than my mom, it was kind of weird.

DAVID   Why can't you remember your mom cooking?

KENNEDY   Because my mother always woke up very early in the morning, left for work. And whenever she made it back, it was always very late at night. So, we had people at home cooking. My sisters could do the cooking. But the only thing I remember is always eating with my mom. She would say, "You're the only one that doesn't argue with me." Because most of my brothers and sisters were always fighting her. I think it's because she was never home that much. So, whenever they had the chance, it was issues and issues and issues and issues. But we [my mom and I] just ate quietly. Talked. She asked me how I was doing. I asked how she was doing. And that almost became our thing until my mom passed away. I think she said more with me than any of my brothers and sisters.

DAVID   How old were you when she passed away?

KENNEDY   She just passed away recently. It was just kind of nice to read a relationship of a mother, you know, [one in which her] kids adore her, you know, just as a backdrop to my own relationship with my mom, and so, I really enjoyed it.

DAVID   This quote summed up the essay. It says, "Very few people see her beauty anymore. Not the people at the clinic—to them, she is sick. Not the people at work—to them she is a worker. Not even the everyday people in my life—to them she is my mother. My father, who I'm sure thinks she is beautiful, doesn't even say it—at least not around us. These strangers, these young Hmong men, are seeing what I've always known to be true." The reason that stood out was this question of, how can we see the beauty in others if our interactions with them might be brief and for a specific purpose?

CHRIS   You know, I'm fascinated by the definition of beauty. These standards are kind of, they're not internal, they're kind of thrust upon you, right? They're external, they're social, they're commercial, you know, all the standards that we've been taught or grew up in. But it also becomes a negotiation with the world—if you're deemed beautiful, what do you owe the world?

WILL   How do you process being commodified?

CHRIS   Yeah, what do you do with it? Feeling beautiful and being beautiful, what's the difference?

WILL   I think that we have this awareness of aesthetic value and aesthetic beauty, and it feels like we might be getting to a better place lately, with body positivity, and just general acceptance of difference, you know, as sort of a social standard, but how much of this stuff is still just programmed into us, you know, where the images that we see in advertising and media [are pushed on us] and [there is] sort of the collective pressure of our social group to see certain people a certain way?

DAVID   People in the essay, they weren't curious. Like the people at the clinic, they weren't curious to hear her story. For example, you know, recently [when I visited] the computer lab, there was a drawing there of a woman. And I just said, "Hey, I like this drawing, who is it?" And this led to one of the workers there, he said, "Oh, that's my wife." If I wasn't curious about that picture, about that artwork, I never would have known that. And then, that became a whole story all of its own because how many prison workers have a drawing of their wife where they work?

JEN   David, you made me think of one of my favorite quotes by Simone Weil—"Attention is the same thing as prayer."

DAVID   Oh, that's beautiful.

JEN   "It presupposes faith and love."

DAVID   I think some people have an easier time with [being atten-tive] than other people. Some people are just naturally attentive—I think it's the way their brains are wired. They're just naturally wired to their environment. And I don't think it means that they care about other people more; they just might be more curious. And I think curiosity is like attention in that it can be developed, like love and faith.

JEN   I don't know. I mean, maybe it does mean that they are just more loving if they're taking the time to see folks? Maybe.
    I like the question you asked, Chris. I don't know if this is how you said it, but you asked, "What is beauty for? What do you do with it?" I thought that was a really compelling question, especially com-ing out of COVID, and in the midst of these conversations around pre-carity. What is the role of beauty?

WILL   Beauty and happiness are ephemeral, nonsense concepts.

DAVID   I think attention, curiosity, and happiness [are each] a form of beauty.

CHRIS   Wonderment.

WILL   I struggle with happiness a lot, because of the way that people would ascribe such value to being "happy." I understand most people when they describe happiness as having an attachment to this brief, sort of fleeting experience of [being] not sad, not stuck, not frus-trated. Whereas, like, more involved concepts, such as joy or satisfac-tion or meaning, are things that get conflated with ideas of happiness. But [happiness is] often not grounded, and it's similar to the aesthetic concept of beauty and that it's fleeting, and it is all subjective.

JEN   If you take the conversation to include beauty that's not just physical, then I wonder how that changes [our understanding of beauty].

CHRIS   Can we be conditioned? Maybe. Or do we choose what we're drawn to?

WILL   We can be *programmed* to be drawn to certain things.

JEN   That's marketing.

DAVID   But I think part of being a human being on this planet is to find what your own idea of beauty is. And I think it's really hard when you let other people define what is beautiful, instead of you defining it for yourself. And that's what I don't like about marketing. And that's why I think there's almost something immoral about marketing. Because you're taking away from a person's . . . if you want to call it—their quest.

JEN   The Buddhists would say that's where the disconnect comes from. So, you're constantly chasing and wanting. But Chris's question is about what you legitimately find beautiful, not what the marketers train us to find beautiful. Can we help that?

WILL   I think that if you cultivate your eye, and your experience, your aesthetic experience, your understanding of visual or texture [or] whatever, just you deepen your experience of being in the world, like you open yourself up more to, to more opportunities for wonderment, to be awestruck.

CHRIS   I understand what you mean. I think what we're talking about has to do with things that choose you versus the things that you choose.

JEN   Will, you're saying you can cultivate yourself to certain types of beauty, and I'm saying you can cultivate yourself to encounter it more. But within that you still can't change what strikes you *genuinely.* Like, because I'm visually illiterate, my artist son explicitly gave me a color scheme to decorate my living room after I got my teal couch, [and now] I have become capable of saying teal and orange look good together, and the next time I see it, I will say, "Yes, that *is* nice." But it doesn't genuinely strike me in the way that certain things do.

WILL   So, think about it this way—

CHRIS   I really appreciate that you will die on a hill, Will. You will die on a fucking molehill. I like that. You keep defending your position.

WARREN   I wouldn't say cultivating, but more interrogating—finding out, understanding why you are drawn to something or something is drawn to you. Like, if I ever walk out of here, I've got an acreage that is absolutely one hundred percent freaking gorgeous from its solar gain to its south-facing horseshoe with a small seep in the middle of it.

WILL   Can utility be beautiful?

WARREN   Oh, God, yes!

JEN   That's the most excited I've ever seen you, Warren!

WARREN   Well, that's my engineering background.

WILL   So, does Warren find utility beautiful because he's an engineer, or does he find engineering to be his passion because he finds utility beautiful?

JEN   One and the same.

WARREN   There's nothing more to me both aesthetically pleasing and beautiful—using them as separate terms—as a well-worn tool, or a well-designed piece of machinery.

JEN   Nature is nothing if not brilliant design, right?

WARREN   Well, it's also chaos, because it has to exploit every opportunity to make more of itself.

JEN   Ah, so true. I'm thinking of the Fibonacci sequence.

WARREN   And that's through how many tens of millions of generations of experiments and failures?

JEN   So that's why [it has] beauty? Because it's efficient?

DAVID   What's useful is beautiful. That's another definition of beauty.

WARREN   One of the arguments that I had with my mother was that she had this old-style religious view that the world was perfect. I said, "You know why the world is perfect?" And she says, "Why is that?" "It's because what is imperfect gets killed." . . . She was angry at me for years over that.

KENNEDY   I was just gonna say that my experience of the American presidency is that the ugly one always loses.

[Laughter]

RUBY   I was having a conversation with a friend of mine recently. I'm personally really drawn to musical voices that have a lot of strength to them, or like a lot of vibrato, because my mom and my grandma sing with a lot of vibrato. And they have really strong voices. And my friend is more drawn to like voices that are softer and breathy. And I'm just wondering—the way that we favor different types of voices. How does that fit in this scenario of cultivating? What is beautiful and what is not beautiful? Is that something that is just innate to us? Or have we learned that based off of our environment?

DAVID   I think this could be a big, multiple-book research project.

RUBY   Do I like a voice because it reminds me of my mom? Or is it because I was born with this, you know, inclination to like those types of voices? I wonder where that fits in [with] what we're talking about.

JEN   I wonder if it has something to do with innate animal survival. It would be wise, from a biological standpoint, to love the sound of your mother's voice in utero—the tenor, the tone of the voice that you're swimming inside of, that's keeping you alive.

How to Slowly Kill Yourself and Others in America: A Remembrance

by Kiese Laymon

I've had guns pulled on me by four people under central Mississippi skies—once by a white undercover cop, once by a young brother trying to rob me for the leftovers of a weak work-study check, once by my mother, and twice by myself. Not sure how or if I've helped many folks say yes to life but I've definitely aided in a few folks dying slowly in America, all without the aid of a gun.

✦✦✦

I'm seventeen, five years younger than Rekia Boyd will be when she is shot in the head by an off-duty police officer in Chicago. It's the summer after I graduated high school and my teammate, Troy, is back in Jackson, Mississippi. Troy, who plays college ball in Florida, asks me if I want to go to McDonald's on I-55.

As Troy, Cleta, Leighton, and I walk out of McDonald's—that Filet-o-Fish grease straight cradling my lips—I hold the door open for a tiny, scruffy-faced white man with a green John Deere hat on.

"Thanks, partner," he says.

A few minutes later, we're driving down I-55 when John Deere drives up and rolls his window down. I figure that he wants to say something funny since we'd had a cordial moment at McDonald's. As soon as I roll my window down, the man screams, "Nigger lovers!" and speeds off.

On I-55, we pull up beside John Deere and I'm throwing finger-signs, calling John Deere all kinds of clever "motherfuckers." The dude slows down and gets behind us. I turn around, hoping he pulls over.

Nope.

John Deere pulls out a police siren and places it on top of his car. Troy is cussing my ass out and frantically trying to drive his mama's Lincoln away from John Deere. My heart is pounding out of my chest, not out of fear, but because I want a chance to choke the shit out of John Deere. I can't think of any other way of making him feel what we felt.

Troy drives into his apartment complex and parks his mama's long Lincoln under some kind of shed. Everyone in the car is slumped down at this point. Around twenty seconds after we park, here comes the red, white, and blue of the siren.

We hear a car door slam, then a loud knock on the back window. John Deere has a gun in one hand and a badge in the other. He's telling me to get out of the car. My lips still smell like Filet-o-Fish.

"Only you," he says to me. "You going to jail tonight." He's got the gun to my chest.

"Fuck you," I tell him and suck my teeth. "I ain't going nowhere." I don't know what's wrong with me.

Cleta is up front trying to reason with the man through her window when, all of a sudden, in a scene straight out of *Boyz n the Hood*, a Black cop approaches the car and accuses us of doing something wrong. Minutes later, a white cop tells us that John Deere has been drinking too much and he lets us go.

Sixteen months later, I'm eighteen, three years older than Edward Evans will be when he is shot in the head behind an abandoned home in Jackson.

Nzola and I are walking from Subway back to Millsaps College with two of her white friends. It's nighttime. We turn off of North State Street and walk halfway past the cemetery when a red Corolla filled with brothers stops in front of us. All of the brothers have blue rags covering their noses and mouths. One of the brothers, a kid at least two years younger than me with the birdest of bird chests, gets out of the car clutching a shiny silver gun.

He comes toward Nzola and me.

"Me," I say to him. "Me. Me." I hold my hands up encouraging him to do whatever he needs to do. If he shoots me, well, I guess bullets enter and hopefully exit my chest, but if the young nigga thinks I'm getting pistol whupped in front of a cemetery and my girlfriend off of State Street, I'm convinced I'm going to take the gun and beat him into a burnt cinnamon roll.

The boy places his gun on my chest and keeps looking back and forth to the car.

I feel a strange calm, an uncanny resolve. I don't know what's wrong with me. He's patting me down for money that I don't have since we hadn't gotten our work-study checks yet and I had just spent my last little money on two veggie subs from Subway and two of those large chocolate chip cookies.

The young brother keeps looking back to the car, unsure what he's supposed to do. Nzola and her friends are screaming when he takes the gun off my chest and trots goofily back to the car.

I don't know what's wrong with him, but a few months later, I have a gun.

A partner of mine hooks me up with a partner of his who lets me hold something. I get the gun not only to defend myself from goofy brothers in red Corollas trying to rob folks for work-study money. I guess I'm working also on becoming a Black writer in Mississippi and some folks around Millsaps College don't like the essays I'm writing in the school newspaper.

A few weeks earlier, George Harmon, the president of Millsaps, shut down the campus paper in response to a satirical essay I wrote on communal masturbation and sent a letter to over twelve thousand, overwhelmingly white, Millsaps students, friends, and alumnae. The letter states that the "Key Essay in question was written by Kiese Laymon, a controversial writer who consistently editorializes on race issues."

After the president's letter goes out, my life kinda hurts.

I receive a sweet letter in the mail with the burnt up ashes of my essays. The letter says that if I don't stop writing and give myself "over to right," my life would end up like the ashes of my writing.

The tires of my mama's car are slashed when her car was left on campus. I'm given a single room after the Dean of Students thinks it's too dangerous for me to have a roommate. Finally, Greg Miller, an English professor, writes an essay about how and why a student in his Liberal Studies class says, "Kiese should be killed for what he's writing."

I feel a lot when I read those words, but mainly I wonder what's wrong with me.

It's bid day at Millsaps.

Nzola and I are headed to our jobs at Ton-o-Fun, a fake ass Chuck E. Cheese behind Northpark Mall. We're wearing royal blue shirts with a strange smiling animal and Ton-o-Fun on the left titty. The shirts of the other boy workers at Ton-o-Fun fit them better than mine. My shirt is tight in the wrong places and slightly less royal blue. I like to add a taste of bleach so I don't stank.

As we walk out to the parking lot of my dorm, the Kappa Alpha and Kappa Sigma fraternities are in front of our dorm receiving their new members. They've been up drinking all night. Some of them have on black face and others have on Afro wigs and Confederate capes.

We get close to Nzola's Saturn and one of the men says, "Kiese, write about this!" Then another voice calls me a "Nigger" and Nzola a "Nigger bitch." I think and feel a lot but mostly I feel that I can't do anything to make the boys feel like they've made us feel right there, so I go back to my dorm room to get something.

On the way there, Nzola picks up a glass bottle out of the trash. I tell her to wait outside the room. I open the bottom drawer and look at the hoodies balled up on the top of my gun. I pick up my gun and think about my grandma. I think not only about what she'd feel if I went back out there with a gun. I also think about how, if my grandma walked out of that room with a gun in hand, she'd use it. No question.

I am her grandson.

I throw the gun back on top of the clothes, close the drawer, go in my closet, and pick up a wooden T-ball bat.

Some of the KA's and Sigs keep calling us names as we approach them. I step, throw down the bat, and tell them I don't need a bat to fuck them up. I don't know what's wrong with me. My fists are balled up and the only thing I want in the world is to swing back over and over again. Nzola feels the same, I think. She's right in the mix, yelling, crying, fighting as best she can. After security and a dean break up the mess, the frats go back to receiving their new pledges and Nzola and I go to work at Ton-o-Fun in our dirty blue shirts.

I stank.

On our first break at work, we decide that we should call a local news station so the rest of Jackson can see what's happening at Millsaps on a Saturday morning. We meet the camera crew at school. Some of the boys go after the reporter and cameraman. The camera gets a few students in Afros, black face, and Confederate capes. They also get footage of "another altercation."

I don't know what's wrong with me. My fists are balled up and the only thing I want in the world is to swing back over and over again.

A few weeks pass and George Harmon, the president of the college, doesn't like that this footage of his college is now on television and in newspapers all across the country. The college decides that two individual fraternity members, as well as Nzola and I, will be put on disciplinary probation for using "racially insensitive language" and that the two fraternities involved will get their party privileges taken away for a semester. If there was racially insensitive language that Nzola and I could have used to make those boys feel like we felt, we would have never stepped to in the first place. Millsaps is trying to prove to the nation that it is a post-race(ist) institution and to its alums that all the Bid Day stuff is the work of an "adroit entrepreneur of racial conflict."

A few months later, Mama and I sit in President George Harmon's office. The table is an oblong mix of mahogany and ice water. All the men at the table are smiling, flipping through papers, and twirling pens in their hands, except for me. I am still nineteen, two years older than Trayvon Martin will be when he swings back.

President Harmon and his lawyers don't look me in the eye. They zero in on the eyes of Mama, as Harmon tells her that I am being suspended from Millsaps for at least a year for taking and returning *Red Badge of Courage* from the library without formally checking it out.

He ain't lying.

I took the book out of the library for Nzola's brother without checking it out and returned the book the next day. I looked right at the camera when I did it, too. I did all of this knowing I was on parole, but not believing any college in America, even one in Mississippi, would kick a student out for a year, for taking and returning a library book without properly checking it out.

I should have believed.

George Harmon tells me, while looking at my mother, that I will be allowed to come back to Millsaps College in a year only after having attended therapy sessions for racial insensitivity. We are told he has given my writing to a local psychologist and the shrink believes I need help. Even if I am admitted back as a student, I will remain formally on parole for the rest of my undergrad career, which means that I will be expelled from Millsaps College unless I'm perfect.

Nineteen-year-old Black boys cannot be perfect in America; neither can sixty-one-year-old white boys named George. Before going on the ride home with Mama, I go to my room, put the gun in my backpack, and get in her car.

On the way home, Mama stops by the zoo to talk about what just happened in George Harmon's office. She's crying and asking me over and over again why I took and returned the gotdamn book knowing they were watching me. Like a Black mother of a Black boy, Mama starts blaming Nzola for asking me to check the book out in the first place. I don't know what to say other than I know it wasn't Nzola's fault and I had left my ID and I wanted to swing back, so I keep walking and say nothing. She says that Grandma is going to be so disappointed in me. "Heartbroken" is the word she uses.

There.

I feel this toxic miasma unlike anything I've ever felt, not just in my body but in my blood. I remember the wobbly way my grandma twitches her eyes at my Uncle Jimmy and I imagine being at the end of that twitch for the rest of my life. For the first time in almost two years, I hide my face, grit my crooked teeth, and sob.

I don't stop for weeks.

The NAACP and lawyers get involved in filing a lawsuit against Millsaps on my behalf. Whenever the NAACP folks talk to me or the paper, they talk about how ironic it is that a Black boy who is trying to read a book gets kicked out of college. I appreciate their work, but I don't think the irony lies where they think it does. Even if I'd never read a book in my life, I shouldn't have been punished for taking and bringing back a library book, not when kids are smoking that good stuff, drinking themselves unconscious, and doing some of everything imaginable to nonconsenting bodies.

That's what I tell all the newspapers and television reporters who ask. To my friends, I say that, after stealing all those Lucky Charms, Funyuns, loaves of light bread, and over a hundred cold dranks out of the cafeteria in two years, how in the fuck do I get suspended for taking and returning the gotdamn *Red Badge of Courage*?!

The day that I'm awarded the Benjamin Brown award, named after a twenty-one-year-old truck driver shot in the back by police officers during a student protest near Jackson State in 1967, I take the bullets out of my gun, throw it in the Ross Barnett Reservoir, and avoid my grandma for a long, long time.

I enroll at Jackson State University in the spring semester, where my mother teaches Political Science. Even though I'm not really living at home, every day Mama and I fight over my job at Cutco and her staying with her boyfriend and her not letting me use the car to get to my second job at an HIV hospice since my license is suspended. Really we're fighting because she raised me to never ever forget that I was on parole, which means no Black hoodies in wrong neighborhoods, no jogging at night, hands in plain sight at all times in public, no intimate relationships with white women, never driving over the speed limit or doing those rolling stops at stop signs, always speaking the king's English in the presence of white folks, never being outperformed in school or in public by white students, and most importantly, always remembering that, no matter what, white folks will do anything to get you.

Mama's antidote to being born a Black boy on parole in central Mississippi is not for us to seek freedom; it's to insist on excellence at all times. Mama takes it personally when she realizes that I realize she is wrong. "There ain't no antidote to life," I tell her. "How free can you be if you really accept that white folks are the traffic cops of your life?" Mama tells me that she is not talking about freedom.

She says that she is talking about survival.

One blue night, my mother tells me that I need to type the rest of my application to Oberlin College after I've already handwritten the personal essay. I tell her that it doesn't matter whether I type it or not since Millsaps is sending a dean's report attached to my transcript. I say some other truthful things I should never say to my mother. Mama goes into her room, lifts up her pillow, and comes out with her gun.

It's raggedy, small, heavy, and black. I always imagine the gun as an old dead crow. I'd held it a few times before, with Mama hiding behind me.

Mama points the gun at me and tells me to get the fuck out of her house. I look right at the muzzle pointed at my face and smile the same way I did at the library camera at Millsaps. I don't know what's wrong with me.

"You gonna pull a gun on me over some college application?" I ask her.

"You don't listen until it's too late," she tells me. "Get out of my house and don't ever come back."

I leave the house, chuckling, shaking my head, cussing under my breath. I go sit in a shallow ditch. Outside, I wander in the topsy-turvy understanding that Mama's life does not revolve around me and that I'm not doing anything to make her life more joyful, spacious, or happy. I'm an ungrateful burden, an obese weight on her already terrifying life. I sit there in the ditch, knowing that other things are happening in my mother's life, but I also know that Mama never imagined needing to pull a gun on the child she carried on her back as a sophomore at Jackson State University. I'm playing with pine needles, wishing I had headphones—but I'm mostly regretting throwing my gun into the reservoir.

When Mama leaves for work in the morning, I break back in her house, go under her pillow, and get her gun. Mama and I haven't paid the phone or the light bill so it's dark, hot, and lonely in that house, even in the morning. I lie in a bathtub of cold water, still sweating and singing love songs to myself. I put the gun to my head and cock it.

I think of my grandma and remember that old feeling of being so in love that nothing matters except seeing and being seen by her. I drop the gun to my chest. I'm so sad and I can't really see a way out of what I'm feeling but I'm leaning on memory for help. Faster. Slower. I think I want to hurt myself more than I'm already hurting. I'm not the smartest boy in the world by a long shot, but even in my funk I know that easy remedies like eating your way out of sad, or fucking your way out of sad, or lying your way out of sad, or slanging your way out of sad, or robbing your way out of sad, or gambling your way out of sad, or shooting your way out of sad, are just slower, more acceptable ways for desperate folks, and especially paroled Black boys in our country, to kill ourselves and others close to us in America.

I start to spend more time at home over the next few weeks since Mama is out of town with her boyfriend. Mama and I still haven't paid the phone bill so I'm running down to the pay phone every day, calling one of the admissions counselors at Oberlin College. He won't tell me whether they'll accept me or not, but he does say that Oberlin might want me because of, not in spite of, what happened at Millsaps.

I drop the gun to my chest. I'm so sad and I can't really see a way out of what I'm feeling, but I'm leaning on memory for help.

A month passes and I haven't heard from Oberlin. I'm eating too much and dry humping a woman just as desperate as I am and lying like it's my first job and daring people to fuck with me more than I have in a long time. I'm writing lots of words, too, but I'm not reckoning. I'm wasting ink on bullshit political analysis and short stories and vacant poems that I never imagine being read or felt by anyone like me. I'm a waste of writing's time.

The only really joyful times in life come from playing basketball and talking shit with O. G. Raymond "Gunn" Murph, my best friend. Gunn is trying to stop himself from slowly killing himself and others, after a smoldering break up with V., his girlfriend of eight years. Some days, Gunn and I save each other's lives just by telling and listening to each other's odd-shaped truth. One black night, Ray is destroying me in Madden and talking all that shit when we hear a woman moaning for help outside of his apartment on Capitol Street. We go downstairs and find a naked woman with open wounds, blood and bruises all over her Black body. She can barely walk or talk through shivering teeth, but we ask her if she wants to come upstairs while we call the ambulance. Gunn and I have taken no sexual assault classes and we listen to way too much *The Diary* and *Ready to Die,* but right there, we know not to get too close to the woman and to just let her know we're there to do whatever she needs.

She slowly makes her way into the apartment because she's afraid the men might come back. Blood is gushing down the back of her thighs and her scalp. She tells us the three men had one gun. When she makes it up to the apartment, we give the woman a towel to sit on and something to wrap herself in. Blood seeps through both and, even though she looks so scared and hurt, she also looks so embarrassed. Gunn keeps saying things like, "It's gonna be okay, sweetheart," and I just sit there, weakly nodding my head, running from her eyes, and getting her more glasses of water. When Gunn goes in his room to take his gun in his waistband, I look at her and know that no one man could have done this much damage to another human being. That's what I need to tell myself.

Eventually, the ambulance and police arrive. They ask her a lot of questions and keep looking at us. She tells them that we helped her after she was beaten and raped by three Black men in a Monte Carlo. One of the men, she tells the police, was her boyfriend. She refuses to say his name to the police. Gunn looks at me and drops his head. Without saying anything, we know that whatever is in the boys in that car, has to also be in us. We know that whatever is encouraging them to kill themselves slowly by knowingly mangling the body and spirit of this shivering Black girl, is probably the most powerful thing in our lives. We also know that whatever is in us that has been slowly encouraging us to kill ourselves and those around us, is also in the heart and mind of this Black girl on the couch.

A few weeks later, I get a letter saying I've been accepted to Oberlin College and that they're giving me a boatload of financial aid. Gunn agrees to drive me up to Oberlin and I feel like the luckiest boy on earth, not because I got into Oberlin, but because I survived long enough to remember saying "yes" to life and "no"—or at least "slow down"—to a slow death.

My saying "yes" to life meant accepting the beauty of growing up Black, on parole, in Mississippi. It also meant accepting that George Harmon, parts of Millsaps College, parts of my state, much of my country, my heart, and mostly my own reflection, had beaten the dog shit out of me. I still don't know what all this means but I know it's true.

This isn't an essay or simply a woe-is-we narrative about how hard it is to be a Black boy in America. This is a lame attempt at remembering the contours of slow death and life in America for one Black American teenager under central Mississippi skies. I wish I could get my Yoda on right now and surmise all this shit into a clean, sociopolitical pull-quote that shows supreme knowledge and absolute emotional trans-formation, but I don't want to lie.

I want to say and mean that remembering starts not with pre-dictable punditry, or bullshit blogs, or slick art that really asks noth-ing of us; I want to say that it starts with all of us willing ourselves to remember, to tell and accept those complicated, muffled truths of our lives and deaths and the lives and deaths of folks all around us over and over again.

Then I want to say and mean that I am who my grandma thinks I am. Yet, I am not.

I'm a walking regret, a truth-teller, a liar, a survivor, a frowning ellipsis, a witness, a dreamer, a teacher, a student, a joker, a writer whose eyes stay red, and I'm a child of this nation.

I know that as I've gotten deeper into my late twenties and thirties, I have managed to continue killing myself and other folks who love me in spite of me. I know that I've been slowly killed by folks who were as feverishly in need of life and death as I am. The really confusing part is that a few of those folks who have nudged me closer to slow death have also helped me say yes to life when I most needed it. Usually, I didn't accept it. Lots of times, we've taken turns killing ourselves slowly, before trying to bring each other back to life. Maybe that's the necessary stank of love, or maybe—like Frank Ocean says—it's all just bad religion, just tasty watered-down cyanide in a Styrofoam cup.

I don't even know.

I know that, by the time I left Mississippi, I was twenty years old, three years older than Trayvon Martin will be when he is murdered for wearing a hoodie and swinging back in the wrong American neighborhood. Four months after I leave Mississippi, San Berry, a twenty-year-old partner of mine who went to Millsaps College with Gunn and me, would be convicted for taking Pam McGill, a social worker, in the woods and shooting her in the head.

San confessed to kidnapping Ms. McGill, driving her to some woods, making her fall to her knees, and pulling the trigger while a seventeen-year-old Black boy named Azikiwe waited for him in the car. San says Azikiwe encouraged him to do it.

Even today, journalists, activists, and folks in Mississippi wonder what really happened with San, Azikiwe, and Pam McGill that day. Was San trying to swing back? Were there mental health issues left unattended? Had Ms. McGill, San, and Azikiwe talked to each other before the day? Why was Azikiwe left in the car when the murder took place?

I can't front, though. I don't wonder about any of that shit, not today.

I wonder what all three of those children of our nation really remember about how to slowly kill themselves and other folks in America the day before parts of them definitely died under the blue-black sky in central Mississippi.

How to Slowly Kill Yourself and Others in America: The Conversation

JEN   Our country is a country that asks people to push and push and push and push and push to succeed in all the ways we just talked about with [Kiese Laymon's] essay, and still [after so much success] this author finds himself in the bathtub feeling like he failed, ready to shoot himself. The literal—not the metaphorical, not the philosophical—the literal. This is what America does to people, especially people of color.

CHRIS   Yeah, I mean, this shit's real. My homeboy in Rush City just killed himself. I just found out last week, and I started approaching my mental health issues because my other homeboy killed himself. So, I mean, this shit's real. So, it's not just race, but mental health too. Race and poverty compound it, obviously.

JEN   Did you see it coming?

CHRIS   Not really. One homeboy a little bit. It was back in the day before mental health was a thing to talk about, so not a lot of us were talking about it. But we knew we both had an issue. So, yes. But no, not the little homeboy just recently though. He had a bunch of time. He'd done twelve and he had fourteen left but nobody really saw it coming. Because he's just such a young dude. He was in his mid-twenties. I don't know; I respect people choosing to leave and choosing to just, you know, walk away. I don't think life's as precious as we think or we like to say it is, and I think that that's sad. But I don't view it as precious, which is kind of sad too. But I think your values are more important.

WILL   I think a lot of us with longer sentences have thought seriously about killing ourselves at some point. It creeps up on you in ways that you didn't expect.

WARREN   It's like the metaphor of the train in the tunnel. If you have a light in front of you, if you have a light behind you, you know about where you are. If one goes out, you still know where you are. If both go out, you don't. And there have been times in my time where I didn't know where I was. During the only counseling that I got from the mental health professional at another prison, she said, "You did time in North Carolina, right?" I said, "Yes." And she said, "Well, then you've obviously had it worse than you have now." I said, "Thank you," and then I said something to the effect of, "You'll know where to find the body." And I walked out. But I thought about it later, and that was a very clear red flag. Nobody checked on me. So many things are so much more distilled—the rage, the isolation, just the pressures of existence.

There are times when I'm taking advantage of the privilege I have to sit down with a pen and paper and write and know that I have somebody at the other end who will tell me I'm either doing well or full of shit. And there are sometimes I will literally sit in my bunk and cry, because it's such a relief to know there's that honesty there. And [Laymon] does not have that [in this essay].

KENNEDY   To answer your question, "why a guy in a bathtub could put a gun to his head"—I think, you know, a lot of white Americans don't understand when a Black person claims racism is being practiced again, it's not just one incident. It is a multitude of incidents. It's at the psychologist; it's in the classroom. Take a Black guy or Black woman like Obama or Kamala, who's done everything right. You know, he's driving nicely to work, then some racist jackass stops them under the guise of *you look like somebody else.* And they stop them there for forty-five minutes to even an hour, and he is not looking for anything. We know that. But what he's actually doing is making this guy late to work. And this smart person, I'm telling you, will go to tell his boss a white cop stopped me for an hour, [and the boss] won't listen to that. He'll think, "This is just a lazy guy that didn't want to show up to work on time." And he will take his promotions away and take his earning capacities away. When people talk about the angry Black person, you know, they don't understand all those things. When my family was in this country, you know, I had to spend more money to go and get a second or third opinion to make sure that the proper care was being given. But what people don't understand is that I'm paying three times for a service that I should have received the first time. So, basically, racism is a system that's making me poor. Talk about precarity.

JEN   For sure. I wasn't wondering why, I was saying look at [what] our country does to people of color.

KENNEDY   Exactly, like, when I teach young men [in prison classes], I tell them to work very hard. So, if you really want to be smart, or you want to succeed, or just to survive, you got to do things two, three times better than most people.

CHRIS   I think [this essay] is touching, too, on the aspect of gun culture. And I mean, I like how [Laymon] starts with, you know, the gun pull. The first time I ever had a gun pulled on me, I was fifteen and we were in a trailer court just doing dumb kid shit—breaking into cars, taking what's in the glove box. It's stupid shit, but I remember when the cops pulled up, I was running and he said, "Stop or I'll shoot," and I just knew he was serious. I was a good fifteen feet away. I could have gotten away. But it's that shit: *Stop or I'll shoot.* Shoot me in the back! But growing up and being in these cultures, you're in these situations where you're powerless; somebody else has a gun or there's been a couple of times where I've had situations where I didn't have a gun, and I knew I was in a precarious situation. So, what? Do you call the cops? What am I gonna do? I'm gonna get a gun. That's part of our culture. We have guns around because we have to take care of ourselves. I was raised in an outlaw culture, that was, you didn't call the police, you called your people. And when you're old enough, it was part of a rite of passage, you get yourself a gun.

But I want to ask [about] this other thing where he talks about when he does find the girl and they call the cops, he talks about what's inside of us is inside of her too. Do you [Jen and Ruby] feel like that? Like, obviously, we're sitting in this room and we've all done terrible shit, right? Does most of the American population really believe that they're capable of such violence? [That] they're capable of these things that we've fallen into?

JEN   At this moment in my life, I don't carry around the sense of anger or danger. Like, I don't feel at risk of wanting to hurt anybody. But I recognize that there could be other moments in my life, under other circumstances, where I wouldn't have a stable base. So, as of this moment, do I feel like I'm a danger? No. But, do I think any human over the course of their life could become dangerous because of any number of things? I don't think any of us are immune to that. I don't think there's a single solitary human on the planet that is not capable of that, under the right circumstances. I have food. My children are healthy. I have a great support system. All my basic needs on Maslow's hierarchy are fulfilled, and then some. It's easier to come from a place of compassion or patience when you are not yourself exhausted from the world, under siege, terrified, or starving. And I'm not making excuses for anyone, I'm just saying. My early childhood was certainly not stable, but I can imagine . . . if the circumstances of my early childhood were persisting and were not even remotely different now? Absolutely. I'd be in a different place. Think of the nicest human you know, the most wonderful, compassionate, kindest human you know . . . I would argue that person is capable of violence under circumstances [different] than perhaps the ones they're currently in.

CHRIS   You're kind of on that list of mine actually.

JEN   Aww, thank you, Chris. But I've been at more fragile points in my life, where I know I have been brittle. And that would look different maybe for me, because I will not own a gun. But I think grace and patience come easier when your resources are met.

WILL   What does darkness look like for someone who is definitively nonviolent in conventional external ways?

JEN   I mean, that presupposes that there must be darkness. And I'm not certain that there has to be, but it can be sadness; it can be self-sabotage; it can be all kinds of things. I think, hopefully, ideally, we become better at being human as we get older and keep trying. I came to this realization one day as I was writing about aging—holy shit!—sometimes we don't get better as we get older, we get worse.

WILL   You've got to do that on purpose.

JEN   Yeah.

WILL   I don't mean to imply some sort of intrinsic darkness in each person, but more in the ebb and flow of everything that goes on. I mean, we find ourselves in dark places and things happen. But when that shift happens, and when that turn happens, like, you might not be someone who grabs a gun and goes for violence, or [someone] who would necessarily start something on fire and burn something down. But there's a manner in which that shit expresses itself in everybody. And I think we all—meaning us incarcerated folk—have a more immediate and tangible experience and expression of that for different reasons. We don't have any of the resources or the upbringing or, we don't start from homeostasis, we start from a negative event, and the things that we do out of what we believe to be necessity or even what we think is the right thing to do at the time, [it's] because it's the best we can do with what we have in the moment. And sometimes it turns inward, you know—[and the best you can do is to] crawl into the bathtub and start saving up your migraine medication [to overdose]. Figure out what time the garbage truck comes through the [industrial] area in Stillwater, you know, maybe throw your head under the wheel. Sometimes it goes outward—you know, that guy said something to me for the last fucking time, so I'm gonna go out there and sneak in behind him. We don't always act on those things. But, you know, those are expressions when starting from a darker shade.

KENNEDY   I think the potential is always there, Chris. It's just a question, I think, of getting to a point whereby you make the choice not to. He could have chosen to pick up that gun and just remain in the hood, you know, but at some point he realized, *I don't have to do that. I can be a writer.* And he made that choice.

JEN   Where does that strength come from? Prisons, for instance, love to talk about character. Yeah, *character counts,* but so do fucking mashed potatoes when you're hungry.

KENNEDY   No, I think for me, that falls into like people doing bad charity. You know, [charity] that doesn't help people for very long. So, for somebody like Chris, or the guys in this room, or me, you know, we could get into all those programs. If you don't go into those programs and [instead] come to the table and play cards, your character isn't gonna work very much. But [if] you give somebody a canvas and you put things there like Chris puts there, that is something that gives a character what it needs to survive. Then, if Chris writes a story, or anybody here writes a story, they have something to protect. They get stronger by that.

JEN   I like the subtext of that, Kennedy. Art is one answer.

Tell Me How It Ends

by Valeria Luiselli

Often, my daughter asks me:

So, how does the story of those children end?

I don't know how it ends yet, I usually say.

My daughter often follows up on the stories she half-hears. There is one story that obsesses her, a story I only tell her in pieces and for which I have not yet been able to offer a real ending. It begins with two girls in the courtroom. They're five and seven years old, and they're from a small village in Guatemala. Spanish is their second language, but the older girl speaks it well. We sit around the mahogany table in the room where the interviews take place, and their mother observes from one of the benches in the back. The little girl concentrates on her coloring book, wielding a crayon in her right hand. The older one has her hands crossed as an adult might, and she answers the questions I ask one by one. She is a little shy but tries to be clear and precise in her answers, delivering all of them with a big smile, toothless here and there.

Why did you come to the United States?

I don't know.

How did you travel here?

A man brought us.

A coyote?

No, a man.

Was he nice to you?

Yes, he was nice, I think.

And where did you cross the border?

I don't know.

Texas? Arizona?

Yes! Texas Arizona.

I realize it's impossible to go on with the interview, so I ask the lawyers to make an exception and allow the mother to meet with us, at least for a while. We go back, and the mother responds for the girls, filling holes, explaining things, and also telling her own version of the story.

When the younger of her daughters turned two, their mother left them in the care of their grandmother. She crossed two national borders with no documents. She wasn't detained by the Border Patrol, and she managed to cross the desert with a group of people. After a few weeks, she arrived in Long Island, where she had a cousin. That's where she settled. Years passed, and the girls grew up. Years passed, and she remarried. She had another child.

One day the woman called her mother—the grandmother of the girls—and told her that the time had come, that she had saved up enough money to bring the girls. I don't know how the grandmother responded to the news of her granddaughters' imminent departure, but she noted the instructions down carefully and later explained them to the girls: in a few days, a man was going to come for them, a man who would help them get back to their mother. She told them that it would be a long trip, but that he would keep them safe. The man had taken many other girls from their village safely across the two borders to their mothers, and everything had gone well. So, everything would go well this time, too.

The day before they left, their grandmother sewed a ten-digit telephone number on the collars of the dress each girl would wear throughout the entire trip. It was a ten-digit number the girls had not been able to memorize, as hard as the grandmother tried to get them to, so she had decided to embroider it on their dresses and repeat, over and over, a single instruction—they should never take this dress off, not even to sleep, and as soon as they reached America, as soon as they met the first American policeman, they had to show the inside of the dress's collar to him. He would then dial the number and let them speak to their mother. The rest would follow.

The rest did follow. The two girls made it to the border, were kept in ICE custody for an indefinite time period (they didn't remember how many days, but they said that they were colder there than they had ever been, even colder than they were in the winter we were in the middle of). After that, they went to a shelter, and, a few weeks later, they were put on a plane and flown to JFK, where their mother, baby brother, and stepfather were waiting for them.

That's it? my daughter asks.

That's it, I tell her.

That's how it ends?

Yes, that's how it ends.

But, of course, it doesn't end there. That's just where it begins, with a court summons—a first Notice to Appear.

Once children receive a Notice to Appear, they have to present themselves in immigration court. If they don't show up—because they fear going to court, or, perhaps, because they have since changed address, or because they simply didn't get the notice—they are usually "removed in absentia." An immigration judge, assisted by a translator, informs the ones who do show up that they have the right to an attorney, but at no expense to the US government. In other words, it is the children's responsibility to find and pay for a lawyer, or to find a free lawyer, who can help them defend their case against the US government attorney seeking to deport them.

A typical immigration hearing begins with the judge stating the basic facts:

This is September 15, 2014, New York, state of New York. This is Immigration Judge [name of judge].

This is in the matter of [name of the child respondent].

Then come a few questions directed at the accused (the child), such as if they respond to Spanish, if they are enrolled in school, and whether they live at the given address. Then the judge states that the child will be speaking to the attorney and asks:

How do you plead?

We admit the charges.

And what are the charges? Fundamentally, it is that the child came to the United States without lawful permission. Admitting these charges alone leads to deportation unless the child's attorney can find the potential avenues of relief that form a defense against it. The admission of guilt, then, is a kind of door that the law holds half open. It is the only way for the accused to begin defending themselves against a categorical sentence and seeking legal avenues to immigration relief. Yet is also the way to deportation.

The most common forms of immigration relief are political asylum or a special visa for child immigrants known as the Special Immigrant Juvenile Status (sijs). If the child is eligible for either of these permits, they may remain in the United States legally and can later apply for lawful permanent residency, and even citizenship.

Usually, the kind of harm the children are fleeing makes them eligible for asylum or sijs. The sijs can be obtained in two steps. First, a family court must determine that they are impeded from reunification with their parents because of abuse, abandonment, neglect, or a similar basis under state law, and, moreover, that reunification in their home country is not in their best interests. Once the family court makes this ruling, the minor can request the sijs visa in the immigration court.

Asylum, on the other hand, is granted to people who are fleeing persecution—or who have a fear of future persecution—based on their race, religion, nationality, and/or association with a particular social or political group. It is very difficult to be granted asylum because it is not enough that these children have suffered unspeakable harm, and even that they will continue to fall victim to the systematic and targeted violence of criminal groups. The harm or persecution *must* be proved to be because of at least one of those four classifications. The main problem with political asylum, and the reason lawyers often consider it a secondary choice, is that if it's granted, the children can never return to their home country, where they fear being persecuted, without jeopardizing their immigration status in the United States. Less common are the u visa, which can only be granted to victims of certain crimes, and the t visa, for victims of human trafficking.

If the child answers the questionnaire "correctly," they are more likely to have a case strong enough to increase their chances of being placed with a pro bono attorney. An answer is "correct" if it strengthens the child's case and provides a potential avenue of relief. So, in the warped world of immigration, a correct answer is when, for example, a girl reveals that her father is an alcoholic who physically or sexually abused her, or when a boy reports that he received death threats or that he was beaten repeatedly by several gang members after refusing to acquiesce to recruitment at school and has the physical injuries to prove it. Such answers—more common than exceptional—may open doors to potential immigration relief and, eventually, to legal status in the United States. When children don't have enough battle wounds to show, they may not have any way to successfully defend their cases and, therefore, are most likely to be "removed" back to their home country, often without a trial.

The interpreters have no control over the type of legal assistance a child receives. We listen to their stories in Spanish and note down key points in English. We must simultaneously pay close attention to the details and find ways to distribute them into categories. On the one hand, it's important to record even the most minor details from every story because a good lawyer can use them to strengthen a case in ways that might not have occurred to an interpreter. On the other, although it's not in the protocol, we must look for more general categories for each story that may tip the legal scale in favor of the future client in a future trial—categories such as "abandonment," "prostitution," "sex trafficking," "gang violence," and "death threats." But we cannot make up the answers in their favor, nor can we lead the children to tell us what is best for their cases, as much as we would like to. It can be confusing and bewildering, and I find myself not knowing where translation ends and interpretation starts.

During the interviews, I sometimes note children's answers in the first person and sometimes in the third:

I crossed the border by foot.
She swam across the river.
He comes from San Pedro Sula.
She comes from Tegucigalpa.
She comes from Guatemala City.

He has not ever met his father.

Yes, I have met my mother.

But she doesn't remember the last time she saw her.

He doesn't know if she abandoned him.

She sent money every month.

No, my father didn't send money at all.

I worked in the fields, ten or maybe fifteen hours a day.

The MS-13 shot my sister. She died.

Yes, my uncle hit me often.

No, my grandmother never hit us.

As predictable as the answers start to become after months of conducting the interviews, no one is ever prepared for hearing them.

If the children are very young, in addition to translating from one language to another, the interpreters have to reconfigure the questions, shift them from the language of adults to the language of children. When I interviewed the girls with the dresses, for example, I transformed question twenty-two on the questionnaire—"Did you stay in touch with your parents?"—into a succession of various questions until I touched on something that produced a memory, which in turn produced a response:

When you were there, how did you contact your mother?

What?

Did you talk to your mother when she was here and you were there?

Back where?

Did your mother call you on the phone?

Finally, the girl nodded, looking at me in silence. Then she searched for her mother's eyes, found them, and smiled. She relaxed a little and began to speak.

Yes, she told me. She had talked to her mother on the phone, and her mother had told them stories about snowstorms, and big avenues, and traffic jams, and, later, stories about her new husband and their new baby brother. After that, we asked her mother to return to the area reserved for relatives of the children.

Questions twenty-three through twenty-six are a little less complicated, though quite redundant, and the girl was able to respond to them less hesitantly.

Twenty-three: Did you go to school in your country of origin?

No.

Twenty-four: How old were you when you started going to school?

I didn't go to school.

Twenty-five: When did you stop going to school?

I already told you; I never went!

Twenty-six: Why not?

I don't know.

I didn't know how to ask questions twenty-seven, twenty-eight, and twenty-nine: "Did you work in your home country?"; "What sort of work did you do?"; "How many hours did you work each day?" But I knew that I had to find a way to do it. We were already halfway through the questionnaire, and I still didn't feel sure that a lawyer would take on the case. I reworded, translated, interpreted.

What kinds of things did you do when you lived with your grandmother?

We played.

But besides playing?

Nothing.

Did you work?

Yes.

What did you do?

I don't remember.

I went on to questions thirty, thirty-one, thirty-two, and thirty-three. The older girl answered them while the little one undressed a crayon and scratched its trunk with her fingernail.

Did you ever get in trouble at home when you lived in your home country?

No.

Were you punished if you did something wrong?

No.

How often were you punished?

Never.

Did you or anyone in your family have an illness that required special attention?

What?

The girls' answers weren't really working. They weren't working in their favor, that is. What I needed to hear, though I didn't want to hear it, was that they had been doing hard labor, labor that put their safety and integrity in danger; that they were being exploited, abused, punished, maybe even threatened to death by gangs. If their answers didn't align with what the law considers reason enough for the right to protection, the only possible ending to their story was going to be a deportation order. It was going to be very hard, with the answers they were giving me, to even find them a lawyer willing to take on their case. The girls were so young, and even if they had a story that secured legal intervention in their favor, they didn't know the words necessary to tell it. For children of that age, telling a story—in a second language, translated into a third—a round and convincing story that successfully inserts them into legal proceedings working up to their defense, is practically impossible.

But how does the story about those girls end? my daughter asks.

I don't know how it ends, I say.

She comes back to this question often, demanding a proper conclusion with the insistence of very small children.

But what happens next, Mamma?

I don't know.

After a few months working with the Door in court cases like this one, feelings of frustration and defeat began to settle over my niece, another interpreter, and me. The numbers weren't adding up. There were so many more children awaiting interviews than there were interpreters and lawyers to conduct them. The ones we had interviewed now faced a shrinking window of time to find legal representation. It was clear that our only role in the court was to serve as a fragile and slippery bridge between the children and the court system. We could translate their cases, but we couldn't do anything to help them. It was like watching a child crossing a busy avenue, about to be run down by any of the many speeding cars and trucks. The two of us were powerless to stop it from happening, our hands and feet tied. One day, while we were walking to the train station, my niece said:

You know, I think I'm going to major in law instead of social work.

Why law? I asked.

My question was unnecessary. I already knew the answer. It's lawyers that are desperately needed. According to a comprehensive report issued in October 2015 by the Migration Policy Institute, the majority of children who find a lawyer do appear in court and are granted some form of relief. All the others are deported, either in absentia or in person.[1] What is needed in particular, and urgently, are lawyers who are willing to work pro bono.

Child refugees in court proceedings, because they are considered "illegal aliens," are not entitled to the free legal counsel that American law guarantees its citizens. In other words, that third sentence in the well-known Miranda rights—"You have the right to consult an attorney . . ." does not apply to them. Therefore, volunteer organizations have stepped in to do the job. Either pro bono or at very low cost, non-profit organizations find attorneys to represent alien children. A handful of non-profit organizations are responsible for all the work being done to help undocumented child migrants, and what they have accomplished is impressive. But they can provide only patchwork support and cannot cover all the gaps.

I realized after several months of working in the court that it was better to write the children's answers in my notebook before copying them down neatly on the intake questionnaire. He says, The gang followed me after school, and I ran, with my eyes closed, I ran. So I write all that down, and then, in the margin, make a note: Persecution? He says more, And they followed me to school and later they followed me home with a gun. So I write that down, too, and then make a note: Death

---

1 Sarah Pierce, "Unaccompanied Child Migrants in us Communities, Immigration Court, and Schools," Migration Policy Institute, October 2015.

threats? Then he says, They kicked my door open and shot my little brother. So I write that down, too, but then I'm not sure what note to make in the margin: Home country poses life-threatening danger? Not in child's best interest to return? What words are the most precise ones? And all too often I find myself not wanting to write anymore, wanting to just sit there, quietly listening, wishing that the story I'm hearing had a better ending. I listen, hoping that the bullet shot at this boy's little brother had missed. But it didn't. The little brother was killed, and the boy fled. And now he was being screened, by me. Later, his screening, like many others, is filed and sent away to a possible lawyer: a snapshot of a life that will wait in the dark until maybe someone finds it and decides to make it a case.

My niece and I almost always leave immigration court in silence. We leave the brutal and exceptional reality of the stories we heard and translated that day, and step into the business-as-usual reality of the city: the hum of crowded streets, the sirens, the subway's screeching when it comes to a halt. Sometimes, only sometimes, while we ride the subway back, we tell each other pieces of the stories we heard during a day's screenings. Telling stories doesn't serve a purpose, doesn't solve anything, doesn't reassemble broken lives, but perhaps it is a way of understanding the unthinkable. If a story haunts us, we keep telling it to ourselves, perhaps replaying it in silence while we shower, while we walk alone down streets, or in our moments of insomnia.

The story that obsesses me is the first one I had to translate. It lives with me now, grows in me, all its details clear in my mind and constantly revisited. It's a story I know well and follow closely, but for which I still cannot see a possible ending.

This is how it starts. A boy and I are seated at one end of the long mahogany table. It is obvious that both of us are new to the scenario, both still uncomfortable with reducing a story to the blank spaces between questions.

First, I fill in biographical information. Next to "name," "age," and "nationality," I write: Manu Nanco, sixteen years old, Honduras. Then, next to the words "guardian," "relationship," and "current residence," I

write: Alina Nanco, aunt, 42 Pine Street, Hempstead, Long Island, NY.
I look at the two questions that float halfway down the page: "Where
is child's mother?"; "Father?" Manu answers with a shrug, and I write:
? and ?

Why did you come to the United States?

He says nothing and looks at me, shrugs a little. I reassure him.

I'm no policewoman; I'm no official anyone; I'm not even a lawyer.
I'm also not a *gringa,* you know? In fact, I can't help you at all. But I
can't hurt you, either.

So why are *you* here then?

I'm just here to translate for you.

And what are you?

What do you mean?

I mean, where are you from?

I'm a *chilanga.*

Well, I'm a *catracho,* so we're enemies.

And in a way, he's right. I'm from Mexico City and he's from
Honduras, and in many ways, that makes us hostile neighbors.

Yeah, I say, but only in football, and I suck at football anyway, so
you've already scored five goals against me.

He smiles, perhaps almost laughs. I know he's going to let me go
on with the questions now. I haven't won his trust, of course, but
at least I have his attention. We proceed, slowly and hesitantly. He
delivers his answers in a whisper or a murmur and looks down at his
clasped hands or turns around to find his aunt and baby cousin. I
try to convey my words neutrally, but every question seems to either
embarrass or annoy him. He answers in short sentences or with silent
shrugs. No, he has never met his father. No, he did not live with his
mother in his home country. He has met her, yes, but she came and
went as she pleased. She liked the streets, perhaps. He doesn't like
talking about her. He grew up with his grandmother, but she died last
year. Everyone was dying or going north. Six months now, exactly,
since she died. She used to take care of them, in Honduras, but it was
his aunt, the same aunt now sitting in the back of the courtroom, who
had always sent money.

How do you like living with your aunt?

He likes her. But even though she is family, he's never really known her. She has always been just a voice inside the telephone. She called in regularly, from New York, to see how they were all doing. I ask who "they" were, to get a clearer picture. Or, in other words, question nineteen, with its respective branches, which in turn branch out, into always more and more complex stories:

Who did you live with in your home country?

With my grandmother and my two cousins.

How old are they?

Nineteen and thirteen. No, wait, nineteen and fourteen.

Names?

Patricia and Marta—why do you need their names?

I just do. Are the two of them still there now?

No.

So where are they?

Somewhere, on their way here.

On their way to the us?

Yes.

With whom?

A coyote—who else?

Paid by?

My aunt, sitting over there.

Is she their aunt too?

No, she's their mother. If they're my cousins, she's their mother, right?

The reason for the trip that the two girls are also now making, following Manu's path, doesn't become clear to me until we finally arrive at the last ten questions. They're the most difficult to ask because they refer to the gangs directly, and it's at this point that many of the children, especially the older ones, begin to break down. Smaller children look back at you with a mixture of bewilderment and amusement if you say "bands of organized criminals," maybe because they associate the word "bands" with musical groups. But the majority, even the littlest ones, have heard the words *ganga* or *pandillera* before, and saying them is like pressing the button on a machine that produces nightmares. Even if they don't have direct experience with the gangs, the threat lurks constantly, a monster under the bed or on the street corner—something they'll meet with sooner or later.

The teenagers have all been touched in one way or another by the tentacles of the MS-13 and Barrio 18, or other groups like them, though the degree of their contact and involvement with *pandilleros* varies. The teenage girls, for example, are not usually coerced into gangs but are often sexually harassed by them or recruited to be girlfriends of gang members. Boys are told that their little sister, cousin, or girlfriend will be raped if they don't man up and join.

I ask Manu question thirty-four, the one that often opens Pandora's box but also gives the interviewer the most valuable material for building the minor's case: Did you ever have trouble with gangs or crime in your home country?

Manu tells me a confusing, fragmented story about the MS-13 and their ongoing fight against the Barrio 18. One was trying to recruit him. The other was going after him. One day some boys from Barrio 18 waited for him and his best friend outside their school. When Manu and his friend saw them there, they knew they couldn't fight. There were too many of them. He and his friend walked away, but they were followed. They tried running. They ran, ran for a block or two, until there was a gunshot. Manu turned around—still running—and saw that his friend had fallen. More gunshots followed, but he kept running until he found an open store and went inside.

Questions thirty-five and thirty-six:

Any problems with the government in your home country? If so, what happened?

My government? Write this down in your notebook: They don't do shit for anybody like me, that's the problem.

It's then that, from his pocket, he pulls out the piece of paper that haunted me for so long—a copy of the police report he filed against the gang. He filed it months before his friend was killed, but the police never did anything. And Manu knew, because everyone knows that this is how it is, that the police wouldn't do anything to prevent a second incident, or a third.

That night, after the confrontation with the gang, he called his aunt in New York. They decided he would leave the country as soon as possible. He didn't leave his house during the weeks that followed. He didn't attend his friend's funeral.

Miguel Hernández has a poem called "Elegy" about the death of a childhood friend. It's not so much a distant remembrance as an obsessive conjuring of his friend's buried corpse. A few lines drive themselves into the mind the way only the sharpest images can:

> I want to gnaw at the earth with my teeth,
> I want to take the earth apart bit by bit
> with dry, burning bites.
>
> I want to mine the earth till I find you,
> and kiss your noble skull,
> and un-shroud you, and return you.[2]

The instructions had been not to leave his house until the day the coyote arrived at his door. In the interview, Manu repeated twice that he wasn't at his friend's funeral. He didn't leave his house until the morning the coyote knocked on his door and they slipped down streets of Tegucigalpa together.

His aunt paid the coyote $4,000. They left at dawn. Manu explains that boys cost $4,000 and girls $3,000.

Why?

Because boys are the worst, he says, smiling wide.

We go over the rest of the story: from Tegucigalpa to Guatemala by bus, to the Mexican border, to Arriaga and then aboard La Bestia, to the us-Mexico border. No serious problems along the way, although I imagine there are serious things that don't seem serious to him anymore. From there to the icebox, the shelter, the airplane to JFK, and

---

2 Miguel Hernández, *The Selected Poems of Miguel Hernández,* edited and translated by Ted Genoways (Chicago: University of Chicago Press, 2001).

finally to Long Island. We're about to finish the session when he suddenly reveals an unexpected turn—the reason his two cousins, Patricia and Marta, set off on the same journey.

Why did they leave?

Something in his body language softens and becomes milder, as if the thought of his two cousins has momentarily stripped away some of his toughness—an attitude that, with practice like this, may turn into personality. When he left, he explains, the two girls began to be harassed by the same gang that had killed his best friend. That's when his aunt decided that she'd rather pay the $3,000 for each of her daughters and put them through the dangers of the journey than let them stay. The dangers the girls will face multiply in my head as Manu tells me all this.

Beyond the dangers posed by organized gangs and criminals in Mexico, there are also the federal, state, and municipal police forces, the army, and the immigration officials who operate under the umbrella of the Ministry of the Interior and whose role has been reinforced by new and more severe policies. Shortly after the unaccompanied child migrant crisis was declared in the United States, and after a meeting between President Barack Obama and President Enrique Peña Nieto, the Mexican government introduced its new anti-immigration plan— the Programa Frontera Sur.[3] The objective of the program, which was granted an initial budget of 102 million pesos from federal funds, was to halt the immigration of Central Americans through Mexico.

To justify Programa Frontera Sur, the Mexican government maintains that Mexico must protect the "safety and rights" of migrants. But the reality is something else entirely. In fact, since the program was implemented, the safety of immigrants has been compromised to an even greater extent, their lives put in even greater danger.

---

3 "Assessing the Alarming Impact of Mexico's Southern Border Program," Washington Office on Latin America, May 28, 2015; "Así Planea México Domar a la Bestia," *La Tribuna,* September 6, 2016; Joseph Sorrentino, "How the US 'Solved' the Central American Migrant Crisis," *In These Times,* May 12, 2015; "Programa Frontera Sur: Una Cacería de Migrantes," *Animal Político*/CIDE.

Anti-immigrant strategies included in the program, mostly to be implemented along the routes of La Bestia, include drones; security cameras and control centers in strategic locations (trains, tunnels, bridges, railway crossings, and city centers); fences and floodlights in the rail yards; private security teams and geolocation technology in trains; alarm systems and motion detectors on the tracks; and, last but not least, the notorious Grupos Beta, which, under the guise of a humanitarian aid organization, locates and then reports migrants to immigration officials, who can then "secure" them—a Mexican euphemism for "capture and deport." Programa Frontera Sur is the Mexican government's new augmented-reality videogame: the player who hunts down the most migrants wins. As the Mexican government has progressively increased its hold on La Bestia, travel aboard the trains has become more and more risky and new routes have been improvised. There are now maritime routes that begin on the coasts of Chiapas, along which the migrants travel with coyotes aboard rafts and other precarious vessels. We've heard the many stories about migrants crossing the Mediterranean—that massive cemetery of a sea—so it's easy to imagine what kinds of stories we'll hear in the next few years of migrants amid the enormous waves of the Pacific Ocean.

Since Programa Frontera Sur was launched in 2014, Mexico has massively deported Central American migrants, many of whom would have had the legal right to request political asylum in either Mexico or the United States. In 2016, for example, Mexico registered the largest number of applications for asylum in recent history. That same year saw a radical increase in deportation rates of Central Americans. This of course begs the question of whether migrants' right to due process is being honored.

Most Mexicans, when asked about immigration issues, talk like they have either a PhD in Mexico-US relations or direct experience with migrating illegally across the border. Mexicans are eager and tireless critics of US immigration policies. And though most critiques of their northern neighbor are probably more than justified, Mexicans are far too lax and self-indulgent when it comes to evaluating their own immigration policies, especially where Central Americans are concerned.

Under Programa Frontera Sur, the emphasis of border control for the Central American exodus is shifting from the Río Grande on the US-Mexico border to the Suchiate and Usumacinta Rivers on the Mexico-Guatemala border. The United States, of course, not only endorses this shift but has been generously financing it: the State Department has paid the Mexican government tens of millions of dollars to filter the migration of Central Americans.[4] In other words, following the old tradition of US-Latin America governmental relations, the Mexican government is getting paid to do the dirty work. And President Peña Nieto—the most well-groomed, cynical, and sinister boy among the subservient Latin American bullies doing the grunt work—has earned his place as the continent's new deporter-in-chief: since 2014, Peña Nieto has deported more Central Americans each year than the United States, more than 150,000 in 2015 alone.[5] The country is now limbo for migrants, an enormous and terrifying customs office staffed as often by white-collar criminals as it is by criminals with guns and pickup trucks.

The next time I see Manu, six months later, we're in a large room on the twentysomethingth floor of a corporate building next to South Ferry. We can see Staten Island from the window, and if we stretch our necks, we can see the Statue of Liberty. The setting is almost unreal, as if we've been thrust into a high-budget production of a bad Hollywood movie.

"Manu says thank you," his aunt tells me to tell the three men in expensive suits who sit across from us at the lacquered table.

I sense his disbelief, and perhaps he senses mine, too. The lawyers who will represent his case work for one of the most powerful and expensive corporate firms in the city. Rarely do these kinds of offices get involved in cases like this one. But thanks to the material evidence Manu has of his statements—the folded slip of paper—the Door was able to find a large firm willing to take his case pro bono. With that

---

4 Sonia Nozario, "Outsourcing a Refugee Crisis: US Paid Mexico Millions to Target Central Americans Fleeing Violence," *Democracy Now,* October 13, 2015.

5 "Mexico Now Detains More Central American Migrants than the US," Washington Office on Latin America, June 11, 2015; Natalia Gómez Quintero, "México Deporta 150 Mil Migrantes en 2015," *El Universal,* February 12, 2016.

kind of material evidence, it would be impossible for them to lose. The lawyers at the Door transformed a dead document into legal evidence for a case.

Sometimes, when cases advance to this second phase, the organizations that work in the court ask the interpreter who did the first interview to rejoin them. Since Manu's new lawyers don't speak Spanish, I was asked to continue translating for him.

I don't hesitate to show Manu my enthusiasm for our reunion. I tell him about another coincidence: I'm now working at a university in Hempstead, the same city in Long Island where he lives. He receives my enthusiasm without a word, maintaining his cool adolescent posturing. We sit around a large black table: Manu, his aunt, three lawyers, and me. We are offered coffee and snacks. Alina and I say yes to the coffee. Manu says he'll have some of everything, if it's free. I translate:

Just a cookie please, thanks, that's very kind of you.

The meeting serves the sole purpose of preparing Manu's SIJS application, though he's probably more likely eligible for asylum. We go through the lawyers' contract and then through his application. Everything runs smoothly until the lawyers ask if Manu is still enrolled in school. He is, he says. He's at Hempstead High School, but he wants to leave as soon as possible.

Why? they want to know. They remind him that if he wants to be considered for any type of formal relief, he has to be enrolled in school. He hesitates then suddenly opens his mouth wide, showing his teeth and gums. He's missing two teeth on the top row. He closes his mouth again and says:

I used to laugh at my grandma 'cause she had no front teeth, and now I look in the mirror and I laugh at me.

He talks slowly and in a low voice, but perhaps more confidently than when I first met him in court, months ago. He periodically looks down at his clasped hands as he talks. Hempstead High School, he tells us, is a hub for MS-13 and Barrio 18. I turn cold at this statement, which he delivers in the tone one might use to talk about items in a supermarket. He's afraid of Barrio 18. They beat his teeth out of his mouth. MS-13 boys saved him from losing the rest of his teeth.

Suddenly, we all suspect Manu, and want to ask question thirty-seven: "Have you ever been a member of a gang (any tattoos)?" No, he has no tattoos. And no, he's never been part of a gang. The MS-13 in Hempstead wants him, but he's not going to fall for it. He'd rather disappear than join them, now more than ever.

What do you mean by now more than ever, Manu? I ask, forgetting for a moment my role as translator.

I mean now that my two cousins are here with us and I have to look out for them.

Look out for them how?

Just look out for them, 'cause Hempstead is a shithole full of *pandilleros,* just like Tegucigalpa.

Between Hempstead and Tegucigalpa there is a long chain of causes and effects. Both cities can be drawn on the same map: the map of violence related to drug trafficking. This fact is ignored, however, by almost all of the official reports. The media wouldn't put Hempstead, a city in New York, on the same plane as one in Honduras. What a scandal! Official accounts in the United States—what circulates in the newspaper or on the radio, the message from Washington, and public opinion in general—almost always locates the dividing line between "civilization" and "barbarity" just below the Río Grande.

A brief, particularly disconcerting article in the *New York Times* in October, 2014, postulated a series of questions and rapid responses about the child migrants from Central America.[6] The questions themselves had a tendentious tone: "Why aren't child migrants *immediately* deported?" one of them said, as if baffled or enraged by the fact that the children are not met at the border with catapults that will return them to their home countries. If the questions themselves showed a light bias, the answers were worse. They seemed like something from an openly racist nineteenth-century magazine or a reactionary anti-immigration serial, not the *Times:* "Under a statute adopted with bipartisan support . . . minors from Central America cannot be

6 Haeyoun Park, "Children at the Border," *New York Times,* October 21, 2014.

deported immediately . . . [but] a United States law *allows* Mexican minors *caught* crossing the border to be sent back quickly." (Note: the majority of children are not "caught"—they turn themselves over to Border Patrol.)

Another question read, "Where are the child migrants coming from?" The answer: "More than three-quarters of the children are from mostly *poor and violent* towns in three countries: El Salvador, Guatemala, and Honduras." The italics are mine, of course, but they underscore the less than subtle bias in the portrait of the children: children *caught* while crossing illegally, laws that *permit* their deportation, children who come from the *poor and violent* towns. In short: barbarians who deserve subhuman treatment.

The attitude in the United States toward child migrants is not always blatantly negative, but generally speaking, it is based on a kind of misunderstanding or a voluntary ignorance. Debate around the matter has persistently and cynically overlooked the causes of the children's exodus. When causes are discussed, the general consensus and underlying assumption seem to be that the origins of the children's crisis are circumscribed to "sending" countries and their many local problems. No one suggests that the causes of the children's exodus are deeply embedded in our shared hemispheric history and are therefore not a local problem in some foreign country that no one can locate on a map, but in fact a transnational problem that includes the United States—not as a distant observer or a passive victim that must now deal with thousands of unwanted children arriving in the southern border, but rather as an active historical participant in the circumstances that generated that problem.

The belief that the migration of all of those children is "their" problem (the southern barbarians) is often so deeply ingrained that "we" (the northern civilization) feel exempt from offering any solution. The devastation of the social fabric in Honduras, El Salvador, Guatemala, and other countries is often thought of as a Central American "gang violence" problem that must be kept on the far side of the border. There is little said, for example, of arms being trafficked from the United States into Mexico or Central America, legally or not; little mention of the fact that the consumption of drugs in the United States is what fundamentally fuels drug trafficking in the continent.

But the drug circuits and their many wars—those openly declared and those that are silenced—are being fought in the streets of San Salvador, San Pedro Sula, Iguala, Tampico, Los Angeles, and Hempstead. They are not a problem circumscribed in a small geographical area. The roots and reach of the current situation branch out across hemispheres and form a complex global network whose size and real reach we can't even imagine. It's urgent that we begin talking about the drug war as a hemispheric war, at least, one that begins in the Great Lakes of the northern United States and ends in the mountains of Celaque in southern Honduras.

It would surely be a step forward for our governments to officially acknowledge the hemispheric dimensions of the problem, to acknowledge the connection between such phenomena as the drug war, Central American gangs, the trafficking of arms from the United States, the consumption of drugs, and the massive migration of children from the Northern Triangle to the United States through Mexico. No one, or almost no one, from producers to consumers, is willing to accept their role in the great theater of devastation of these children's lives. To refer to the situation as a hemispheric war would be a step forward because it would oblige us to rethink the very language surrounding the problem and, in doing so, imagine potential directions for combined policies. But, of course, a "war refugee" is bad news and an uncomfortable truth for governments, because it obliges them to deal with the problem instead of simply "removing the illegal *aliens.*"

When I ask Manu after the meeting what he thinks of Hempstead, he says it is almost as ugly as Tegucigalpa but at least it was home to Method Man, from the Wu-Tang Clan, and you could get good CDs there. Before we say good-bye, he promises to show me around one day. He doesn't.

In a later web search, to corroborate the random fact about Method Man, I find that Hempstead is also where Walt Whitman lived for a while, and where the fourth most obese man in the world was born.

In the weeks that follow, I buy some books and start reading about the town. It is a broken community that has served as a stage for the Bloods and the Crips for more than forty years. The rapper A+ released a 1999 album called Hempstead High. The hit single from the album is called "Enjoy Yourself," and in the final stanza A+ says, "Actin' all wild, unprofessional / Who got beef, I knock teeth out ya smile / But my lyrical lubricant keeps the crowd movin'." I listen to the song on repeat as I ride the Long Island Railroad one day on my way to Hempstead—the irony of those words pounding in my head. Certainly, the 18 of Tegucigalpa would have done much worse than knock out Manu's front teeth, as the Hempstead 18 had done. But I imagine that, in his nights of adolescent rage and desperation, Manu wonders why, why this story all over again, why he ever came to the United States.

One day in court I tried to explain the phrase "de Guatemala a Guatepeor"—from Guatebad to Guateworse—to a lawyer. In translation the phrase loses some of its meaning, but it can be glossed this way: almost five thousand kilometers separate Tapachula, the Guatemala-Mexico border town from which La Bestia departs, from New York. Hundreds of thousands of kids have made the journey, tens of thousands have made it to the border, thousands to cities like Hempstead. Why did you come to the United States? we ask. The kids might ask us a similar question: Why did we risk our lives to come to this country? Why did they come when, as if in some circular nightmare, they arrive at new schools, in their new neighborhoods, and find there the very things they were running from?

Thirty-eight: "What do you think will happen if you go back home?" Some months later, in a phone interview with Alina in which I am still trying to put some pieces of the story together, she tells me that she saved up for years to bring her two daughters and Manu to New York. But she decided to stop saving and go into debt to bring Manu as soon as she realized it was no longer a joke.

No longer children's games, she says. They killed his friend in front of him, you know, and I knew he'd be next.

Thirty-nine: "Are you scared to return?" In this same conversation, Alina also tells me that she brought the girls over after some *pandilleros* from the gang that killed Manu's friend started waiting outside her eldest daughter's school every day, following her slowly back home on motorbikes as she walked along the side of the road, trying not to look back.

Up until then, the idea of letting the children travel alone with a coyote had been unimaginable—crossing borders, mounting La Bestia. Suddenly the idea of allowing them to stay in Tegucigalpa became even more unimaginable.

Forty: "Who would take care of you if you were to return to your home country?" If the answer is no one, the only option you have is to leave and never go back.

Alina contacted the same coyote that brought Manu to the United States and asked him to bring her daughters over. At nineteen, one daughter was put in jail instead of the icebox after she crossed the border because she was not a minor, and Alina had to pay $7,500 to get her out. I don't ask where she's getting all the money. I suppose that her entire life savings, and her husband's, have all gone into bringing their three teenagers over.

The children who cross Mexico and arrive at the US border are not "immigrants," not "illegals," not merely "undocumented minors." Those children are refugees of a war, and, as such, they should all have the right to political asylum. But not all of them have it.

Tell me how it ends, Mamma, my daughter asks me.

I don't know.

Tell me what happens next.

Sometimes I make up an ending, a happy one. But most of the time I just say:

I don't know how it ends yet.

Tell Me How It Ends: The Conversation

JEN   Kennedy, why did you leave Kenya to come to the US?

KENNEDY   Education. That was the only reason I came here. But the thing that struck me about this essay is it took me back. And I think the United States has a legacy, a very long legacy, of mistreating children that I don't think any other nation on earth has a history of. You go on to the 1600s when children were taken from their moms and sold to other households during slavery. The [white] fathers from that same period, who sold their own kids to slavery, or even ended up sleeping with their own daughters, because now they are cuter than their mothers. It's one of the legacies of white fathers in America that nobody ever talks about, which is a very sad part of the history of the United States. But at the same time, when this issue came up recently about immigrant children being locked up . . . it's almost like everybody forgot that the United States has been locking up its own kids, you know, for a very long time. This is the only country on earth where an eleven-year-old is treated like an adult and given an adult sentence. I mean, everybody says this is a Christian nation. [But] when you really come down to the human level, they're very cruel. You know, people talk about freedoms, or treating people fairly. Like right now, who is treating women fairly in America? It's not happening. It's hard for societies to change. The only thing I always ask myself is: "Don't the leaders of this country have children?" You know, we have about sixty thousand politicians. Everybody knows what kids need. I remember my own kids, when I had them in the summer, around me as their father, they could make jokes about me, or talk about me, but the nice lady that babysat them, they couldn't even talk to her.

JEN   Why is that?

KENNEDY   Familiarity. Kids are more comfortable around somebody they know—family, you know, they open up more, you know, they could make fun of me and they were developing a sense of humor that way, you know, and it takes a long time for kids to be acclimated to the new person. So, when you put children in a place like detention centers—I mean, a lot of people need to be pissed about it, and just go down and fix it.

DAVID   How would you fix it?

KENNEDY   Children need to be with their moms. You can't berate kids for being here. You got to be a very stupid person, or an idiot, to think that a kid traveling five thousand or eight thousand miles through three countries, isn't doing that for a good reason. You know, everybody knows what they're coming from. And I think you have to be responsive to that. I mean, why are we spending all the billions of dollars in Ukraine, when a fraction of that actually could fix all the problems down there [in Central America]? And those disparities like that just annoy me a lot. Because I think, as human beings, we owe each other some kindness, a sort of empathy that just comes naturally with these kids. I haven't seen that, even from both parties. They talk too much. They want to help but they don't do much to help them at all.

DAVID   It can really affect them [the children] later on.

JEN   The trauma's never going to go away. It changes the very structure of their brain. That's not the scientific way of saying it.

CHRIS   Now, I know it's a dead horse, but isn't race always a central issue? People will flinch. I mean, they're like, "Yeah, it's sad." But how do you get people to feel like it's their responsibility? Like, even us, I feel like my responsibility to me is my people. Like you guys are my people. This program's my people. When I hear about problems around the facility, I'm like, "Eh, *whatever*. It's not my people." I think it's so easy just to not give a shit. And then you're insulated by your wealth, and you're insulated by the bureaucracy of it.

DAVID   It's because people don't identify with them.

JEN   To Kennedy's point with Ukraine, they saw white kids, essentially, fleeing in clothes that look somewhat similar to what our own kids wear, and that seemed impossible to imagine. But there absolutely is not the same reaction when a brown child comes across the border. There's a failure to even perceive, or as Steve would say, *regard,* a brown child at the border, as opposed to a light-skinned Ukrainian kid running off in a puffy jacket and Levi's.

CHRIS   Right, what do you do about that? How do you confront that? How do you do that without making them angry? *[mockingly]* "I'm not racist. I'm not racist."

WARREN   It's so ingrained. Like those short stories and poems we read, I cannot remember her name, but when she gave her credit card to the waiter, and then he returned with the credit card and gave it back to her white friend. But I mean, this is so ingrained in human nature that you have to consciously look, not really so much past, but through it. Because, you know, so many of these stories in here, so many of these lives in here, I, as a white, cisgender, heterosexual Christian male, represent the enemy. Because I was raised conservative. We used to be Blue Dog Democrats. But, you know, just looking past that, and looking through it, to see the person behind it. And even efforts to make people more visible are gratuitous, because we look at the same message all the time, and then just flip somewhere else.

CHRIS   It's callous.

WARREN   Yeah, it's not so much callousness as it is, "Okay, what more do you want me to do?" I either won't or can't get myself to do it. It's hard to do.

DAVID   I think the only thing that breaks through that callousness is stories. I think that's one of the dangers where people who only get their news from the newspaper or the news because it just gives statistics or it gives the same narrative again and again and again and you read an essay like this or any piece of journalism that goes a step beyond that explains, "Hey, look, these are people's lives," and then it permeates you emotionally, in ways you might not get just seeing the same images over and over again.

CHRIS   The people that have the most control aren't going to read this shit anyway. I just feel like there's a part of me that feels really dismayed by the whole effort. Because, you know, there's that part where she makes the example of watching the kids running through traffic, that's how it feels, and like knowing you can't save them. I feel like, that's the strategy with stories. But I feel like people are insulated by their wealth so much that they never even get the information. Even people that are close enough to it, Fox News, or even CNN—they are these identity politics people that help people confirm their own opinions. How do you, how do you cultivate empathy?

DAVID   I'm not saying this is a solution. But you know, those children's stories you gave me—and, Warren, I know that you're working on a children's book—they had really adult themes to them, you know, whether it's the environment, or racism, or precarity. And [while] I'm reading these books, I'm thinking to myself [about how] this is at a whole different level than the books that were available when I was a child. You start them young. Empathy has to be cultivated, just like throwing a baseball needs to be cultivated. And it's just, that's why I think like, our schools are so important. And then you have this whole battle in schools with critical race theory [CRT].

CHRIS   Yeah, with the CRT thing—how do you get parents to understand any of this shit anymore? It's just this great divide. I think we should go to civil war. [The room laughs.]

JEN   You're not alone in that. I know that we've talked about this a little bit, but I think it's worth asking if empathy does create change.

Empathy is a feeling; it's not an action. *Is* empathy the solution? There are people who suggest that empathy may be harmful, because it makes us feel something and then we think, "Oh, I'm a good person. I felt something. It hurt me to see that child put through that."

RUBY   Well, I was listening to the *Ezra Klein Show* and Ezra Klein was interviewing Ibram X. Kendi. He was saying that typically people think that minds have to change in order for policy to change, but it's actually the opposite. Like, in terms of interracial marriage, approval for interracial marriage increased after the policy actually allowed it.

JEN   So, in one way, society can force change.

WARREN   Well, you see it all the time here: guys are looking for somebody or something to follow. They don't really, I don't know if it's a lack of confidence or self-knowledge or self-recognition, but there's so many people that are just, they're lost unless they have somebody else's goal. You know, and that's where the politicians just cash in, because as soon as they find enough people to get them elected, then the people who got them elected can tell their friends that this is somebody we can follow. He believes in us. We're notoriously short-sighted. Change, even a good change, can be so temporary unless it becomes embedded in, in the society and in the political sphere, and that's hard to do.

JEN   Do you want to say more about civil war, Chris?

CHRIS   I'd want to circle back to what Dave was saying about the creative class and how, you know, people just wanted to come home from work and consume content and just be told what to believe, because I think a lot of people just don't give a shit. You know, a lot of people are mediocre. They're just mediocre.

JEN   What does that mean?

CHRIS They don't have the vision to do much. They want to just live in a comfortable home. And a lot of people, they have to create shit to care about. A lot of these people are fighting against abortion, [they are fighting against] these social causes that aren't necessarily economic and don't affect them personally. So, one of the main ladies fighting the CRT thing, she didn't even have kids! She was this seventy-year-old that was going to these panels, and was one of the [prominent] voices against CRT.

DAVID *[joking]* Maybe she's a patriot.

CHRIS She's *obviously* a patriot. *[Laughter.]* I just think this, this is a personal thing. You wake up and you have a fucking knee on your neck. And you inherit that shit. Just like people inherited comfort. I know plenty of people that don't really want for shit.

JEN That's interesting. I've thought about epigenetics and inheriting trauma. But I've never thought about the idea of inheriting comfort or complacency.

CHRIS And that just leads to individualism, which leads to "That's not my problem. I do this dog rescue program, so, that's how I contribute to the world."

[With this essay], though, there's a degree of allyship that's perplexing to me. Because, like Luiselli is dealing with the system, she's the translator, so she's an ally to [the kids]. But she's also servicing the system. She's still getting paid by the system. You're trying to do what you can, but you're still operating within shitty confines.

DAVID But you need both. We need people outside the system, and we need people within the system.

CHRIS I think the United States is not a good idea. I hate the fact that it's this red-blue bullshit. And then we have this idea that we're a union. We're not a union. We've never been a union. The North has never been an ally. The South has never been the enemy. People look out for their own interests, and they create shit to keep the people of their own interests safe. And it's not even about racism. It's capitalism; it's wealth; it's looking out for your own. And I'm guilty of the same shit.

DAVID   A person only has so much time and energy; they pick their issues.

CHRIS   You have to. How can we care about trees, the environment, racism? It's too overwhelming. So, we don't care about shit then.

DAVID   And then you just tune out. You watch your TV shows; you consume your products.

CHRIS   And you rely on politicians.

DAVID   But what about Minnesota Legacy politicians. I mean . . . that amendment has done so much.[1]

CHRIS   [The amendment is] a product of a lobbyist. That's one thing that lobbyists have [that] maybe helped us within a sea of terrible shit that lobbyists do.

JEN   Or maybe it goes back to Ruby's point—morality *can* be legislated. This idea that you can create change through the policy.

CHRIS   It's the only way to do it within the confines of the system.

RUBY   Going back to your question, Jen, about whether or not empathy actually creates action. I think anger is a lot more actionable,

---

1 The amendment increased the state sales tax by three-eighths of 1 percent in 2009. The additional sales tax revenue is distributed between a clean water fund, an outdoor heritage fund, an arts and cultural heritage fund, and a parks and trails fund, thereby making Minnesota a national leader in arts and environment funding.

and empathy can often spark anger; and also suffering can do the same. And I think that is when those two things collide and there is actual movement. But that would never necessarily be effective in like, a bureaucratic system, or [with] someone working on the inside. Outside forces would have to put that together.

JEN   That makes me think of George Floyd. Some theorize that one of the reasons George Floyd's murder created such active resistance was because the pandemic made space for the anger. Anger because we saw the video, right? But also, [because] he was murdered during a pandemic. Folks who had, perhaps, paid no attention to police brutality were sitting still. And in the relative silence of that, they saw [and] heard what Black folks have been saying forever—that a cop always has a knee on their neck. And some [people] finally felt something, got angry, and joined those who've been marching forever.

KENNEDY   Valeria writes this book—and she's brave to write this book—because she has empathy and she does really care, not because she wants to get rich. I can assure you that somebody who's sold a million books out there won't be able to write an essay like this for fear of offending. I'm thinking if a renowned singer could sing about those kids, people *might* hear it, bureaucracy *might* act, the politicians *might* act, because they will see a lot about the cause. Like the Floyd video. The songs that live in us will carry us through the cause. That is what is missing.

DAVID   Sometimes people choose art—movies or the songs, in order to *forget* about their lives.

KENNEDY   Empathy does create change. I want to argue that point. You know, it's everything that makes somebody talk about the suffering of others, you know, and if you're a singer, or a writer, or a painter, and your message goes out there, things change.

CHRIS   *[to Ruby]* I'm most excited about you guys taking over the world.

DAVID   This is one thing I think is so interesting—when following the news, you can get really numb to it. The news doesn't make a difference. But this essay? All these essays . . . That is one thing that's really cool about paying attention to the world—it's just one big story.

Acknowledgments

As Epictetus said, "No great thing comes into being all at once." This collection is no exception. We'd like to recognize the many humans who made this book possible.

We're grateful to Kevin Lindsey and the MHC team for the good work they do. Thank you for your support of this project.

Kristi Maher, thank you for keeping this project a priority and not letting anything, not even a pandemic, shut it down. Thank you also to DOC staff who made communications possible: John Landretti, Matt Hosmer, Tamra Newham, Nancy Rosman, Ann Deiman, Jeremy DeAngelo, and countless others.

Enormous gratitude to the team at Coffee House Press who made this book possible despite a shortage of hours in their days. Lizzie Davis, Abbie Phelps, Zoë Koenig, Quynh Van, Carla Valadez, Daley Farr, we appreciate your heart and passion. Making a book is always hard; making a book from prison requires saintly patience and flexibility.

Chris Fischbach, thank you for your enthusiasm and counsel, always, and for believing in and launching this book from its inception.

For writers in the Twin Cities and beyond, who visit us, who join our readings, and who read for us and on our behalf. The energy you bring is very much appreciated and remains long after our events end.

We want to thank the entire Minnesota Prison Writing Workshop community.

MPWW writing instructors past and present: your commitment to cultivating our creativity has added so much meaning in our lives day after day, year after year, decade after decade. We thank each and every one of you: Mike Alberti, Deborah Appleman, Bill Breen, Jennifer Bowen, Wendy Brown-Baez, Matt Burgess, Michael Kleber-Diggs, Antonio Duke, Dain Edward, Amy Fladeboe, David Lawrence Grant, April Gibson, Joe Horton, Su Hwang, Kelly Hansen Maher, Abbey Mei Otis, Jeannine Ouellette, Rachel Moritz, Junauda Petrus-Nasah, Peter Pearson, Matt Rasmussen, Katie Robinson, Erin Sharkey, Sun Yung Shin, Mary Stein, Elizabeth Tannen, Nico

Taranovsky, Michael Torres, Nell Ubbelohde, Adam Levy, Alida Winternheimer, Chaun Webster, Chavonn Williams Chen, Sam Stokley, Claire Schwartz, Vincent Cheng.

MPWW mentors: the quiet constancy behind our writing. Thank you for all the time and work you spend giving us feedback, critiques, directions, and reading material catered to our artistic aims. We thank each of you, and extend a special thank-you to those who have both mentored and coordinated the mentor program: Anika Eide, Kate Shuknecht, Mike Manerowski, Mike Alberti, and Ari Tison.

Ruby Haack, for transcribing and helping edit the conversations, for your keen insights, for your joyful personality, and for your brilliance. You've been a gift to our community.

Deborah Appleman, MPWW's unofficial godmother and tireless force behind our success against headwinds we cannot weather on our own.

Elizabeth Tannen and Rachel Moritz, for teaching us anthology work through the prison journals without having any idea what would eventually become of it.

Kelly Hansen Maher, for sowing the seeds that generated the editors.

Ari Tison, for being a crucial link between all of us and our mentors.

Su Hwang, thank you for keeping the world aware that we exist through your outreach. You are truly the world's best hype woman.

Mike Alberti, for all the good work you do with the best of intentions and a magnitude that can't be measured.

Jennifer Bowen, for being present in all our struggles and triumphs.

And personally, we'd like to add:

For Jen Bowen, thank you so much for the time, energy, and never-flagging cheerleading on our behalf. Without your support, my writing would never have dragged itself from where it lay hidden. I'm grateful to my family for their words of wisdom, support, and belief. Without them, I would've remained buried in the doldrums. And finally, to my first and greatest writing mentor, Alida; you taught me when to use the hatchet, when to use the bulldozer, and when to use the scalpel. (Mark "Red" Altenhofen)

Bismillah-ir Rahim (In the Name of Allah, Most Gracious, Most Merciful). Thank you, Samantha Thelma Pereira, for giving your life to ferry me across the Rubicon; Barb Louise Portinga, for providing the existential gravitas around which I slingshot; Jake Nyberg, for having always been my friend in clutch and incredible ways; everyone who stayed for their intuitive belief in possible worlds. (Will Anderson)

Thank you, Clyde, for your endless fountain of stubborn; Carol, for your quiet, gentle reminder that I am not alone; and Alice, please play the music louder and keep moving. (Warren Bronson)

Thank you, Justine Hill, for allowing me time to work on this project. My friend, Steven Horowitz, for your support and encouragement during hard times; Scott Sayer, for rooting for me in reality; Julie Gubbin and Caitlin Noone, for reminding me what is important and to smile often. (Kennedy Amenya Gisege)

I want to give a lot of thanks and recognition to MPWW, the director Jen Bowen, and all of the instructors who have dedicated so much of their time and effort. I also want to recognize my family members, who have lived within multiple classes, in and out of America. (Ronald L. Greer II)

Thank you, Ron Reed, for your wise words during the many days they were needed; Sarith Peou, for your kindness and compassion; my mother, for having happiness; my wife, Pauline, for her love and devotion. (David Janisch)

This work is funded in part by the Minnesota Humanities Center with money from the Arts and Cultural Heritage Fund that was created with the vote of the people of Minnesota on November 4, 2008.

Coffee House Press began as a small letterpress operation in 1972 and has grown into an internationally renowned nonprofit publisher of literary fiction, essay, poetry, and other work that doesn't fit neatly into genre categories.

Coffee House is both a publisher and an arts organization. Through our *Books in Action* program and publications, we've become inter-disciplinary collaborators and incubators for new work and audience experiences. Our vision for the future is one where a publisher is a catalyst and connector.

LITERATURE
is not the same thing as
PUBLISHING

Funder Acknowledgments

Coffee House Press is an internationally renowned independent book publisher and arts nonprofit based in Minneapolis, MN; through its literary publications and *Books in Action* program, Coffee House acts as a catalyst and connector—between authors and readers, ideas and resources, creativity and community, inspiration and action.

Coffee House Press books are made possible through the generous support of grants and donations from corporations, state and federal grant programs, family foundations, and the many individuals who believe in the transformational power of literature. This activity is made possible by the voters of Minnesota through a Minnesota State Arts Board Operating Support grant, thanks to the legislative appropriation from the Arts and Cultural Heritage Fund. Coffee House also receives major operating support from the Amazon Literary Partnership, Jerome Foundation, Literary Arts Emergency Fund, McKnight Foundation, and the National Endowment for the Arts (NEA). To find out more about how NEA grants impact individuals and communities, visit www.arts.gov.

Coffee House Press receives additional support from Bookmobile; the Buckley Charitable Fund; Dorsey & Whitney LLP; the Gaea Foundation; the Matching Grant Program Fund of the Minneapolis Foundation; Mr. Pancks' Fund in memory of Graham Kimpton; the Schwab Charitable Fund; and the U.S. Bank Foundation.

The Publisher's Circle of Coffee House Press

Publisher's Circle members make significant contributions to Coffee House Press's annual giving campaign. Understanding that a strong financial base is necessary for the press to meet the challenges and opportunities that arise each year, this group plays a crucial part in the success of Coffee House's mission.

Recent Publisher's Circle members include many anonymous donors, Kathy Arnold, Patricia A. Beithon, Andrew Brantingham, Kelli & Dave Cloutier, Theodore Cornwell, Mary Ebert & Paul Stembler, Kamilah Foreman, Eva Galiber, Jocelyn Hale & Glenn Miller Charitable Fund of the Minneapolis Foundation, Roger Hale & Nor Hall, Randy Hartten & Ron Lotz, Carl & Heidi Horsch, Amy L. Hubbard & Geoffrey J. Kehoe Fund of the St. Paul & Minnesota Foundation, Kenneth & Susan Kahn, the Kenneth Koch Literary Estate, Cinda Kornblum, the Lenfestey Family Foundation, Sarah Lutman & Rob Rudolph, Carol & Aaron Mack, Gillian McCain, Mary & Malcolm McDermid, Daniel N. Smith III & Maureen Millea Smith, Robin Chemers Neustein, Vance Opperman, Alan Polsky, Robin Preble, Steve Smith, Paul Thissen, Grant Wood, and Margaret Wurtele.

For more information about the Publisher's Circle and other ways to support Coffee House Press books, authors, and activities, please visit www.coffeehousepress.org/pages/donate or contact us at info@coffeehousepress.org.

About the Editors

Zeke Caligiuri is a writer from South Minneapolis and author of *This Is Where I Am,* published by University of Minnesota Press. He is cofounder of the Stillwater Writers Collective, the first of its kind in the country. Zeke's work has been featured by LitHub and PEN America, and is anthologized in *Prison Noir* (Akashic Books, 2014), edited by Joyce Carol Oates, and *The Sentences That Create Us: Crafting a Writer's Life in Prison* (Haymarket Books, 2022). He is directly impacted by over two decades of incarceration and is currently helping to build the Re-Enfranchised Coalition, empowering system-impacted people and reinvesting in the humanization of those still stuck within the captivity business. He misses the days riding around Minneapolis looking for pick-up baseball games.

Fong Lee is an artist and storyteller based in Saint Paul, Minnesota. He is a celebrated poet—published through the Minnesota Prison Writing Workshop and Asian American Writers' Workshop—a beloved painter, and a published photographer. He is a dedicated restorative justice practitioner and enjoys traveling. Fong and his family immigrated to the US as Hmong refugees when Fong was a child, and after his family were displaced from their borrowed homeland in Laos.

B. Batchelor is a poet and member of the Stillwater Writers Collective and Minnesota Prison Writing Workshop. His poetry has been published in *The Nation, Columbia Journal,* and *Cream City Review,* among others. He was a 2022 finalist for Milkweed's Ballard Spahr Poetry Prize for his manuscript *Disfigured Hours.* B.'s first spoken sentence was, "I want a cookie!"

C. Fausto Cabrera is a multi-genre artist and writer incarcerated since 2003. He is coauthor, with photographer Alec Soth, of *The Parameters of Our Cage* (MACK, 2020). His work has been anthologized in Modern Language Association's *Teaching in Prison.* His poetry, prose, and visual art appear in *Washington Post Magazine,* the *Missouri Review, California Quarterly, descant,* the *Woodward Review* (Pushcart nomination), the *Colorado Review,* the *Antioch Review,* and *Puerto del Sol,* among others. When frightened as a child, he'd sneak into his mother's room and sleep on the floor next to the bed. In the morning, she always stepped on him.

Will Anderson is a transgender/nonconforming writer, artist, and musician currently incarcerated in Faribault, Minnesota. They are a member of the MPWW Writers' Collective. Their writing has appeared or is forthcoming in *Territory, Chatham Review, Stillpoint Magazine,* and *Ecologies of Justice.* Links to music and written work at www .linktr.ee/wma9455.

Warren Bronson has been a marine, a husband, and a father, and was a miserable failure at all three; his heart remembers the rolling flatlands of southern Minnesota and hopes to return to them some day. He has been a member of the Minnesota Prison Writing Workshop (MPWW) since its inception, writes mainly in the speculative, and has edited several MPWW incarcerated writers' anthologies. His work first appeared in *So It Goes: The Journal of the Kurt Vonnegut Museum and Library.*

David Janisch is a writer whose work is forthcoming in *Nightmare Magazine.* As a child, he loved to carry around a can of spinach, believing that if needed, it could turn him into Popeye.

Kennedy Amenya Gisege is an accomplished visual artist and poet whose work appears in *Agni* and *Bangalore Review,* among others. His chapbook *The Liturgy of Smell* was published by Red Bird Chapbooks. He has written several books under the pen name Ken Amen. Gisege is incarcerated in the Minnesota Correctional Facility–Faribault.

Mark "Red" Altenhofen is a PEN Prison Writing Award winner in fiction and an honorable mention in CNF. He has served on numerous editorial boards, editing *The 27th Letter* and *Words in Grayscale,* among others. He is currently working on his second novel and first collection of short stories. As a boy, he once thought it wise to bring a squirrel to show-and-tell.

Jeff Young is a journalist, poet, fiction writer, and memoirist. Jeff is currently one of two incarcerated law students in the nation through Mitchell Hamline School of Law and The Legal Revolution. His awards include a Pamela J. Caligiuri Broadside Award, a PEN Prison Writing Award, and more. His work appears in the *Minnesota Spokesman-Recorder,* among others. He moved to Minneapolis from Boston when he was eight years old, leaving behind cherished trips to cranberry bogs and the ocean, where he collected dead horseshoe crabs.

Ronald L. Greer II is a multi-genre writer from Detroit, MI. He is a poet by nature and a daydreamer by necessity. His latest work is published in *A Darker Wilderness: Black Nature Writing from Soil to Stars* (Milkweed, 2023). He is a long-standing member of Minnesota Prison Writing Workshop and is in partnership with the SEEN Project. As a young man, he enjoyed eating concord grapes and strawberries out of his grandfather's personal garden.

LaVon Johnson is a writer whose works appear in *Poetry Magazine* and *Midwest Journal,* among others. LaVon, a dog lover, spent his early years training Alaskan Malamutes in Chicago.

About the Contributors

Eula Biss is the author of four books: *Having and Being Had* (Riverhead Books, 2020), *On Immunity* (Graywolf Press, 2014), *Notes from No Man's Land* (Graywolf Press, 2009), and *The Balloonists* (Hanging Loose Press, 2002). Her work has been translated into a dozen languages and has been recognized by a National Book Critics Circle Award, a Guggenheim Fellowship, and a 21st Century Award from the Chicago Public Library. As a 2023 National Fellow at New America, she is at work on a collection of essays about how private property has shaped our world.

Michael Torres was born and brought up in Pomona, California, where he spent his adolescence as a graffiti artist. His debut collection of poems, *An Incomplete List of Names* (Beacon Press, 2020) was selected by Raquel Salas Rivera for the National Poetry Series and named one of NPR's *Books We Love.* His honors include awards and support from the National Endowment for the Arts, the McKnight Foundation, the Bread Loaf Writers' Conference, CantoMundo, VONA Voices, the Minnesota State Arts Board, the Jerome Foundation, the Camargo Foundation, and the Loft Literary Center. Currently he's an assistant professor in the MFA program at Minnesota State University, Mankato, and a teaching artist with the Minnesota Prison Writing Workshop. Visit him at: michaeltorreswriter.com.

Alice Paige is an author, performing artist, and creative writing teacher from Chicago, Illinois. She has her MFA in creative writing from Hamline University and her BSc in biology from Iowa State University; she is a LOFT Mentor Series fellow, a Digital Pedagogical Lab fellow, and a McNair Scholar. Her work can be found in *Coffin Bell, Take a Stand, Art Against Hate: A Raven Chronicles Anthology, Luna Station Quarterly,* and plenty of other strange journals.

Inara Verzemnieks has written for *New York Times Magazine, Tin House*, the *Atlantic*, the *Iowa Review*, and *Creative Nonfiction*. She is the recipient of a Pushcart Prize and a Rona Jaffe Writers' Award, and was named a finalist for the Pulitzer Prize in feature writing. After working for thirteen years as a newspaper journalist, she received her MFA from the University of Iowa's Nonfiction Writing Program, where she now teaches as an assistant professor.

Sarith Peou, a Khmer Rouge Genocide survivor, is a prolific prison writer. He has authored two books, among them his poetry collection, *Corpse Watching* (Tinfish Press, 2007).

Kristin Collier is a high school teacher and organizes with the Debt Collective. Her work has appeared in publications such as *Longreads* and *Fourth Genre*. Her first book, *What Debt Demands*, a mix of memoir and reportage, is forthcoming with Grand Central Press.

Angela Pelster was a 2021 McKnight Artist Fellow judged by Hanif Abdurraqib. Her first essay collection, *Limber*, won the Great Lakes Colleges Association Award for nonfiction and was a finalist for the PEN/Diamonstein-Spielvogel Award. Her work has appeared or is forthcoming in *Orion*, LitHub, *Ploughshares, Tin House, Granta*, the *Kenyon Review*, and the *Gettysburg Review*, among others. She's been a Bread Loaf Fellow in nonfiction and a Minnesota State Arts Board grantee, and has an MFA from the University of Iowa. She's currently at work on her new book, *The Evolution of Fire: Meditations on Crises*.

Lauren Markham is a writer based in California whose work has appeared in outlets such as *Guernica, Harper's*, the *New York Review of Books, New York Times Magazine*, and *VQR*, where she is a contributing editor. She is the author of *The Far Away Brothers: Two Young Migrants and the Making of an American Life* (Crown, 2017) and the forthcoming *A Map of Future Ruins*.

Lacy M. Johnson is a Houston-based professor, curator, and activist, and is author of *The Reckonings* (Scribner, 2018) and *The Other Side* (Tin House Books, 2014)—both National Book Critics Circle Award finalists—and *Trespasses* (University of Iowa Press, 2012). She is editor, with the designer Cheryl Beckett, of *More City Than Water: A Houston Flood Atlas* (University of Texas Press, 2022). She teaches creative nonfiction at Rice University and is the founding director of the Houston Flood Museum.

Steve Almond is the author of a dozen books, including the *New York Times* bestsellers *Candyfreak* (Algonquin Books, 2004) and *Against Football* (Melville House, 2014). His novel *All the Secrets of the World* (Zando, 2022) has been optioned for TV by 20th Century Studios. Almond teaches at the Nieman Fellowship at Harvard and Wesleyan. He lives outside Boston with his family.

TM "Redd" Warren is an artist and writer who has, thankfully, participated in several Minnesota Prison Writing Workshops. His craft has appeared on many walls and in his notebooks, and has been published in *Drop a Kite* and *J Journal: New Writing on Justice*, among others. Warren spent his formative years exploring the lakes and woods of northern Minnesota. Regretfully incarcerated since 1994, he hopes to reunite with his family, marry his beloved Chelsea, swim in clear blue lakes, and hug healthy trees very soon.

Kao Kalia Yang is a Hmong American writer of memoir and children's literature, a librettist, a public speaker, and a teacher. Her first book, *The Latehomecomer: A Hmong Family Memoir* (Coffee House Press, 2008), was a National Endowment for the Arts Big Read title and remains the only Asian American title adapted for the stage by Literature to Life. Her second memoir, *The Song Poet: A Memoir of My Father* (Metropolitan Books, 2016), was a finalist for the National Book Critics Circle Award, the Chautauqua Prize, the PEN America Literary Awards, and the Dayton's Literary Peace Prize. The Minnesota Opera commissioned a libretto by Yang for an opera of the same name, which had a sold-out premiere run in 2023. Her collective refugee memoir, *Somewhere in the Unknown World* (Metropolitan Books, 2020), was one of Kirkus's Best Books of the Year. Yang has received the American Library Association's Asian/Pacific American Literary Award for Children's Literature and four Minnesota Book Awards, among many other awards, for her writing across genres. She is a Soros, McKnight, and Guggenheim fellow.

Kiese Laymon is a Black southern writer from Jackson, Mississippi. The Libby Shearn Moody Professor of Creative Writing and English at Rice University, Laymon is the author of *Long Division* (Agate Bolden, 2013), which won the 2022 NAACP Image Award for fiction, and the essay collection *How to Slowly Kill Yourself and Others in America* (Agate Bolden, 2013), named a notable book of 2021 by the *New York Times*. Laymon's bestselling *Heavy: An American Memoir* (Scribner, 2018) won the Andrew Carnegie Medal for Excellence in Nonfiction and the Christopher Isherwood Prize for Autobiographical Prose, and was named one of the "50 Best Memoirs of the Past 50 Years" by the *New York Times*. Laymon was awarded a MacArthur Fellowship in 2022.

Valeria Luiselli is the author of the award-winning novels *The Story of My Teeth* (2015) and *Faces in the Crowd* (2013) and the books of essays *Sidewalks* (2013) and *Tell Me How It Ends* (2017), the latter of which was a finalist for the National Book Critics Circle Award for Criticism in 2017—all published by Coffee House Press. Her second novel, *Lost Children Archive* (Knopf, 2019), was a winner of the 2020 Andrew Carnegie Medal for Excellence in Fiction and the 2020 Folio Prize. It was a 2019 Kirkus Prize finalist; was longlisted for the Booker Prize, the Women's Prize for Fiction, and the Aspen Words Literary Prize; and was shortlisted for the Simpson Family Literary Prize. Luiselli is the recipient of a 2020 Guggenheim Fellowship and a MacArthur Fellowship.

American Precariat was designed by
Bookmobile Design & Digital Publisher Services.
Text is set in Adobe Garamond Pro.